Curriculum Wisdom

Educational Decisions in Democratic Societies

James G. Henderson
Kent State University

Kathleen R. Kesson
Long Island University

Upper Saddle River, New Jersey
Columbus, Ohio

Library of Congress Cataloging-in-Publication Data
Henderson, James George.
  Curriculum wisdom : educational decisions in democractic societies / James G. Henderson,
Kathleen R. Kesson.
    p. cm.
  Includes bibliographical references and index.
  ISBN 0-13-111819-6
    1. Curriculum planning—Philosophy. 2. Education—Curricula—Social aspects.
  3. Education—Aims and objectives. 4. Democracy.   I. Kesson, Kathleen R. II. Title.

LB2806.15.H45 2004
375'.001—dc22

                                                      2003059610

Vice President and Executive Publisher: Jeffery W. Johnston
Executive Editor: Debra A. Stollenwerk
Editorial Assistant: Mary Morrill
Production Editor: Kris Robinson-Roach
Production Coordination: nSight
Design Coordinator: Diane C. Lorenzo
Cover Designer: Ali Mohrman
Cover Image: Ali Mohrman
Production Manager: Pamela D. Bennett
Director of Marketing: Ann Castel Davis
Marketing Manager: Darcy Betts Prybella
Marketing Coordinator: Tyra Poole

This book was set by Laserwords. It was printed and bound by R. R. Donnelley & Sons Company. The cover
was printed by Coral Graphic Services, Inc.

Pearson Education Ltd.
Pearson Education Singapore Pte. Ltd.
Pearson Education Canada, Ltd.
Pearson Education—Japan

Pearson Education Australia Pty. Limited
Pearson Education North Asia Ltd.
Pearson Educación de Mexico, S.A. de C.V.
Pearson Education Malaysia Pte. Ltd.

10 9 8 7 6 5 4 3 2 1
ISBN: 0-13-111819-6

Foreword

One of the most attractive features of teaching as a profession is that it provides opportunities for the intellectual stimulation and growth of teachers. Henderson and Kesson invite teachers to seek wisdom and to apply that wisdom to a wide array of problems in teaching and professional life.

Consider a problem that emerges with some regularity in high schools—tardiness to class. Anyone who has served on a high school faculty can testify that the problem is a familiar one. Some members of the faculty demand strict rules and penalties harsh enough to "let the kids know we mean business!" Perhaps, sadly, most high school teachers react this way.

But a few teachers counsel reflection and careful analysis. These teachers ask what the faculty is trying to accomplish besides on-time attendance. What will the use of rules and penalties tell students about our aims for their education? One teacher, Ms. A., describes a method she has found effective. She tells her students that she will always start class on time and that she expects them to be present and ready to participate with her. Then, acknowledging that circumstances sometimes cause lateness, she suggests that a couple of the seats nearest the door be left vacant for latecomers. When a student is unavoidably late, she or he should take one of those seats and wait for a break in classroom activity before asking others what was missed. Obviously, the teacher can see who is late and, if the problem occurs frequently, she can speak to the tardy student.

In defending her method of handling tardiness, Ms. A. argues that the respect she shows students is reciprocated. Students are rarely late to her classes. She points out also that her aim is to prepare students for responsible participation in a democracy. Their behavior should be governed by an internal sense of responsibility, not by rules and penalties. She does not reject all rules and penalties, but she advises that every rule be subjected to the sort of analysis she has described.

Henderson and Kesson provide teachers with some strategies for approaching such problems. Each problem should be considered in context. Wise teachers look beyond the problem at hand to see how both problem and proposed solution fit into the whole picture of educating young people in a liberal democracy. Do we want graduates who will obey authority under all circumstances? Or do we want to encourage both critical thinking and a commitment to a democratic way of life?

Wise teachers will continue to reflect on the aims of education. Is happiness such an aim? If so, how should we choose our curriculum and conduct our classes so that students will learn something about the various views of happiness? If, for example, we teach poetry because it may provide lifelong delight and wisdom, should it not be presented in a way that induces both delight and wisdom now?

Advising teachers to pursue and use wisdom is, today, both frightening and heartening. It is frightening because the professional lives of teachers are now so tightly controlled. How can one use wisdom if she cannot even choose the content of her lessons or the method by which she will present them? It is heartening because it reminds us that, if we acquire wisdom, we may prevail—that the pursuit is worthwhile in itself, and it may give us the tools to build a more enlightened future for schooling.

All teachers should be committed to the quest for wisdom: to the analysis of means and ends, to the evaluation of topics for the curriculum, to the investigation of collateral learning that may accompany the choice of various methods, and to the assessment of their own growth in delight and wisdom. This book points the way.

Nel Noddings
Teachers College, Columbia University and Stanford University

Foreword

Clawing its way out of an open, post–World War II grave dug by social critics and academics, the field of curriculum studies resurfaced as a genuinely fascinating and lively intellectual arena of work during the 1970s and 1980s, challenging not only its own somnambulism but increasingly conservative and other-directed efforts to control public education in this country. To succeed, however, our field had to disconnect in many respects from its very roots in public schooling (symbolized in contemporary times by the decades-old "Tyler Rationale") so that curriculum workers could distance themselves from the increasing strictures of "curriculum making" promoted by the overwhelming institutionalized cultures of schooling and formal education.

Today, curriculum studies is once again a truly vibrant and exciting place to locate oneself as an educator, though one is likely to be identified and placed within one or more "camps" within the field (postmodernists, traditionalists, feminists, critical pragmatists, technologists, etc.). The thickest line of separation among and between these camps is drawn between those who remain focused on curricular problems and decisions relevant to schools and school people (theirs is called the "institutionalized" curriculum conversation) and those who do not. Curriculum studies has, nonetheless, slowly and purposefully worked its way of late toward a praxis of theoretical understanding and contextualized problem solving and decision making. *Curriculum Wisdom* represents this attempt at praxis better than any curriculum book I've read.

Unfortunately, this well-established theory/practice curriculum divide remains alive in the university classroom. Like many others who locate themselves within the field of curriculum studies, I teach graduate classes populated, for the most part, by school people—serious and committed educators (classroom teachers, administrators, counselors, special education teachers, school librarians, etc.) who care about themselves and the students they serve. Some take my classes to move up on the pay scale or to accumulate their state-mandated "professional development" credits (to remain certified), some take my classes as requirements toward a specific certificate or degree, and some take my curriculum classes out of genuine interest in learning more about curriculum studies (and perhaps, themselves). In truth, I meet few graduate students who arrive in my classes with a distinctly intellectual desire to more deeply understand curriculum theory or philosophy. I meet even fewer who represent the mindless practitioners we often read about in the media and some professional texts—educators who have abandoned all hope and desire for improving their world and the world of their students. Most educators I encounter are relatively open-minded pragmatists.

As such, these educators, regardless of their graduate student course needs and intentions, have shown a consistent willingness to read and discuss multiple and often challenging texts, to seriously engage complex curriculum thoughts and ideas, and to share their understandings and questions with others in class presentations, small-group discussions, and formal projects. I believe that much of this willingness has to do with their deeply personal and professional appreciation for having a space within which they can both criticize the books and ideas they encounter and acknowledge their own frustrations and concerns with the "institutional" state of curriculum affairs. For years now, my personal challenge has been to steer these educators away from simple, formulaic, "how to" curriculum monologues toward more complex historical, philosophical, and theoretical curriculum discourses—hoping at the same time to advance personal/professional interest and meaning without diminishing the desire to remain tethered to their lives in schools. Said differently, what I try to do within a curriculum class is to provide educators with a space to *explore* (their own and others' issues, stories, etc.), *explode* (sometimes about the readings and ideas they encounter, other times about the situations in which they work), and *envision* (what possibilities seem worthwhile for and creatable by themselves and others). Like Nel Noddings, I believe that teaching, for these graduate students, represents an opportunity for intellectual (and emotional) stimulation and growth. Because of this belief, I'm convinced that *Curriculum Wisdom* is a book that will help me foster these same opportunities.

Since the mid-1980s, conversations *across* and *within* our field's curriculum divide have become more compelling and sophisticated thanks to persistent scholars like James Henderson and Kathleen Kesson. Together and separately, their commitment has been to develop and represent complicated curriculum thinking and understanding within complex pragmatic contexts, to coax institutionally oriented (i.e., school-based) educators into our "remarkably complex curriculum conversation." With its focus on wise judgments through multidimensional arts of inquiry, *Curriculum Wisdom* is the high water mark in their ongoing project.

Henderson and Kesson use the phrase *curriculum wisdom* here as an image to "convey the subtle and complex challenges of approaching curriculum work as *envisioning and enacting a good educational journey.*" They invite us to move away from routine thoughts and talk of "knowledge" in order to consider, instead, images and conversations about the *wisdom* of curriculum work, because "all curriculum decisions are, at their heart, moral decisions. They touch the core of what it means to be human, to live in community with others, to find meaning and purpose, and to create a more just and peaceful world."

Most educators with whom I've worked know this to be true and yet manage to hold this truth in abeyance within their increasingly restrictive and performance-dominated professional contexts. They are willing to consider philosophical and theoretical discussions about a good educational journey so long as the discussions pertain to life within their workplaces. What *Curriculum Wisdom* offers these educators is an open embrace of "the pragmatic turn"—the authors' consistent efforts to present curriculum wisdom within a context of "practical efficacy and adaptability." Said differently, this book is about educational *actions* (i.e., solving curricular problems and making curricular decisions) taken by wisdom-seeking educators.

Having said that, let me be clear that *Curriculum Wisdom* will never be identified as a "how to" book. For example, the authors explain that curriculum wisdom reflects a "doubled" problem solving that begins with the practical and moves to the moral, incorporating a shared understanding of "good" conduct within the "good" life. That is, curriculum decision making must include "a critically informed moral vision" that, in this text, centers on "democracy as a moral way of living." Furthermore, because "democracy" is an interpretive notion, pragmatic curriculum decision making must be multifaceted and collaborative in nature. "Simply stated," say the authors, "the best way of proceeding is to be democratic about democratic morality." Most educators I know bear grave concerns about their decreasing opportunities to engage in curriculum conversations at all, let alone curriculum decisions of a practical or moral nature. Because of this, they will, I feel, resonate with these ideas. As the authors note, "Curriculum matters cannot be handled through simple technical procedures; they require sophisticated professional judgment." My sense is that a great many educators ache to know more about exercising such judgments and to actively participate in the curriculum conversations that surround them. They seek a voice beyond their closed classroom doors and their clandestine conversations with like-minded colleagues and school friends.

Most compelling about this book is the authors' ability to explain how curriculum wisdom is, at its core, a "philosophy of being" for educators—a way of cocreating meaning for others and ourselves through educational action that is "as much a matter of 'degree' as it is a matter of 'moment.' ' Henderson and Kesson use images throughout the book, such as "fragile enterprise" and "never-ending cycle of educational effort," to convey this philosophical perspective, making clear that accepting such a difficult challenge will require us to live with "doubt on our shoulders" and the need to find comfort within our "cultivated ignorance." Curriculum wisdom, like nirvana, heaven, and enlightenment, is an aspiration rather than a tangible end. As Nel Noddings points out, "Advising teachers to pursue and use wisdom is, today, both frightening and heartening." Yet many educators seem poised for this very pursuit.

I've come to believe that educators who take graduate courses in curriculum have the seeds of such philosophical thinking sprouting within them, that they resonate with ideas such as vision, moral relevance, uncertainty, collaboration, deliberation, and a right to be heard. They know (or can accept) such ideas because these educators have an already strong social commitment or calling to the welfare and future of their students, and it is this teacher/student relationship that permeates *Curriculum Wisdom*. Whether the authors are taking us on long and complex journeys into the history of philosophical thought or recent public policy, they always bring us back to the daily interactions among and between educators and students. Henderson and Kesson are direct in their belief that for educators, the overall purpose for leading an inquiry-based life is to continuously self-examine the "goodness" of our interactions with others (students, their parents, other teachers, administrators, etc.). It is this basic intention that will resonate with the educators I'll continue to meet in my classroom, for I believe, like these authors, that

> [C]urriculum work begins with the professionals but culminates with the students' learning experiences. At the heart of an educational calling, and at the heart of the professional guidance in this book, is the recognition of this teaching-learning reciprocity.

J. Dan Marshall
Pennsylvania State University

THREE WORKING ASSUMPTIONS

Three basic assumptions have guided the creation of this book. First, we believe that it is possible to approach curriculum work as an exercise in "practical wisdom." As you will read in Chapter 1, human wisdom is defined in the *Oxford English Dictionary* as "the capacity of judging rightly in matters relating to life and conduct; soundness of judgment in the choice of means and ends; sometimes, less strictly, sound sense, especially in practical affairs." Curriculum workers who adopt a wisdom orientation are, therefore, challenging themselves

- To consider the "good conduct" and "enduring values" implications and consequences of their decisions;
- To think about the relationship between educational means and ends; and
- To engage in sophisticated practical reasoning.

Aristotle's philosophy is an important foundational source for understanding practical wisdom. He writes that the practically wise person is someone who can carefully deliberate over the concrete specifics of individual matters while keeping an eye on what is "the best for man of things attainable by action" (Aristotle, 1941, p. 1028). Aristotle continues, "Nor is practical wisdom concerned with universals only—it must also recognize particulars; for it is practical, and practice is concerned with particulars" (p. 1028). Practical wisdom requires a doubled problem solving. The intent is to solve an immediate problem while advancing enduring values. This is a "means/end" **and** "means/visionary end" way of operating. The problem solving is situated in both the immediate present and the visionary future. The search for the resolution of a particular problem is, at the same time, an aspiration to advance a critically informed moral vision. Sensitive perception and venturesome imagination are equally important. Though this is a very demanding professional standard for curriculum decision making, we think many educators are capable of working in this way.

Egan (2002) clarifies this standard for curriculum work. He notes that "it is always easier and more attractive to engage in technical work under an accepted paradigm than do hard thinking about the value-saturated idea of education" (p. 181). To avoid this trap, Egan writes, educators must think very broadly and deeply; they must make their conceptions of education "more elaborate and comprehensive" (p. 181), and as part of their decision making, they must carefully consider what "is the best way to be human, the best way to live" (p. 182). Approaching curriculum work in this way requires educators' best efforts to enact practical wisdom.

Second, we will approach curriculum wisdom from a *love of wisdom* perspective—the frame of reference that serves as the etymological source for philosophy. To love wisdom is not the same as assuming that one is wise. In fact, it is its humble opposite. To love wisdom is to practice an open-hearted and open-minded life of inquiry. Hadot (2002) presents a Western history of the practice of the love of wisdom from Socrates through Kant and Nietzsche to the present and describes Socrates' insight into this practice:

> In the *Apology,* Plato reconstructs, in his own way, the speech which Socrates gave before his judges in the trial in which he was condemned to death. Plato tells how Chaerephon, one of Socrates' friends, had asked the Delphic oracle if there was anyone wiser (*sophos*) than Socrates. The oracle had replied that no one was wiser than Socrates. Socrates wondered what the oracle could possibly have meant, and began a long search among politicians, poets, and artisans—people…who possessed wisdom or know-how—in order to find someone wiser than he. He noticed that all these people thought they knew everything, whereas in fact they knew nothing. Socrates then concluded that if in fact he was the wisest person, it was because he did **not** think he knew that which he did not know. What the oracle meant, therefore, was that the wisest human being was "he who knows that he is worth nothing as far as knowledge is concerned." This is precisely the Platonic definition of the philosopher in the dialogue entitled the *Symposium:* the philosopher knows nothing, but he is conscious of his ignorance. (pp. 24–25) (author's emphasis)

The love of wisdom is "a never-ending quest" (Hadot, 2002, p. 280), and we provide guidance for this disciplined way of working through the introduction of seven modes of inquiry. There is a phrase that captures the design of this book. In an essay on the critical foundations of pedagogy, Greene (1986) writes, "To do philosophy with respect to teaching…is [in part] to stimulate reflections about the intentions in which teaching begins, the values that are espoused, the ends that are pursued" (p. 479). Greene envisions doing "philosophy with respect to teaching." This book alters this perspective in a subtle but important way. We envision doing curriculum in the spirit of philosophy.

To approach curriculum work in this spirit is very challenging, requiring "arts" that cannot be reduced to rules or procedures; we will consistently use the phrase *arts of inquiry* to refer to the practice of curriculum wisdom. Because Western insights into the love of wisdom trace back to ancient Greece, we will describe the seven modes of inquiry using both English and ancient Greek terminology. We do this to remind our readers that the arts of inquiry in this book, though applied to current, postmodern societies with democratic ideals, have a premodern heritage that traces back to Greece and other ancient civilizations.

This brings us to our third and final working assumption. We believe that an important, enduring focus for curriculum wisdom is the "democratic good life." When we use this phrase, we have in mind the exercise of responsible freedom in daily educational affairs. Our concern is with the quality of curriculum conduct, not with any particular form of government—though, of course, we don't want to deny the important relationship between curriculum and politics. This commits us to an interpretation of liberalism that is cogently summarized by Fleischacker (1999):

> Most Americans are liberals … as are, at least nominally, most people in democracies throughout the modern world. It has been plausibly argued that liberalism in the sense of a concern for liberty is the *only* appropriate mode of politics in the modern age. What marks modernity…is the loss of any substantial agreement about what constitutes the purpose of human life, and in that context it is essential that individuals have the liberty to explore that question, and pursue the answers they find on their own. (p. 3)

We believe educators should have the freedom or, more precisely, the professional liberty to responsibly pursue "democratically liberating" educational purposes. They do this by practicing an inquiry-based curriculum decision making focused on students' inquiry-based decision making; the seven inquiry modes in this book have been designed to encourage this teacher-student reciprocity.

Fleischacker provides philosophical and political insights into human freedom interpreted as responsible decision making, and these insights inform this curriculum text. Drawing on the work of Adam Smith and Immanuel Kant, he notes that a responsible decision requires a sophisticated judgment informed by a "free play of the faculties" (1999, p. 24). Human freedom is realized through the cultivation of this capacity for judgment:

> It may sound unexciting to announce that one wants to make the world free for good judgment, but this quiet doctrine turns out to be the most sensible, most decent, and at the same time richest concept of liberty we can possibly find.... A world where everyone can develop and use their own judgment as much as possible is closer to what we really want out of freedom.... (p. 243)

This understanding of freedom is a middle way between the libertarian right, with its focus on governmental noninterference and private choice, and the egalitarian left, with its focus on multicultural inclusiveness and community solidarity (Fleischacker, 1999, p. 267). This middle ground draws on both the "negative" and "positive" conceptions of freedom, nicely summarized by Fleischacker (1999):

> Berlin [1969] described two concepts of liberty: a negative one, by which I am free *from* constraint insofar as other people refrain from interfering with me, and a positive one, by which I am free to act insofar as I am included in the political units managing my environment. (p. 3) (author's emphasis)

Our focus is on the cultivation of responsible curriculum judgments centered on the facilitation of responsible student judgments. We believe that curriculum workers' professional freedom is bound up with students' personal freedom. Both educators and their students need to be included in informed curriculum decision making, but they should not be required to conform to any ideological script or agenda. Their inquiry capacities should be nurtured, without them being dictated to about how they should think. This delicate balancing act between active support and noninterference is the territory of "freedom" staked out by this book. We have created this book in a particular emancipatory, postideological spirit. Dewey (1963/1938) articulates this spirit: "The only freedom that is of enduring importance is freedom of intelligence, that is to say, freedom of observation and judgment exercised in behalf of purposes that are intrinsically worthwhile" (p. 61).

It is interesting to note that one of the defining characteristics of human wisdom—soundness of judgment in the choice of means and ends—is clearly operative in our middle position. Inquiry-based judgment is both the "means" for deciding how to educate for democratic living and its "end in view." The curricular means is integrally linked to the educational ends; or, in more colorful metaphorical terms, what is good for the goose (the curriculum worker) is also good for the gander (the student).

This understanding of the integrity between means and ends in education is, of course, a central principle in Dewey's writings. Doll (2002) notes that this principle is based on an "emergent," as distinct from an "externally imposed," sense of control (p. 39). Doll (2002) explains:

> External ends were anathema to Dewey. He felt that dichotomously separating the ends in activity from the activity itself reduced the activity (and the one doing the activity) to a mere means. To counteract this, he argued that ends or "aims fall within an activity instead of being furnished from without" (Dewey 1966/1916, p. 101). In his famous phrase on this point, he says (1974/1923):
>
> > Ends arise and function within action. They are not as current theories too often imply, things lying beyond activity at which the latter is directed. They are not strictly speaking ends or termini of action at all. They are terminals of deliberation, and so turning points *in* activity. (p. 70) (author's emphasis)
>
> Dewey calls these turning points in activity "ends-in-view." (p. 39)

The heart of this book is the practice of certain arts of curriculum inquiry, and this disciplined inquiry requires the internal, emergent orientation described by Dewey and Doll.

We can summarize our three working assumptions by describing a set of possible alternative titles for this text. If we had based our book only on the first assumption, we might have titled it *Curriculum Work as Practical Wisdom* or, perhaps, *Curriculum Work as Moral Deliberation* or, more simply, *Curriculum Deliberation*. If we had based our book only on the second assumption, we might have titled it *Curriculum Work as a Love of Wisdom* or, perhaps, *The Arts of Curriculum Inquiry* or, more simply, *Curriculum Inquiry*. If we had based our book only on the third assumption, we might have titled it *Curriculum Decision Making for Democratic Liberty* or, perhaps, *Curriculum Judgment for Student Freedom* or, more simply, *Curriculum Judgment*.

Because we are working with all three assumptions, we have titled the book the way we have. Keep in mind, however, that when we use the title *Curriculum Wisdom*, we have in mind a Socratic love for pragmatic wisdom in curriculum affairs; and when we use the subtitle *Educational Decisions in Democratic Societies*, we have in mind the exercise of professional and student freedom through the cultivation of responsible, inquiry-based judgment.

THE DESIGN OF THE BOOK

The text's design carefully reflects our three working assumptions. Curriculum wisdom is enacted at the intersection of theory and practice, and this book reflects this balanced approach. Chapters 1 and 2 have a more theoretical flavor. Chapter 1 makes the case for the importance of curriculum wisdom as understood in this text. Because this chapter presents the rationale for the text, it has a more conceptual emphasis and draws on a wide range of literature for its support. Chapter 2 provides a brief overview of the history of American pragmatism, which is a philosophical tradition that provides a great deal of insight into curriculum wisdom. Because Chapter 2 focuses on philosophical foundations, it also taps into a broad body of literature.

Chapter 3 is the heart of the book and it is positioned between theory and practice. As mentioned above, it presents seven modes of inquiry that serve as a guide for the practice of curriculum wisdom. Each mode is carefully defined (through the use of theoretical literature) and then illustrated in one or more specific curricular contexts. The arts of practicing these seven modes of inquiry are depicted in a holographic image that serves as the organizing concept for the chapter. This strategy is used to stress the point that the seven inquiry modes are embedded in one another. "All is one and one is all" might serve as an appropriate motto for Chapter 3. Curriculum wisdom is a holistic challenge, and though the seven modes are presented separately to simplify explanation and illustration, they are deeply and playfully connected in practice. Chapter 4 discusses the kinds of personal and institutional obstacles that can inhibit, suppress, and/or overtly prohibit the practice of the arts of inquiry described in Chapter 3.

The practice of curriculum wisdom is explored in Chapters 5–9. Chapter 5 presents three perspectives on the enactment of curriculum wisdom: as a paradigm shift, as a disciplined way of living, and as systemic reform. In Chapter 6, a classroom teacher, a teacher educator, and a public school superintendent comment on these perspectives. The classroom teacher's commentary is the longest because it provides the most in-depth analysis. The other two commentaries are deliberately shorter owing to space limitations and to avoid unnecessary redundancies. The teacher educator's commentary has an additional feature in that it is based on two years of research into the challenges of teaching the arts of inquiry described in Chapter 3 to future teachers.

Chapters 7 and 8 present four practitioner narratives. The stories in Chapter 7 are teacher narratives because a kindergarten teacher and a college teacher wrote them. Two educational administrators, a director of professional development and an elementary school principal, wrote the stories in Chapter 8. The narratives in Chapters 7 and 8 are a little different than the commentaries in Chapter 6. The practitioners in Chapter 6 were asked to directly address the central concepts of this book, while the practitioners in Chapters 7 and 8 were asked only to keep the concepts in mind as they told their story. The Chapter 6 commentaries were written to clarify and illustrate, while the narratives in Chapters 7 and 8 were written to extend and elaborate.

Chapter 9 presents three international commentaries on the feasibility of practicing curriculum wisdom in three distinctive cultural contexts: Australia, sub-Saharan Africa, and India. These commentaries are quite different from the three practitioner commentaries in Chapter 6. The three international commentaries help bring the subtitle of this book, *Educational Decisions in Democratic Societies,* into better focus. Though this book is co-authored by two American curriculum workers, many countries in the world are self-identified democracies and are, presumably, concerned about educating for enduring democratic values. We want to acknowledge, honor, and encourage this global aspiration.

OUR INTENDED AUDIENCE

We have in mind a general audience of curriculum workers composed of both university academics and practitioners in school and other educational settings. We envision these educators as open-minded professionals who are comfortable with an inquiring, postideological approach to curriculum decisions. We imagine them being "multitextual" in their orientation, as articulated by Pinar, Reynolds, Slattery, and Taubman (1995): "Curriculum is intensely historical, political, racial, gendered, phenomenological, autobiographical, aesthetic, theological, and international.... Curriculum is an extraordinarily complicated conversation" (pp. 847–848).

Given the audience we have in mind, we are careful to maintain a theory-practice balance; our topic (curriculum wisdom) requires such diligence. This is neither a theoretical book nor a practical book. It is both. If it had been one or the other, it would have been written differently. We therefore envision an audience that is concerned about the integration of theory and practice in the curriculum field.

This is certainly a curriculum theory book in the spirit of Walker's (2003) definition:

> Curriculum theories...are about ideals, values, and priorities. They employ reason and evidence, but in the service of passion. Curriculum theories can be analytical as well as partisan, but unlike scientific theories, they are not curriculum theories unless they are about ideals. Curriculum theories make ideals explicit, clarify them, work out their consequences for curriculum practice, compare them to other ideals, and justify or criticize them. (p. 60)

In this book we advance the *ideal* of the arts of curriculum inquiry; we passionately feel that if these arts were to be widely practiced, curriculum workers would be in a better position to ask, and even demand, that their educational decisions be trusted. A central theme in the history of curriculum work in the United States and other countries is the dominance of management strategies predicated on a direct or indirect distrust of educators' judgments. We are very critical of this history. We think this is a terrible error that must be corrected, *but only if* educators are willing to cultivate the necessary inquiry capacities to earn the public's trust.

This is also a curriculum practice book. We provide a glossary of theoretical terms, several schematics and illustrations, numerous examples, and seven practitioner commentaries and narratives. We want this book to be used by educators who want to improve the quality of their curriculum decisions. Our focus is on action, not on theoretical conversation. We are pragmatists to the core, and we firmly believe that the ultimate meaning of ideas is located in the consequences of enacting those ideas. Simply stated, we believe that actions speak louder than words.

Because the heart of this book is the practical guidance in Chapter 3, we conclude with an "Afterword" that focuses on getting started with the seven inquiry modes. What are good ways to develop these inquiry capacities? Who should be involved? How can curriculum workers support one another? How should such key terms in current educational literature as "standards," "accountability," and "empowerment" be interpreted in light of the arts of inquiry in this book?

TWO FOREWORDS

We have included two forewords to provide further insight into our purposes for writing this book. As stated earlier, we believe it is important to practice curriculum in the original spirit of philosophy, which, as we discussed, involves embracing a "love of wisdom." In this spirit, we asked Nel Noddings, a leading American educational philosopher, to provide a brief comment on the purpose of this text. Hers is the first foreword.

Because this book is an attempt to contribute to the curriculum studies literature, we asked leading curriculum scholar J. Dan Marshall to provide a historical context for understanding the text. Dr. Marshall is coauthor of *Turning Points in Curriculum: A Contemporary American Memoir* (Marshall, Sears, & Schubert, 2000) and is well qualified to situate this book in the tradition of American curriculum theory and practice. Because Dr. Marshall wrote his foreword after reading Dr. Noddings' foreword, he does not begin with the usual overview of the text, and his essay should be read as an extension of Dr. Noddings' commentary.

ACKNOWLEDGMENTS

Thanks to Linda Wolf, Mary Toepfer, Elizabeth Goldthwait, doctoral students at Kent State University, for their assistance with editing the manuscript.

We also want to thank the reviewers of this manuscript: Sue R. Abegglen, Culver-Stockton College; Karen Bosch, Virginia Wesleyan College; India Broyles, University of Southern Maine; Valerie J. Janesick, University of South Florida, Tampa; and Dan Marshall, Pennsylvania State University.

Our thanks to Mark Corsey and his nSight team for their excellent production and editing work and to Debbie Stollenwerk, our Merrill/Prentice Hall editor, for her many insights and steady support. We would also like to thank the many colleagues in the curriculum studies field who have offered useful comments during our conference presentations on various aspects of this book. We particularly have in mind our friends at the annual Curriculum and Pedagogy Conference.

With deepest gratitude to Janis McGowan and George and Jeanne Henderson for the inspiration and support to practice a love of wisdom.

References

Aristotle. (1941). Nicomachean ethics (W. D. Ross, Trans.). In R. McKeon (Ed.), *The basic works of Aristotle* (pp. 927–1112). New York: Random House.

Berlin, I. (1969). *Four essays on liberty.* Oxford, England: Oxford University Press.

Dewey, J. (1963). *Experience and education.* New York: Collier Books. (Original work published in 1938)

Dewey, J. (1966). *Democracy in education.* New York: Free Press. (Original work published in 1916)

Dewey, J. (1974). The nature of aims. In R. D. Archambault (Ed.), *John Dewey on education: Selected writings* (pp. 70–80). New York: Random House. (Original work published in 1923)

Doll, W. E., Jr. (2002). Ghosts in the curriculum. In W. E. Doll, Jr. & N. Gough (Eds.), *Curriculum visions* (pp. 23–70). New York: Peter Lang.

Egan, K. (2002). *Getting it wrong from the beginning: Our progressivist inheritance from Herbert Spencer, John Dewey, and Jean Piaget.* New Haven, CT: Yale University Press.

Fleischacker, S. (1999). *A third concept of freedom: Judgment and freedom in Kant and Adam Smith.* Princeton, NJ: Princeton University Press.

Greene, M. (1986). In search of critical pedagogy. *Harvard Educational Review, 56*(4), 427–441.

Hadot, P. (2002). *What is ancient philosophy?* (M. Chase, Trans.). Cambridge, MA: The Belknap Press of Harvard University Press.

Marshall, J. D., Sears, J. T., & Schubert, W. H. (2000). *Turning points in curriculum: A contemporary American memoir.* Upper Saddle River, NJ: Merrill/Prentice Hall.

Walker, D. F. (2003). *Fundamentals of curriculum: Passion and professionalism* (2nd ed.). Mahwah, NJ: Lawrence Erlbaum Associates.

Contributing Authors

The following contributing authors served as theoretical discussants, text commentators, and professional narrators. Their work enriches this book in many ways, and we wish to offer a special word of gratitude.

Theoretical Discussion (Chapter 4)
Rosemary Gornik

Text Commentary (Chapter 6)
Dana Keller
Richard Ambrose
Douglas Hiscox

Teacher Narratives (Chapter 7)
Sheri Leafgren
Thomas Kelly

Administrative Narratives (Chapter 8)
Michelle Thomas
Rebecca McElfresh

International Commentary (Chapter 9)
Ian Macpherson
Issaou Gado
Geeta Verma

Educator Learning Center: An Invaluable Online Resource

Merrill Education and the Association for Supervision and Curriculum Development (ASCD) invite you to take advantage of a new online resource, one that provides access to the top research and proven strategies associated with ASCD and Merrill—the Educator Learning Center. At **www.EducatorLearningCenter.com** you will find resources that will enhance your students' understanding of course topics and of current educational issues, in addition to being invaluable for further research.

How the Educator Learning Center will help your students become better teachers

With the combined resources of Merrill Education and ASCD, you and your students will find a wealth of tools and materials to better prepare them for the classroom.

Research

- More than 600 articles from the ASCD journal *Educational Leadership* discuss everyday issues faced by practicing teachers.
- A direct link on the site to Research Navigator™ gives students access to many of the leading education journals, as well as extensive content detailing the research process.
- Excerpts from Merrill Education texts give your students insights on important topics of instructional methods, diverse populations, assessment, classroom management, technology, and refining classroom practice.

Classroom Practice

- Hundreds of lesson plans and teaching strategies are categorized by content area and age range.
- Case studies and classroom video footage provide virtual field experience for student reflection.
- Computer simulations and other electronic tools keep your students abreast of today's classrooms and current technologies.

Look into the value of Educator Learning Center yourself

Preview the value of this educational environment by visiting **www.EducatorLearningCenter.com** and clicking on "Demo." For a free 4-month subscription to the Educator Learning Center in conjunction with this text, simply contact your Merrill/Prentice Hall sales representative.

Brief Contents

Contents

Chapter 1

Curriculum Wisdom in Democratic Societies

THE QUALITY OF CURRICULUM JUDGMENTS

The quality of education in the United States and many other democratic societies is a regular topic in newspapers, magazines, and books and on radio and television talk shows. American national polls continually rank education as a vital, pressing social concern; in response to these polls, American politicians generally work hard to be publicly perceived as "pro-education" leaders. Over the past hundred years the United States has spent billions of dollars on the improvement of education, yet many Americans report that they are not satisfied with the results of these reform efforts. What should Americans and citizens in other countries that share similar historical circumstances do? Though there is no simple answer to this complex question, one response to the problem of educational reform is to work on improving the quality of curriculum judgments; this will be the approach taken by this book. **This text has been created to encourage and facilitate wise curriculum decision making in societies with democratic ideals**.

Why is the quality of curriculum judgments so central to education reform? The answer to this question can be found in the etymology of the term *curriculum*. *Curriculum* comes from the Latin *currere*, which literally means "the course to be run" (Eisner, 1994, p. 25). The implication of this Latin phrase is that the educational course that the student will run will be good for him or her. It will energize, galvanize, and provoke growth. Doll (2000) explains, "Curriculum is…a coursing, as in an electric current. The curriculum should tap this intense current within, that which courses through the inner person, that which electrifies or gives life to a person's energy source" (p. xii).

Extending this etymological insight, curriculum work in societies with democratic ideals can be defined as decision making focusing on **envisioning** and **enacting** a good educational journey for **all** students. Educators must be inclusive and they must be generous. They must embrace a loving ethic, which is the philosophy that "everyone has the right to be free, to live fully and well" (hooks, 2000, p. 87). This curriculum work requires the practice of sophisticated professional judgments. Let's think further why this is so.

The process of envisioning a good educational journey for **all** students requires both disciplined searching and caring imagination. The curriculum worker must consciously inquire into the quality of educational experiences in a comprehensive, penetrating, and farsighted way. Gough (2002) writes, "When we generate visions of curriculum futures…[we] call on a wide variety of…resources" (p. 15). Curriculum envisioning involves both personal soul searching and discerning social criticism. It is an affirmation of hope and aspiration: "curriculum [visioning] testifies to the strength of the human spirit to dream and realize imagined possibilities through intentionality; it advocates the use of mind to…map out and traverse paths to the 'land of promise'" (Quinn, 2002, p. 239). The American philosopher John Dewey (1935) provides a vivid description of such a challenging, multi-intelligent undertaking:

> What will it profit a man [or woman] to do this, that, and the other specific thing, if he has no clear idea of why he is doing them, no clear idea of the way they bear upon actual conditions and of the end to be reached? The most specific thing that educators can first do is something general. The first need is to become aware of the kind of world in which we live; to survey its forces; to see the opposition in forces that are contending for mastery; to make up one's mind which of these forces come from a past that the world in its potential powers has outlived and which are indicative of a better and happier future. (p. 7)

The process of enacting an envisioned educational journey is equally challenging. Courage, integrity, and a long-term perspective are central to visionary enactment. It takes boldness, bravery, and a deep sense of responsibility to translate our visions into action. Gough (2002) makes the point that envisioning without "embodiment," which is his term for enactment, results in a superficial "lip-service to abstractions":

> Without the particularities and specificities of location and embodiment, prospective vision in curriculum inquiry is wishful thinking. …If curriculum visions are to be generative—that is, if we are to be in a position to negotiate visions of curriculum futures worth working for—we must accept that we stand at the center of our own histories and fields of visualization as responsible, engaged, embodied actors…. (p. 5)

During curriculum enactment we must stick our necks out in a high-minded, determined, and consistent way. We must act with integrity. We must operate out of a deep sense of conscience, principle, and honor; and we must work hard to translate our educational visions into creatively designed programs, meaningful student learning experiences, and authentic forms of assessment. Kesson and Oliver (2002) write, "Enactment requires deep personal involvement and participation…. Enactment is a critical integrative force…because it compresses qualities of experience… into a single unitary apprehension of the whole" (pp. 188, 195).

Curriculum enactment is necessarily grounded in a humble, pragmatic openness. Perhaps our vision of the good journey is mistaken and even if it is not, our imaginative exercises will undoubtedly require midcourse corrections as we honestly proceed with our journey. Our enacting thus inevitably feeds back into our envisioning, and vice versa. It is a never-ending cycle of educational effort. As curriculum workers, we must learn to position ourselves in the space between the processes of envisioning and enacting; this positioning places an enormous challenge on our capacities to exercise good judgment. Again, Dewey (1920/1982) provides an insightful description of this professional challenge:

Let us, however, follow the pragmatic rule, and in order to discover the meaning of the idea ask for its **consequences**. Then it surprisingly turns out that the primary significance of the unique and morally ultimate character of the concrete situation is to transfer the weight and burden of **morality to intelligence**. It does not destroy responsibility; it only locates it. A moral situation is one in which **judgment and choice** are required.... There are conflicting desires and alternative apparent goods. What is needed is to find the right course of action, the right good. (p. 182, emphasis added)

Let's consider what Dewey is saying. When we make curriculum decisions, we must think broadly about the consequences of our actions, which requires a very sophisticated intelligence. Therefore, we must develop our intellectual capacities as completely as we possibly can. In fact, as educators, we are morally bound to cultivate our intellects because our educational decisions must be directed toward courses of action with long-term implications. While doctors are engaged in critical life and death decisions, educators make critical choices about leading a good life. At its best, our curriculum practices are informed by a broad, visionary educational agenda. To work in this way is to engage in a professional art that requires our best judgment.

A RATIONALE FOR THE BOOK'S APPROACH TO REFORM

Before turning to a more in-depth examination of the nature of curriculum judgments, a consideration of the rationale for this approach to educational reform should help you understand this text. Though this book's topic possesses many complexities and nuances, its justification is actually quite straightforward. Sirotnik (2002) defends the importance of elevating professional judgments in education. He begins by distinguishing between responsibility and accountability: "Responsibility certainly includes accountability but, also, according to the dictionary, includes the more layered qualities of being 'able to make moral or rational decisions,' being 'trustworthy or dependable or reliable,' and 'showing good judgment.' (p. 665). Sirotnik is arguing that responsible educators assume the challenge of making informed, publicly defensible judgments, which is precisely the focus of this book.

Why is this a good way to go about the business of improving education? This is, actually, a simple question to answer but difficult to practice. **Curriculum matters cannot be handled through simple technical procedures; they require sophisticated professional judgment**. This is a basic working principle for all complex human endeavors. Sirotnik (2002) writes, "No modern organization would ever use a lone indicator to judge the worth of its operation.... No sensible hospital director would mandate more frequent temperature-taking to cure patients..." (p. 665). Hagstrom (2000) makes a similar point about investment decision making. Specialized knowledge and simplistic business models are too narrow a foundation for good judgments. Therefore, financial advisors must base their decisions on a broad "latticework of understanding."

To return to curriculum decision making, using standardized tests as the basis for professional judgments is too limited. It is, simply, not good educational policy or practice. There is nothing wrong with collecting information about students' educational progress through test scores; in fact, it could be helpful. However, the collection of this information doesn't go far enough. It's not the end of the story. Educators must still make wise curriculum judgments, and this is where this book enters the picture. Coulter and Wiens (2002) write, "There is no more important educational question, however, than how we foster educational judgment in students, teachers, and researchers. How do we learn to exercise our freedom understood as responsibility?" (p. 23). This question serves as the organizing theme of this book.

To summarize our discussion so far, good curriculum judgment demands multidimensional, long-term problem solving. The focus is on envisioning and enacting a good life. Because of the lifelong consequences of their educational activities, educators must cultivate a wide-ranging intellect. Sirotnik (2002) provides a concise description of this long-term thinking, and his questions are an excellent point of departure for this text:

> A responsible accountability system will include many forms of assessment that tap directly into the actual performances that students are expected to demonstrate, especially performances that take place in classrooms. Such performances include reading, writing, speaking, problem solving, experimenting, inquiring, creating, persisting, deliberating, collaborating—abilities that many of today's leaders in both the public and the private sectors say they wish were exhibited more strongly by the people they employ. Moreover, what goes on after school is equally important, including what happens to students after they graduate from high school. Do they become decent people, good parents, good community members? Do they participate constructively in civic deliberation and democratic practice? Are they economically productive citizens? Have they continued to learn in the many ways that are possible to continue learning and growing as human beings? (p. 666)

INTRODUCING THE CURRICULUM WISDOM CONCEPT

When curriculum work is understood as an exercise in human judgment, the question of **wisdom** becomes personally and professionally relevant.[1] Wisdom is defined in the *Oxford English Dictionary* as "the capacity of judging rightly in matters relating to life and conduct; soundness of judgment in the choice of means and ends; sometimes, less strictly, sound sense, especially in practical affairs." **Wisdom is a lofty yet worldly term, denoting a soulful and holistic practical artistry directed toward personal and social goods.** The concept **curriculum wisdom** will be used in this book as a concise way to convey the subtle and complex challenges of approaching curriculum work as envisioning and enacting a good educational journey. Jardine (1997) provides poetic insight into this interpretation:

> ...It is not accumulated curricular knowledge that we most deeply offer our children in educating them. It is not...their mastery of requisite skills or their grade-point average, but literally their ability to live, their ability to be on an Earth that will sustain their lives. ...[Curriculum] is concerned with the knowledge—perhaps we must say the wisdom, even if we find such notions vaguely embarrassing, antiquated, unrigorous, or unclear—that we must pass onto our children so that life on Earth can go on. (pp. 216–217)

---

[1]There is a wide range of definitions of curriculum in the literature, and important examples of these different perspectives will be discussed in the section Acknowledging Other Curriculum Interpretations.

The concept of curriculum wisdom evokes ancient and esoteric traditions of human knowing. Wisdom is an elusive concept (Robinson, 1990). When we think of wise people, we think of sages, philosophers, healers, and mystics—people above the turmoil and complexity of everyday life who possess special, even extraordinary, powers of conception. When we speak of wisdom, we often speak of "wisdom traditions." Most wisdom traditions are grounded in a religious worldview. Scriptures of these traditions contain time-tested moral templates with guidelines on how to live a good life. They often include instructions on how to cultivate the soul in accordance with divine law. For many Christians, wisdom is found in the Ten Commandments as well as in the stories and parables of the New Testament. These instructions, available to all, compose an exoteric, or outward, wisdom tradition.

Some wisdom traditions focus less on providing rules and regulations and more on cultivating a state of mind that is receptive to inner wisdom, or the truth of the spirit. These more inward-focused traditions are considered esoteric traditions and they often contain elements of mystery and initiation into deeper and subtler truths. The Taoist tradition, with its emphasis on discovering the internal "Way" of truth, reflects this nondoctrinaire approach to wisdom:

> When the Way is lost,
>   afterward comes integrity.
> When integrity is lost,
>   afterward comes humaneness.
> When humaneness is lost,
>   afterward comes righteousness.
> When righteousness is lost,
>   afterward comes etiquette. (Lin, 2002, p. 4)

Etiquette here might be thought of as formulae—explicit instructions for living a good life—whereas the "Way" exemplifies the opposite, a deeply felt sense of what is right and what is wrong in specific situations. These two ends of the continuum represent what could be described as "inner" and "outer" approaches to morality. The above sutra from the Tao Te Ching suggests that if we distance ourselves from a more organic and intuitive moral wisdom, we can become too literal and external. Our consciousness can be caught in the letter and not the spirit of the matter.

All wisdom traditions, while they may share kernels of universal truth, reflect the culture they emerged from, embodying the norms and frameworks specific to particular languages, histories, geographies, and customs. The Confucian wisdom tradition, for example, codifies a complex set of kinship relations and patterns of behavior, including behavior toward ancestors. Many indigenous, or tribal, wisdom traditions encode the principle of reciprocity (behavior that mutually benefits all species as well as past and future generations.) You may have heard a reference to the "seven generations" principle—a Native American mandate to assess all actions in terms of their long-term impact on generations to come. This wisdom is usually encoded in stories and rituals that renew the relationships of reciprocity. These are just two examples of wisdom traditions that are rooted in specific cultural contexts.

There are nonreligious wisdom traditions as well. Hermeneutics is a method of truth seeking with roots in early Greek philosophy. In this tradition the god Hermes,

mediator between the gods and mortals, is the archetype for the interpretive movement back and forth between whole and part, metaphoric and literal, spirit and matter.
Hermeneutics, as Smith (1999) says, is the "act of interpreting our lives and the world
around us" (p. 27). It is the art of practical wisdom. In the act of hermeneutics ideas are
analyzed for historical context, differing interpretations are weighed, and analysis shifts
from the big picture to the details and back again as hermeneutic scholars seek the truth
of situations.

In the world of education we seldom talk about wisdom. Of course we talk about knowledge. Knowledge is at the center of the educational project. Increasingly, politicians and policy makers are using more instrumental language when they talk about what teachers and
educational leaders should know: They want educational decisions to be "data driven" and
for teachers and educational leaders to utilize research-based information. The image here is
one of gathering bite-sized facts, especially "scientifically proven" facts, and bringing them
to bear on curriculum decisions. The information or data used to develop curricular plans and
policies is not necessarily generated in specific situations, but at a distance, far removed from
the particular concerns of students, teachers, and local communities. Often missing from this
picture are the more qualitative dimensions of educational judgments: values, aesthetics, justice, and meaning, to name just a few. Thinking in these more expansive terms would require
that we ask different kinds of questions, aside from the instrumental "what works?": Does
this educational decision benefit all people equally, especially those who have been marginalized in the past? What kind of good life does this curriculum policy envision? Does this
curriculum plan add to the beauty, the richness, and the harmony of a community's life? Will
this decision foster generosity, compassion, and benevolence? What will be the effect of this
decision seven generations from now? What does our community really care about? What is
worth doing? How can we create a better world?

These kinds of questions are very complicated, and they involve difficult, value-laden
conversations. Perhaps this is why we seldom ask them, choosing instead to focus on sim-
pler questions of procedure: How can I design a curriculum that meets state guidelines for
what students should know in the fourth grade? How can I align my assessments with the
standardized tests? How can I create a classroom management system that reduces discipline problems?

Asking deeper and more meaningful educational questions and facilitating public discussions around these questions is a challenging task. If we, as educators and curriculum
workers, are to be successful at this task, we will have to develop our own professional
wisdom tradition. This is important, because all curriculum decisions are, at their heart,
moral decisions. They touch the core of what it means to be human, to live in a community with others, to find meaning and purpose, and to create a more just and peaceful world.
To meet these moral challenges, we will need to become morally wise, which will be neither easy nor unproblematic. Moral wisdom is not something that you get and then have. It
is not a thing, but a process; not static, but dynamic; not a technique, but a way of living.
There are no fixed templates, with rights and wrongs laid out for us to follow. There are no
definitive models. There is only, in the words of Pinar, Reynolds, Slattery and Taubman
(1995), "an extraordinarily complicated conversation" (p. 848) that must be engaged in
meeting the curriculum wisdom challenge.

STAYING FOCUSED ON ENVISIONING AND ENACTING

The concept of *curriculum wisdom* is further clarified by briefly considering three general ways that curriculum workers can lose sight of this professional challenge. First, curriculum workers who operate from a traditional frame of reference may lose sight of the envisioning side of their decisions. They may view the contemplation of the good life, with its related critique of contemporary life, as the prerogative and responsibility of authoritative others. These curriculum workers may see their job as the enactment of the received knowledge of a particular moral heritage, and their decisions may be constrained by specific literal and/or fundamentalist interpretations of this tradition (Sears, 1998). In effect, their work is not characterized by a vital envisioning-enacting dialectic. This type of curriculum work can be found in highly authoritarian and dogmatic educational settings.

Curriculum workers who operate from a modern frame of reference may also lose sight of the envisioning side of their decisions, but in a different way. Because our European heritage of modern rationality is based on the separation of church and state and the primacy of precise rational methods (Borgmann, 1992), educators who work from this perspective may unnecessarily separate their reasoning from their intuition, imagination, and emotion (Thayer-Bacon, 2000). As a consequence of becoming too easily encapsulated by a particular rational system, their envisioning efforts may be limited or nonexistent. They become constrained by the need for a methodical, businesslike efficiency. Because their work lacks a compelling moral depth, they may not be able to clearly articulate or publicly defend why they do what they do. They may too easily succumb to the latest educational fads or they may simply present themselves as mere cogs in the bureaucratic machine. The only justification for their actions is that they are simply responding to what the system requires. Much like their traditionalist counterparts, their work is not embedded in a vital envisioning-enacting dynamic. Their work is characterized by a moral superficiality and/or a technical-procedural rigidity. Ironically, what they perceive as the implementation of rational policies may actually be highly irrational in terms of establishing a meaningful educational journey for their students (Eisner, 1994). This type of curriculum work can be found in educational settings that are preoccupied with the implementation of standardized learning performance and assessment systems.

Finally, curriculum workers who operate from a postmodern frame of reference may unnecessarily constrain their envisioning or they may either de-emphasize or entirely overlook the enactment of their critical visions. In either case, they lose sight of the curriculum wisdom challenge. Though there is an enormous diversity of projects that are self-identified as postmodern in focus and intent (Rosenau, 1992), the common ground in all of this work is skepticism about the modern, rational European heritage (Lyotard, 1984). This skeptical positioning can be articulated through a wide range of critical questions on such topics as Western rationalism, sexism, racism, colonialism, social class privilege, homophobia, and so on.

Curriculum workers who base their efforts on one or more postmodern projects may, consciously or unconsciously, delimit their vision of the good life. They become so focused on their particular critical concern that they lose sight of the big picture. They are clear about what they are against, and their critical clarity can be quite penetrating and significant; however, from a wisdom point of view, it would be fair to ask them, What is the good life that you envision? What are your enduring values? What is your sense of good conduct? Fay (1987) argues that a mature critical theory "is a vision of life, and it is only when this vision is made manifest and analyzed that the merits and demerits of the theory can be fully recognized" (p. 1).

Furthermore, these critical curriculum theorists may not sufficiently consider the practical consequences of their critical theories (Wraga, 1999). They do not make the pragmatic turn and properly deliberate over the consequences of enacting their emancipatory ideas in specific educational contexts containing unique, emergent contingencies (Cherryholmes, 1999). As a result, their professional endeavors may lack practical efficacy and adaptability. Walker (2003) notes that "curriculum issues are too many-sided for any single theory to cover… [and] theories may never completely capture all the relevant features of the individual case that we must consider when we make wise curriculum decisions" (p. 214). Thus, curriculum work that is preoccupied with advancing a particular critical theory can too readily result in rigid, narrow, and doctrinaire actions.

CURRICULUM WISDOM AS PROBLEM SOLVING

Curriculum wisdom is identified with a particular kind of educational decision making. It can be described as a "doubled" problem solving. There is, first, the effort to be practical—to solve the immediate problem or problems one is facing. This is a context-specific and fairly straightforward means/end way of operating: Admit there is a problem, work on defining the problem, decide how to solve the problem, work on the solution, and periodically evaluate the results of your actions (Dewey 1910/1933; Grimmett, 1988.)

To undertake the wisdom challenge is to situate this decision making at a deeper level. The focus is still on solving an immediate problem—after all, the concept of wisdom denotes such practicality—but now an effort is made to solve the problem with reference to one's understanding of good conduct, one's conception of a good life. This is a more complicated means/end and means/visionary end way of operating that is based on a particular moral position. At this deeper level, the problem solving becomes infused with critical and imaginative insights. The search for a practical resolution is transformed into the aspiration to advance a critically informed moral vision.

Kekes (1995) provides an insightful analysis of the doubled nature of curriculum wisdom:

> Moral wisdom is thus a "capacity" to judge, but the mere capacity is not sufficient because the judgment needs to be "right," "sound," or "just." …The object of sound judgment in moral wisdom is to evaluate what is true or right from the perspective of life as a whole. …What should I do in this concrete situation, given my overall view of what a good life should be? This question incorporates a double "should." (pp. 4–5)

Curriculum wisdom thus occurs in settings where educational decisions are made with reference to encouraging, facilitating, and cultivating the enduring values of a moral way of living, and this book has been created with this "deep" decision making in mind. To use a geographic metaphor, curriculum wisdom is situated at the confluence of practical, critical, and visionary inquiries, as depicted in Figure 1.1.

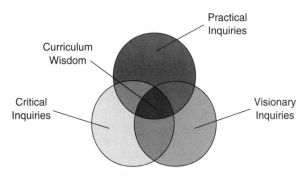

FIGURE 1.1

Situating Curriculum Wisdom

UNDERSTANDING DEMOCRATIC MORALITY

The curriculum wisdom advice in this book is based on a particular moral sensibility. Imagine curriculum workers engaging in a continuous educational envisioning and enacting from the point of view of democracy as a moral way of living. On the eve of World War II—at a very dramatic point in the contest of human civilizations—79-year-old John Dewey (1939/1989), possessing a wealth of life experience, gave voice to this moral sensibility:

> The democratic road is the hard one to take. It is the road which places the greatest burden of responsibility upon the greatest number of human beings. Backsets and deviations occur and will continue to occur. But that which is its own weakness at particular times is its strength in the long course of human history. Just because the cause of democratic freedom is the cause of the fullest possible realization of human potentialities, the latter when they are suppressed and opposed will in time rebel and demand an opportunity for manifestation. We have advanced far enough to say that democracy is a way of life. **We have yet to realize that it is a way of personal life and one which provides a moral standard for personal conduct**. (pp. 100–101, emphasis added)

The practice of curriculum wisdom, as understood in this book, occurs in educational settings where democratic moral wisdom is viewed as a viable professional challenge. These are places where nurturing democratic conduct is the goal of the educational decision making. In such places teachers and other curriculum stakeholders (students, parents, community leaders, and so on) attempt to "walk the talk" of their democratic values. They want their judgments to be testaments to their faith in the democratic way of life.

Democracy is typically understood as a way of government. To approach democracy as a way of life—or as Dewey puts it "a moral standard for personal conduct"—is to extend a democratic outlook to one's daily living. Democracy now becomes a moral referent for good living. It becomes the basis for a wisdom challenge, requiring a sophisticated form of understanding. There is no ultimate definition for "democratic morality"—no final democratic doctrine. At best, there are only informed interpretations, and the interpreter must acknowledge and work with the ambiguity and plurality inherent in his or her search for the "democratic good life."

Tracy (1987) provides insight into this way of working. He argues that moral understanding in the context of religious diversity is best handled as a "plurality of interpretations and methods" (p. 112). He explains,

> We find ourselves with diverse religious classics among many religious traditions. ...The conflicts on how to interpret religion, the conflicts caused by the opposing claims of the religions themselves, and the internal conflicts within any great religion all affect interpreters, whether they will it or not. None of these conflicts is easily resolved, and no claim to certainty, whether religionist or secularist, should pretend otherwise. ...Einstein once remarked that with the arrival of the atomic age everything had changed except our thinking. Unfortunately the remark is true. Perhaps contemporary reflections on interpretation, with their emphasis on plurality and ambiguity, are one more stumbling start, across the disciplines, to try to change our usual ways of thinking. (pp. 112–114)

Interpretations of democratic morality begin at the point where plurality and ambiguity are embraced; otherwise, the resulting understanding cannot be democratic. When religious morality is interpreted in the spirit of plurality and ambiguity, it informs the democratic good life. However, when religious morality is reduced to rigid doctrines and ideological litmus tests (i.e., "true beliefs"), a democratic way of life can only be practiced by carefully separating church and state.

The fact that religious morality can inform democratic morality should not be surprising since the wellspring for both is the call to love. This, of course, is amply clear in religious traditions, but it may not be as clear with respect to democratic morality, which, historically, has no discernible tradition. There is no bible for democracy, no "Koran" for the democratic way of life. There is certainly a wealth of democratic literature tracing back to ancient Greek times, but there is no rich narrative heritage on how democratic ideals are experienced on a daily basis. Dewey's own life makes this point dramatically. The cornerstone for his philosophical arguments was his conception of "experience." Near the end of his life, he realized that, given his underlying sense of democratic morality, he was referring to culture when he argued for experience. Jackson (2002) explains,

> Dewey's choice of the word *culture* to replace *experience* rested on what he had come to understand.... What Dewey found to be attractive about the notion of experience in the first place was its breadth of coverage.... [He was] openly committed to the goal of social betterment through the continued criticism of ongoing social practices and cultural traditions. (pp. 52–54) (author's emphasis)

This "breadth of coverage," which lies at the heart of democratic morality, is the affirmation of a generative and generous life. To be generative is to embrace the love of human growth. According to Dewey (1932/1985), a generative educational experience allows for the continuous "development and fulfillment of self, while [its contrast]...stunts and starves selfhood by cutting it off from the connections necessary to its growth" (p. 302). In a poetic evocation of Dewey's philosophy of continuous growth, Garrison (1997) writes, "Those who are in love with life desire to grow. Those who love to grow, love and care for others, and let others care for them. That is the paradoxical logic of expansive growth. Only the truly tough-minded dare embrace this paradoxical truth" (p. 52). hooks (2000) writes that true love is "a resonance between two people who respond to the essential beauty of each other's individual natures, behind their facades, and who connect on a deeper level" (p. 182). In educational work this love is enacted in teaching-learning relationships.

Teachers realize the beauty of their professional selves by facilitating the unique beauty of their students' selves. Generativity is, thus, manifested through creativity. Garrison (1997) writes, "Growth means the continued creation and creative unification of meanings and values. Evil is the decay of those values that sustain life and growth. Growth is the all-inclusive and supreme value because artistic creation…is the most magnificent activity of the living creature" (p. 49).

To be generous is to be sensitive to, and tolerant of, others' beliefs, styles, and circumstances. Meier (1997) provides an eloquent account of this human virtue:

> Well-developed empathy makes it hard to feel untouched by the misery of others; it enables us to hear their voices inside our own head and to understand their explanations and their "side" of the story. …Empathy subtly broadens our capacity for imagination; our natural childish playfulness is expanded, not obliterated. Good literature, great drama, and powerful art of every kind—all these help a person to develop empathy. Such is the purpose of a good education for democracy. (p. 63)

In her philosophical essay *The Dialectic of Freedom*, Maxine Greene (1988) provides insight into the nature of the generative and generous intellect. She argues that people who develop themselves in this way reject "oppression or exploitation or segregation or neglect" while engaging in authentic creative activities with others (p. 9). Her book is, ultimately, a celebration of such life-affirming individuals: "Looking back, we can discern individuals in their we-relations with others, inserting themselves in the world by means of projects, embarking on new beginnings in spaces they open themselves. We can recall them…opening spaces where freedom is the mainspring, where people create themselves by acting in concert" (p. 134).

When teachers invite their students to study topics of oppression, exploitation, segregation, and neglect, they are encouraging their students to use their intellectual powers in generative and generous ways. They are teaching for democratic living. In parallel fashion, when teachers invite their students to collaborate on creative and meaningful learning projects, they are also encouraging their students to use their intellectual powers in generative and generous ways. They are also teaching for democratic living.

CURRICULUM WISDOM AS AUTHENTIC ENACTMENT

Macpherson, Aspland, Brooker, and Elliott (1999) provide a useful way to understand curriculum wisdom. They introduce the related notions of the "place" and "space" of curriculum decision making. Their notion of place refers to specific locations in classrooms, schools, communities, and other settings where curriculum decisions are made, and they argue that teachers should have a prominent role at these sites. They believe that teachers should have the opportunity to work as curriculum decision makers. Teachers should enact their own decisions, not implement others' decisions. As Snyder, Bolin, and Zumwalt (1992) note, the term *implementation* connotes the image of top-down reform—teachers and their students being asked to implement a prescribed change agenda. The idea of enactment, however, conveys a sense of responsible power sharing: "From the enactment perspective, curriculum is viewed as the educational experiences jointly created by student and teacher. The externally created curricular materials…are seen as tools for students and teacher to use as they construct the enacted experience in the classroom (Snyder et al., 1992, p. 418).

The practice of curriculum wisdom requires a place for enactment, and to assert this is to make a social and political point that will be explored in more detail in Chapter 4. Macpherson et al.'s (1999) notion of space is more psychological and developmental in orientation. It refers to "authentic participation in curriculum decision-making in those places" (Macpherson et al., 1999, p. 2). It is one thing to be invited to participate in curriculum decision making; it is another thing to authentically engage in this process in a responsible manner. This latter consideration will also be explored in more detail in Chapter 4.

To set the scene for this further analysis of the place and space of curriculum wisdom—the politics and psychology of curriculum decision-making—we invite you to consider 5C's of wise curriculum judgments: collaboration, caring, character, challenge, and calling.

Collaboration

There is much to consider when problem solving from the perspective of the democratic good life. Because democracy is an interpretive term—because it has many meanings that are not anchored in any specific moral doctrine—the decision-making process must necessarily be multifaceted. Problem solvers must be playfully light on their feet. They must approach their deliberations in the spirit of Pinar et al.'s (1995) multidimensional curriculum "conversation." Schwab (1978) describes this as the practice of an "eclectic artistry" in curriculum work, which allows for "the serial utilization or even the conjoint utilization of two or more theories on practical problems" (p. 297).

Because there are many theories about the democratic good life, it is best to approach this problem solving in a spirit of collaborative inquiry. There is too much for one person to consider, too much for one person to know. Simply stated, the best way of proceeding is to be democratic about democratic morality. William James, an American philosopher and contemporary of John Dewey, thought a great deal about the democratic good life. In 1899, he published *Talks to Teachers*, in which he argued for a pluralistic approach to educational work: "The truth is too great for any one actual mind, even though that mind be dubbed "the Absolute," to know the whole of it. …There is no point of view absolutely…universal" (James, 1899/1958, p. 19). In democratic decision making no one person has the final say; everyone has a voice. Garrison (2002) captures the spirit of this problem-solving approach by distinguishing between monism and pluralism in educational work:

> The pluralist does not think there is anywhere to stand outside the flux of events to obtain an indubitable perspective; hers is the participant, not the spectator, view of existence. The pluralist thinks that monism is dogmatism. There are always other valuable ways to interpret and connect things and events. (p. 30)

As Alexander (1995) notes, "Democracy cannot merely 'tolerate' diversity; it alone of all forms of civilization *requires* diversity…. There is an initial need to *encounter difference meaningfully*" (pp. 75–76, emphasis in original). Thayer-Bacon (2000) uses the image of a quilting bee to describe this open-minded and open-hearted embrace of diverse perspectives: "A quilting bee metaphor for…thinking reminds us that people construct knowledge, that knowledge is not found out there in the world or inside of ourselves. The quilting bee stands for our social communities and thus helps to highlight the social context within which each of us is embedded" (p. 145).

There is a very basic way to understand democratic decision making. The means used to solve the problem is organically related to the visionary end: The democratic good life is enacted during the decision-making process. The curriculum workers "walk" their moral "talk" during the judgment process.

Caring

To practice this type of collaborative problem solving is a very caring way of working. Noddings (1984) describes educators working as caring professionals who confirm their students' "best selves" through the practice of a cooperative, sensitive dialogue:

> When we attribute the best possible motive consonant with reality to the cared-for, we confirm him; that is, we reveal to him an attainable image of himself that is lovelier than manifested in his present acts. ...Confirmation, the loveliest of human functions, depends upon and interacts with dialogue and practice. I cannot confirm a child unless I talk with him and engage in cooperative practice with him. (pp. 193, 196)

Educating for the democratic good life is all about practicing this ethic of care. It is a loving way of living that celebrates the possibilities of actualizing individual dreams of excellence in an inclusive and synergistic spirit. The democratic union, perhaps, finds its most elegant realization in the respectful interactions between authentically engaged individuals. Greene (1988) celebrates this possibility in educational work: "This is what we shall look for as we move: freedom developed by human beings who have acted to make a space for themselves in the presence of others.... We want to discover how to open spaces for persons in the plurality, spaces where they can become different, where they can grow" (p. 56).

Character

Curriculum wisdom is a personally demanding professional norm. It requires one to be openly self-critical. As Kekes (1995) notes, Socrates felt that moral wisdom was the "greatest" of the human virtues. He explains,

> A just and honorable life is lived according to virtue, and Socrates recognizes five virtues required by such a life: temperance, courage, piety, justice, and...moral wisdom. He held that these virtues are related to each other more intimately than parts are related to a whole, ...although "wisdom is the greatest of the parts." [Plato, 1961, p. 329], ... because no action can be virtuous unless it is based on the knowledge moral wisdom gives. (pp. 32, 37)

The practice of democratic moral wisdom requires a soul-searching honesty. Are my decisions congruent with my beliefs? Do my judgments embody the democratic good life? Am I truly open to diverse others? Do I listen carefully to people with whom I disagree, and am I willing to dialogue with them or, at least, to "agree to disagree"? Am I willing to challenge social policies and institutions that I feel are undemocratic? As an educator, am I committed to facilitating a meaningful educational journey for each of my students? Am I concerned about their personal dreams of excellence? Am I comfortable with the inherent pluralism and idiosyncrasies of the democratic good life?

These are the kinds of personal questions that are essential to the practice of curriculum wisdom as advocated in this book.

Challenge

Because democratic curriculum wisdom is such a multifaceted, pluralistic, personally involving, and personally demanding way of working, it is an enormous professional challenge. It must be treated as an inquiry journey, not a destination. It would be most unwise to attribute wisdom to oneself or to another. Such self-centeredness is a sign that a particular educational worker has not authentically entered the practice of curriculum wisdom. Too much self-regard indicates "self-deception, the desire to present ourselves in a favorable light, and lack of self-knowledge" (Kekes, 1995, p. 13). Such limitations in human consciousness stand in vivid contrast to wisdom as a virtue.

Finally, there is the matter of context and contingency in attributing wisdom to either oneself or another (Cherryholmes, 1999). What might be a wise judgment at one moment in one setting may not be wise at another moment in that setting, let alone in another setting. A good-life orientation requires a supple judgment. Curriculum wisdom is an exercise in human artistry. Schwab (1978) describes this way of working as engaging in the "arts" of the practical:

> The particularities of each practical problem can be sought in the practical situation itself.... The methods by which these ends might be achieved, have, however, a complication of their own. Although they can be described and exemplified, they cannot be reduced to generally applicable rules. Rather, in each instance of their application, they must be modified and adjusted to the case at hand. Because of this complication, I call them *arts*. (p. 323) (author's emphasis)

Curriculum wisdom is also challenging because it requires a disciplined life of inquiry that has no end. Simply stated, curriculum wisdom is cultivated ignorance. It requires what Cherryholmes (1999) characterizes as the disposition of fallibility: "[We realize that] we can be mistaken...about the desirability of our aesthetic tastes, knowledge of the world, and trustworthiness of social and political institutions" (p. 40). We choose to live with "doubt on our shoulders." Concerning this commitment to disciplined inquiry, Davidson (1998) writes,

> Wisdom is knowing how little you know. Ignorance is the beginning of wisdom, Socrates cautioned us. Zen practitioners call it "beginner's mind," which is truly open and fresh, willing to remain innocent and receptive to life, not attached to our knowledge. It is the willingness to be empty, and thus open to learning and growing. This is the source of creativity and innovation, the key to continuous improvement.... (pp. 36–37)

Over two thousand years ago, Socrates worked out a way to practice this cultivated ignorance. It is an open-ended method of questioning that has three stages. The first stage is to question our potential "foolishness" as unwitting followers of cultural patterns and scripts. Kekes (1995) explains,

We are born into a society, and as we grow up we imbibe its conventions and customs, its notions of the good, and its ideals of a good life. To take these for granted is foolish. We have not bothered then to find out whether the conventional notions of the good by which we allow ourselves to be guided are indeed good. (p. 39)

The second stage of the Socratic inquiry method is to move from one's "ignorance of one's ignorance" to a disciplined life of questioning. Now that you know that you are ignorant of the good life, you begin to actively seek out—to construct—your understanding of the good life. You become a "lover of wisdom," which of course, is the etymological source for the word *philosophy*. You take Dewey's advice as quoted near the beginning of this chapter. You "become aware of the kind of world in which we live...survey its forces...see the opposition in forces that are contending for mastery...[and] make up...[your] mind which of these forces come from a past that the world in its potential powers has outlived and which are indicative of a better and happier future" (Dewey, 1935, p. 7).

The third stage of the Socratic method is to practice self-insight—to take on the personal challenge of acquiring the virtue of wisdom. You understand the search for wisdom as a matter of character building, as the cultivation of a virtuous life. Kekes (1995) explains, "The search for moral wisdom, therefore, leads inward; knowledge of the good turns out to be self-knowledge; and the key to a good life is the examination of our own life in which moral wisdom...frees us from internal obstacles to living as we should" (p. 41).

Curriculum wisdom is such an all-embracing professional standard that it is as much a matter of degree as it is a matter of "moment." As Kekes (1995) writes, "The possession of moral wisdom is a matter of degree: more of it makes lives better, and less makes them worse" (p. 1). Like any other human virtue, we may have our good days and our bad days. There may be times when we are more authentically engaged in the democratic wisdom challenge, and there may be moments, or even days, weeks, or months, when we miss the mark. At these times we may have little interest in collaborative inquiry, the ethic of caring, or character building. We may feel too overwhelmed by life, too disconnected from others, too stressed, or too caught up in the rush to judgment.

For these reasons, wisdom is a fragile enterprise. It can easily be lost in the daily pressures and busyness of life. It can too quickly disappear from view. To stay the course of curriculum wisdom is a never-ending venture in the arts of inquiry. Though there is no final destination in our wisdom journey, there is a deep joy that we are, indeed, moving in the right direction—that our path is good. And this, of course, is the etymological source of the Latin word *curriculum*. Whether it's recognized or not, a particular curriculum is not only a specific course of study; it is, at least in a small way, a generative and generous course of life. To envision and enact the democratic good life is to be deliberate about the philosophical direction of our educational actions. It is to think deeply about the long-term consequences of our professional decisions. To take on the curriculum wisdom challenge is to affirm our capacities to create meaning. Though we may not be complete masters of our fate, we can seek a life of vision and purpose.

Calling

Because democratic curriculum wisdom is such a personally and politically challenging matter, it is helpful to think of this type of curriculum practice as a professional calling. Van Manen (1991) provides an insightful account of education as a vocational calling, which he compares to the joys and responsibilities of parenting:

> How does a woman become a mother? A man a father? How does a person become a teacher? …Initially one may only "know" oneself to be a parent or a teacher in a biologi-cal or legal sense. …What makes a person a parent or a teacher is largely a matter of living and existing as a parent or teacher. In actually living with children, in its many small expe-riences, the awareness of oneself as a parent or teacher comes into being. …[It is] impor-tant to realize that our lives with children will only be pedagogically meaningful when we feel animated or inspired by education as a calling. (pp. 24–25)

Van Manen is describing a deep-seated developmental process. What may, at first, be perceived as a professional role and legal responsibility hopefully grows, over time, into something that is much more profound, more personally compelling, and more artful. What may begin as ordinary becomes inspired. Cooper (1994) writes, "The sacred call enters our heart's secret cavity, evoking an awareness that eclipses our normal daily expe-rience, attuning us to a new level of appreciation" (p. 9). This movement from the normal to the sacred is clearly captured in the *Oxford English Dictionary's* definition of *calling* as both an "ordinary occupation, means by which livelihood is earned, business, trade" and a "state of grace and obedience…; duty." This dual meaning of a professional calling is also reflected in the doubled nature of wise problem solving, as discussed earlier in this chapter.

To tackle the wisdom challenge is to make decisions on the basis of one's quest for the good life. Levoy (1997) explains, "Calls are essentially questions. …You want a question that will become a chariot to carry you across the breadth of your life, a question that will offer you a lifetime of pondering, that will lead you toward what you need to know for your integrity, draw to you what you need for your journey…" (pp. 6–7). An educational calling is an inquiry-based way of living. The teacher-as-examiner-of-students lives in a continu-ous state of professional self-examination: How do we learn together? How can we make the most of this educational moment? How is my growth entwined in your growth? What is compelling about our growth? Does our educational journey possess enduring value? How does our teaching-learning relationship stand the test of time?

Finally, to approach any professional work as a vocation means one works out of a deep sense of duty to others, and the *Oxford English Dictionary* also captures this sense of calling by describing it as a compelling sense of "service." Van Manen (1991) writes, "The pedagogical calling is that which calls, summons us to listen to the child's needs" (p. 25). As educators called to a democratic way of living, we strive to confirm the democratic needs of each of our students. We practice Noddings' (1984) "ethic of care" as applied to the moral imperatives of democracy. We recognize that curriculum work begins with the professionals but culminates with the students' learning experiences. At the heart of an ed-ucational calling, and at the heart of the professional guidance in this book, is the recogni-tion of this teaching-learning reciprocity.

A Teacher Reflects on Curriculum Wisdom

A middle school teacher was asked to reflect on the idea and ideal of curriculum wisdom.[2] This is what he wrote:

The pilgrimage to the curriculum wisdom space is complex and personal and is sought for within a complex matrix of social contexts. Further, this pilgrimage, especially in democratic societies, cannot occur outside the boundaries of a personal wisdom space—a search for a deep understanding of self, others, democracy, democratic citizenship, and how they relate to education. In other words, if a teacher is to teach from the curriculum wisdom space, he or she must understand the lives, values, beliefs, customs, governmental complexities, and economic structures and their impact on the culture of the people who form the relationships that nurture education. To teach wisely a teacher must live wisely. In the search for the wisdom space, a teacher must become a student of the world and a serious critic of self.

To explore this further, I define myself in many ways, focusing on my roles as a democratic citizen, husband, father, and teacher. These are, for me, overlapping parts of the same whole or gestalt. I take time daily to evaluate my performance in each part, evaluating if I am indeed acting in a wise manner. For example, if my wife tells me I am not being helpful enough around the house or if my principal tells me I get too worked up in meetings and become unhelpful, I need to evaluate if I am living up to my enduring values and consider making adjustments.

Certainly, this way of living leads to perpetual personal and professional inquiry. Much of this development, for me, comes with deep self-inquiry but also deep inquiry about the nature of learning, the nature of education, the dynamics of the district in which I work, and the community in which my district functions (from the city up to the nation). I ask questions such as "What skills should I be teaching my students, given the nature of the environments in which they live, community expectations, expectations for democratic citizens, etc.? What classroom environment should I create to facilitate the development of those goals?"

This substantial study, careful evaluation, and progressive change—especially when they motivate and inform better living and teaching—become the wisdom challenge, and the goal is to transform a course of study into "instances" of democratic living. Davis (2001) writes, "The full measure of a culture embraces both the actions of its people and the quality of their aspirations. ...What matters is the potency of [their] belief and the manner in which [their] conviction plays out in the day to day life of its people" (p. 52). If this is true, and if a culture is to be truly great, each of its members must make a conscientious study of the driving values of the group and the self. This level of self-inquiry places particular responsibility upon those whose lives are dedicated to the development of the culture's citizens. If teachers carefully create a link between quality aspirations and day-to-day actions, what would life in their classrooms be like?

Should we be satisfied to measure student learning with standardized tests? Even if these tests do accurately measure certain knowledge and skills, what is the value of that knowledge and those skills in an authentic setting like work or the democratic life in general? In other words, do good test scores correlate in any way to the pursuit of the American Dream, either for the individual or our entire culture? Why is the government such a proponent of testing and for whose gain?

(continued)

[2]Reflection written by Dana Keller.

Must a class of students all read the same book? Must all students read on the same schedule? Must all performances be evaluated in the same way? Must the teacher determine reading pace, the vocabulary to be studied, the questions to be considered, the nature of projects, and the points that call for in-depth study?

Once I began questioning my teaching self just a little, it quickly became apparent that there was no end; the questions have a life of their own. In other words, the questions are already out there. Do I have it within me to seek answers?

I am in no way advocating that teachers abandon control or leadership in their classrooms. Teachers certainly have vast knowledge to impart and many skills to teach students. But how that knowledge is imparted, how it becomes valuable to each student's life, and how an environment is crafted that allows for the pluralistic development of solid citizens are challenging questions.

To accept the wisdom challenge, teachers need to accept that their work is progressive and "ecologically" connected. Interestingly, this may go against a notion we have about veteran teachers. A veteran in any field should know well what he or she is doing. This implies stability and the ability to work a bit less hard because he or she already has the game figured out. I would argue that in a work environment that encourages wise curriculum decision making, the exact opposite is true. The veteran would be the teacher who has accepted and adapted and even nurtured the evolutionary nature of education. He or she assumes a deep professional responsibility for curriculum decisions.

I can well imagine a place of curriculum wisdom. It is a changeable, adaptive, sensitive, purposeful location. It is a territory of inquiry. We all know people who reside in this place—at least at moments in their lives—and we are comforted and accepted in their presence. Such people have a feel for the big picture, and every little part of them is connected to it. They exhibit virtue, enterprise, and honor. And when such people are teachers, they are educators in the most elevated and sacred sense of the word.

A PREVIEW OF THE REMAINING CHAPTERS

Now that you have been introduced to the concept of curriculum wisdom, we turn to a brief preview of the remaining chapters. As you undoubtedly noted from the broad use of quotations in this chapter, the rationale for this text's interpretation of curriculum is drawn from a wide range of literature. Because this book is designed to provide practical guidance on curriculum inquiry, we will not be pursuing this foundational literature in any detail. However, we do make one exception. We feel that the tradition of American pragmatism provides important insights into the nature of democratic moral wisdom; in fact, John Dewey, who is a central figure in this tradition, has already been extensively quoted in this chapter. Therefore, Chapter 2 is a synopsis of American pragmatism.

We recognize that American pragmatism is a type of "local knowledge" with its own idiosyncrasies. Gough (2003) writes,

Until relatively recently in human history, the social activities through which distinctive forms of knowledge are produced have for the most part been localized. The knowledges generated by these activities thus bear what Sandra Harding (1994) calls the idiosyncratic "cultural fingerprints" (p. 304) of the times and places in which they were constructed. (p. 59)

Gough makes this point to alert curriculum workers to the problem of "cultural imperialism" when they assume that their knowledge is universal. We do not want to make this mistake, particularly given the fact that respect for pluralism is a central feature of the democratic good life. As indicated in this book's subtitle, *Educational Decisions in Democratic Societies,* our focus is on the practice of curriculum wisdom in diverse societies with democratic ideals. Any local, foundational source of knowledge, which informs an understanding of wise democratic decision making, is a welcome addition.

Chapter 3 is the central chapter of this book. Curriculum wisdom requires the practice of arts of inquiry. Chapter 3 introduces seven modes of inquiry that facilitate democratic decision making and provides a "map" of the place and space of curriculum wisdom. It stakes out the territory of curriculum envisioning and enacting for societies with democratic ideals.[3]

In Chapter 4 we turn to a consideration of the obstacles educators can be expected to confront when undertaking the curriculum wisdom challenge. Given its focus on arts of inquiry, this book can be described as assuming a grass roots or inside-out perspective on educational reform. The reform effort begins with teachers and other curriculum stakeholders who feel called to curriculum wisdom. If a sufficient number of these curriculum workers—a critical mass—emerge in a particular institutional setting, they may be able to politically confront and address the more deeply embedded structural constraints they face. For example, they may find a way to carve out sufficient work time for the necessary collaborative inquiry. Chapter 4 is organized in accordance with this approach to educational reform. We will first discuss the personal and interpersonal challenges of practicing curriculum wisdom and then turn to an analysis of institutional and cultural obstacles.

The implications of practicing curriculum wisdom are the focus of Chapter 5. We will examine the enactment of democratic decision making from three points of view: as a paradigm shift, as a disciplined way of living, and as systemic reform. This latter discussion will highlight the close relationship between curriculum development, professional development, organization development and community development. In Chapter 6 three educators will comment on the practice of curriculum wisdom. These professionals—a public school teacher, a teacher educator, and a public school superintendent—represent key curriculum stakeholders in the educational community; collectively, they provide important perspectives on the practice of curriculum wisdom. Chapters 7 and 8 present four personalized narratives on the application of curriculum wisdom as both a concept and a professional calling. A teacher and a teacher educator tell two teaching stories in Chapter 7, and a central administrator and a principal tell two administrative stories in Chapter 8. These four narratives provide you with a further opportunity to assess the value of practicing curriculum wisdom.

---

[3]As a historical aside, Peter Ramus, a professor of philosophy at the University of Paris, was probably the first person to use the Latin term *curriculum* in a publication (Hamilton, 1990). In 1576 he published a series of logical maps of philosophical knowledge, which he collectively called a "curriculum" for university students. Though Ramus' maps were limited to what he termed "dialectical reasoning" and were highly structured, it is interesting to note that he conceptualized curriculum as a philosophical journey. Unlike Ramus' logical maps, the inquiry artistry map in Chapter 3 incorporates a wide range of intellectual capacities and allows for more flexible case-by-case adaptations appropriate for professional judgments. Ramus' maps were designed to facilitate logical reasoning, while the map in Chapter 3 is designed to support the art of curriculum wisdom.

In Chapter 9 three international educators comment on the feasibility of practicing curriculum wisdom in their cultural contexts. We end this book with a brief Afterword on the future of curriculum wisdom. Can an increasing number of educators undertake the challenge of wise curriculum decision making? Will they receive the necessary social and political support? We don't know the answers to such questions, but we are hopeful. There is an underlying democratic spirit in the affairs of humankind and in the long course of history, democracy as a moral basis of living is making slow, gradual inroads. We are heartened by the many educators we know who are attuned to this spirit.

ACKNOWLEDGING OTHER CURRICULUM INTERPRETATIONS

This book's understanding of curriculum draws on the work of a group of influential curriculum scholars, and we want to acknowledge our indebtedness to these individuals. Without their insights into the theory and practice of curriculum, this book could not have been created. We fully acknowledge that we are standing on their shoulders.

We begin our thanks with Ralph Tyler's (1949) highly influential curriculum decision-making "rationale," which is in effect, a problem-solving approach linking educational purposes, learning experiences, instructional organization, and learning evaluation. Tyler argues that curriculum workers should systematically ask themselves four questions:

1. What educational purposes should the school seek to attain?
2. How can learning experiences be selected that are likely to be useful in attaining these objectives?
3. How can learning experiences be organized for effective instruction?
4. How can the effectiveness of learning experiences be evaluated?

Tyler provides insight into curriculum decision making, but unfortunately, his still very dominant rationale is too limited for the purposes of this book. His book does not address the relationship between democracy and education in any moral or ethical depth, and it is too easily adapted to system-wide implementation strategies that can inhibit or constrain the enactment of curriculum wisdom.

Joseph Schwab's (1978) analysis of the "eclectic arts" of curriculum work has already been cited in this chapter. His scholarship provides insight into the subtle nuances of practicing curriculum judgments. Michael Connelly and Jean Clandinin (1988) extend Schwab's essays by stressing the centrality of teachers' personal-practical knowing in curriculum affairs. Their approach highlights the deeply personal and situational nature of curriculum work. They write, "We believe that curriculum development and curriculum planning are fundamentally questions of teacher thinking and teacher doing. We believe that it is teachers' 'personal knowledge' that determines all matters of significance relative to the planned conduct of classrooms. So 'personal knowledge' is the key term" (p. 4).

We are indebted to Elliot Eisner's (1994) work on the nature and value of imagination in curriculum:

> Curriculum development is the process of transforming images and aspirations about education into programs that will effectively realize the visions that initiated the process.

...Much of what we value, aspire to, and cherish is ineffable; even if we wanted to, we could not adequately describe it. ...Our images of virtue are in flux; because images can never be translated wholly into discourse, to that degree they are always somewhat beyond the grasp of written or verbal expression. (p. 126)

Eisner's further clarification of imaginative practice as an exercise in educational connoisseurship and criticism also provides insight into curriculum wisdom as a professional way of life—a topic we will be exploring in more detail in Chapter 5.

The scholarship of Jim Macdonald and David Purpel (1987) shares many similarities with Eisner's work. Their writings provide insight to the envisioning-enacting dialectic in curriculum work:

We have argued that any model of curriculum planning is rooted in a cluster of visions—a vision of humanity, of the universe, of human potential, and of our relationship to the cosmos. ...What is of the most extraordinary import, of course, is which particular vision we decide to choose, for the choosing of a vision allows us to become that vision. (p. 192)

Edmund Short's (1991) analysis of curriculum work as diversified inquiry informs Chapter 3. He writes, "All fields of practical inquiry, including curriculum inquiry, are in reality composite fields. Several domains of inquiry exist side-by-side within such a field of inquiry, each focusing on a different aspect of the practical activity toward which inquiry may be addressed..." (p. 6). While Short (1991) identifies and describes 17 loosely connected forms of curriculum inquiry, Chapter 3 is organized around 7 integrated modes of curriculum inquiry.

Pinar et al. (1995) present a sophisticated multifaceted understanding of curriculum work as "intensely historical, political, racial, gendered, phenomenological, autobiographical, aesthetic, theological, and international...[as] an extraordinarily complicated conversation" (pp. 847–848). Their work informs the organization of this book and, in particular, our discussions in Chapters 1 and 3. Their "conversational" metaphor is applied to curriculum development by Slattery (1995), who presents "a vision of the postmodern curriculum that is radically eclectic...and ultimately, a...search for greater understanding that motivates and satisfies us on the journey" (p. 267). We are indebted to Slattery's sophisticated, multilayered understanding of curriculum. He helps us appreciate the importance of approaching curriculum work through multiple inquiry lenses.

Though all of the interpretations of curriculum work we have just cited inform this book, none of them incorporates **all** of the components of curriculum wisdom that have been presented in this introductory chapter. You are being introduced to an understanding of curriculum that emerges out of a critical analysis of the strengths and limitations of influential publications in the field. This book assumes a particular position on curriculum work that contrasts with other positions. That this is the case should not be surprising, given the interpretive nature of the curriculum field.

CONCLUSION: A FAITH IN EDUCATORS

We welcome you to the personal and professional journey of this book. You have been introduced to the concept of curriculum wisdom that serves as the focus for this text. We recognize that this concept is also a professional calling, so we hope you will find this text to be personally meaningful and inspiring. Our concern is with a curriculum artistry that we initially described as democratic envisioning and enacting. We feel this artistry could, over time, become a significant professional norm because we have a deep faith in the creative and critical capacities of educators. As an expression of our faith, we end this chapter with an excerpt from John Dewey's *My Pedagogic Creed*. His words celebrate the dignity of teachers and the importance of educating for the democratic good life:

> The community's duty to education is…its paramount moral duty. …Through education, society can formulate its own purposes, can organize its own means and resources, and thus shape itself with definiteness and economy in the direction it wishes to move. …Education thus conceived marks the most perfect and intimate union of science and art conceivable in human experience. The art of thus giving shape to human powers and adapting them to social service is the supreme art, one calling into its service the best of artists; that no insight, sympathy, tact, executive power, is too great for such a service. The teacher is engaged, not simply in the training of individuals, but in the formation of the proper social life. Every teacher should realize the dignity of his [or her] calling; that he [or she] is a social servant set apart for the maintenance of proper social order and the securing of the right social growth. (Dewey, 1897/1997, p. 23)

References

Alexander, T. (1995). Educating the democratic heart: Pluralism, traditions and the humanities. In J. Garrison (Ed.), *The new scholarship on Dewey* (pp. 75–92). Boston: Kluwer Academic.

Borgmann, A. (1992). *Crossing the postmodern divide*. Chicago: University of Chicago Press.

Cherryholmes, C. H. (1999). *Reading pragmatism*. New York: Teachers College Press.

Connelly, F. M., & Clandinin, D. J. (1988). *Teachers as curriculum planners: Narratives of experience*. New York: Teachers College Press.

Cooper, D. A. (1994). Invitation to the soul. *Parabola, 19*(1), 6–11.

Coulter, D., & Wiens, J. R. (2002). Educational judgment: Linking the actor and the spectator. *Educational Researcher, 31*(4), 15–25.

Davidson, L. (1998). *Wisdom at work: The awakening of consciousness in the workplace*. Burdett, NY: Larson.

Davis, W. (2001). *Light at the edge of the world, a journey through the realm of vanishing cultures*. Washington DC: National Geographic Society.

Dewey, J. (1933). *How we think: A restatement of the relation of reflective thinking to the educative process* (2nd ed.). Boston: D. C. Heath. (Original work published 1910)

Dewey, J. (1935). The teacher and his world. *The Social Frontier, 1*(4), 7.

Dewey, J. (1982). Reconstruction in philosophy. In J. A. Boydston (Ed.), *The middle works of John Dewey, 1899–1924* (Vol. 12). Carbondale, IL: Southern Illinois University Press. (Original work published 1920)

Dewey, J. (1985). Ethics. In J. A. Boydston (Ed.), *The later works of John Dewey, 1925–1953* (Vol. 7). Carbondale, IL: Southern Illinois University Press. (Original work published 1932)

Dewey, J. (1989). *Freedom and culture*. Buffalo, NY: Prometheus. (Original work published 1939)

Dewey, J. (1997). My pedagogic creed. In D. J. Flinders and S. J. Thornton (Eds.), *The curriculum studies reader* (pp. 17–23). New York: Routledge. (Original work published 1897)

Doll, M. A. (2000). *Like letters in running water: A mythopoetics of curriculum*. Mahwah, NJ: Lawrence Erlbaum Associates.

Eisner, E. W. (1994). *The educational imagination: On the design and evaluation of school programs* (3rd ed.). Upper Saddle River, NJ: Prentice Hall/Simon and Schuster.

Fay, B. (1987). *Critical social science*. Ithaca, NY: Cornell University Press.

Garrison, J. (1997). *Dewey and eros: Wisdom and desire in the art of teaching*. New York: Teachers College Press.

Garrison, J. (2002). James's metaphysical pluralism, spirituality, and overcoming blindness to diversity in education. In J. Garrison, R. Podeschi, and E. Bredo (Eds.), *William James & education* (pp. 27–41). New York: Teachers College Press.

Gough, N. (2002). Voicing curriculum visions. In W. E. Doll, Jr. & N. Gough (Eds.), *Curriculum visions* (pp. 1–22). New York: Peter Lang.

Gough, N. (2003). Thinking globally in environmental education: Implications for internationalizing curriculum inquiry. In W. F. Pinar (Ed.), *International handbook of curriculum research* (pp. 53–72). Mahwah, NJ: Lawrence Erlbaum Associates.

Greene, M. (1988). *The dialectic of freedom*. New York: Teachers College Press.

Grimmett, P. P. (1988). The nature of reflection and Schon's conception in perspective. In P. P. Grimmett & G. L. Erickson (Eds.), *Reflection in teacher education* (pp. 5–15). New York: Teachers College Press.

Hagstrom, R. G. (2000). *Latticework: The new investing*. New York: Texere.

Hamilton, D. (1990). *Curriculum history*. Geelong, Australia: Deakin University Press.

Harding, S. (1994). Is science multicultural? Challenges, resources, opportunities, uncertainties. *Configuration: A Journal of Literature, Science, and Technology, 2*(2), 301–330.

hooks, b. (2000). *All about love: New visions*. New York: William Morrow.

Jackson, P. W. (2002). *John Dewey and the philosopher's task*. New York: Teachers College Press.

James, W. (1958). *Talks to teachers on psychology: And to students on some of life's ideals*. New York: W. W. Norton. (Original work published 1899)

Jardine, D. W. (1997). "To dwell with a boundless heart": On the integrated curriculum and the recovery of the earth. In D. J. Flinders & S. J. Thornton (Eds.), *The curriculum studies reader* (pp. 213–223). New York: Routledge.

Kekes, J. (1995). *Moral wisdom and good lives*. Ithaca, NY: Cornell University Press.

Kesson, K, & Oliver, D. (2002). On the need for a reconceptualized theory of experience. In W. E. Doll, Jr. & N. Gough (Eds.), *Curriculum visions* (pp. 185–197). New York: Peter Lang.

Levoy, G. (1997). *Callings: finding and following an authentic life*. New York: Three Rivers Press.

Lin, Yi. (2002). Ancient systems thinking in China and its application in Chinese life. Retrieved August 31, 2002, from http://www.newciv.org/ISSS_Primer/asem02yl.html

Lyotard, J-F. (1984). *The postmodern condition: a report on knowledge* (G. Bennington & B. Massouri, Trans.). Minneapolis: University of Minnesota Press.

Macdonald, J. B., & Purpel, D. E. (1987). Curriculum and planning: Visions and metaphors. *Journal of Curriculum and Supervision, 2*(2), 178–192.

Macpherson, I., Aspland, T., Brooker, R., and Elliott, B. (1999). *Places and spaces for teachers in curriculum leadership*. Deakin: Australia Curriculum Studies Association.

Meier, D. (1997). Habits of mind: Democratic values and the creation of effective learning communities. In B. S. Kogan (Ed.), *Common schools, uncommon futures: A working consensus for school renewal* (pp. 60–73). New York: Teachers College Press.

Noddings, N. (1984). *Caring: A feminine approach to ethics and moral education*. Berkeley: University of California Press.

Pinar, W. F., Reynolds, W. M., Slattery, P., & Taubman, P. M. (1995). *Understanding curriculum: An introduction to the study of historical and contemporary curriculum discourses*. New York: Peter Lang.

Plato. (1961). *Protagoras*. In E. Hamilton & H. Cairns, (Eds.), *Plato: The collected dialogues*. Princeton, NJ: Princeton University Press.

Quinn, M. (2002). Holy vision, wholly vision-ing: Curriculum and the legacy of the chariot. In W. E. Doll, Jr. & N. Gough (Eds.), *Curriculum visions* (pp. 232–244). New York: Peter Lang.

Robinson, D. N. (1990). Wisdom through the ages. In R. J. Sternberg (Ed.), *Wisdom: Its nature, origins, and development* (pp. 13–24). New York: Cambridge University Press.

Rosenau, P. M. (1992). *Post-modernism and the social sciences: Insights, inroads, and intrusions*. Princeton, NJ: Princeton University Press.

Schwab, J. J. (1978). *Science, curriculum, and liberal education: Selected essays* (I. Westbury & N. J. Wilkof, Eds.). Chicago: University of Chicago Press.

Sears, J. T. (1998). Crossing boundaries and becoming the other: Voices across borders. In J. T. Sears

(Ed.), *Curriculum, religion, and public education: conversations for an enlarging public square* (pp. 36–58). New York: Teachers College Press.

Short, E. (Ed.). (1991). *Forms of Curriculum Inquiry.* Albany: State University of New York Press.

Sirotnik, K. A. (2002). Promoting responsible accountability in schools and education. *Phi Delta Kappan, 83*(9), 662–673.

Slattery, P. (1995). *Curriculum development in the postmodern era.* New York: Garland.

Smith, D. G. (1999). *Pedagon: Interdisciplinary essays in the human sciences, pedagogy, and culture.* New York: Peter Lang.

Snyder, J., Bolin, F., & Zumwalt, K. (1992). Curriculum implementation. In P. W. Jackson (Ed.), *Handbook of research on curriculum* (pp. 402–435). New York: Macmillan.

Thayer-Bacon, B. J. (2000). *Transforming critical thinking: Thinking constructively.* New York: Teachers College Press.

Tracy, D. (1987). *Plurality and ambiguity: Hermeneutics, religion, hope.* San Francisco: Harper & Row.

Tyler, R. W. (1949). *Basic principles of curriculum and instruction.* Chicago: University of Chicago Press.

van Manen, M. (1991). *The tact of teaching: The meaning of pedagogical thoughtfulness.* Albany: State University of New York Press.

Walker, D. F. (2003). *Fundamentals of curriculum: Passion and professionalism* (2nd ed.). Mahwah, NJ: Lawrence Erlbaum Associates.

Wraga, W. G. (1999). "Extracting sun-beams out of cucumbers": The retreat from practice in reconceptualized curriculum studies. *Educational Researcher, 28*(1), 4–13.

Chapter 2

Pragmatism: A Philosophy for Democratic Educators

INTRODUCTION

In these early years of a new millennium, it is clearer than ever that we need an education organized around the principles and practices of democracy. Faced with great uncertainty about our future, our political system faces some tests as we grapple with external threats such as the terrorist bombings of September 2001 and the resultant economic instability and domestic dissent over foreign policy and the moral direction of our country. We like to think that our political system is unshakable; indeed, it has weathered a civil war without undergoing a change in its basic structure and function, a multitude of other large and small wars in the intervening century, and cycles of economic depression and recession. But it is sometimes easy to forget that the world's first constitutional democracy, barely 200 years old, is still, in the larger scheme of things, an experiment and, therefore, fragile.

Many theorists of democracy point to a current "crisis of democracy" (Trend, 1996). It is important to recognize and understand the challenges that confront our democratic way of life if we are to become "democratically wise" in the way we are proposing. It is also important to acknowledge the signs of hope that tell us that this grand experiment that was birthed on our soil will flourish in the new century. These signs of hope include a revitalization of communities as well as of civil society. They include citizen mobilization around important issues such as food safety, foreign policy, and the globalization of the economy. Another sign of hope can be found in the new direction in democratic theory that furthers Thomas Jefferson's contention that the solution for the problems of democracy is more democracy. We will look at both the challenges to democracy and at some signs of hope in this chapter.

First, however, we will take a brief historical journey and explore the uniquely American philosophy that has provided an important intellectual foundation for the

Portions of this chapter appeared previously in "Democratic Education and the Creation of the Loving and Just Community" (Kesson, Koliba, & Paxton), in *Creativity and Collaborative Learning* (Thousand, Villa, & Nevin [2002]). Baltimore: Paul H. Brookes.

development of democratic theory and practice in the United States and, to some extent, in other modern industrial countries. Significantly for educators, it has also provided the foundation for an understanding of the complex relationship between democracy and education. This philosophy is called American pragmatism. John Dewey (1859–1952) is perhaps the most influential American pragmatist, a point brought home by the current international resurgence of interest in his ideas. His hundreds of books and articles furnish us with a comprehensive set of ideas about how people learn, how they think, the nature of experience, and how to educate students for active participation in democratic life. Teachers, whether they have studied Dewey or not, are teaching in accord with his ideas when they practice inquiry-based learning, school/community projects, whole language, or cooperative learning. In this section we will touch briefly on the contributions of Dewey and other early pragmatists to our evolving understanding of democratic living. We will also look at some of the contemporary criticisms of pragmatism and think about ways that a revitalized, reconceptualized pragmatism can deepen our understanding of the arts of democratic inquiry.

Pragmatists would applaud this rethinking of their ideas; pragmatism is a fluid and evolving philosophy, not a rigid, formulaic way of thinking. It is uniquely designed to respond to an ever-changing and uncertain world. It is future oriented and looks to results, offering as Cleo Cherryholmes suggests, "a discourse that attempts to bridge where we are with where we might end up" (1999, p. 3). It thus provides a philosophical scaffold for what critical theorists have termed a "language of possibility" (Giroux, 1991, p. 52) or a "pedagogy of hope" (Freire, 1995). Unlike some postmodern philosophies, it is not relativist (a point of view that suggests that any one set of ideas is as good, or as useful, or as true as another). Instead, it offers a normative framework—a set of ideas and commitments and practices around which to develop a moral approach to democratic living. However, it is a normative framework that is unusually accommodating to differences in time, place, and circumstance.

PRAGMATISM AND THE PRAGMATISTS

This uniquely American philosophical tradition, with roots in the nineteenth century, is, according to Cornell West, "an attempt to reinvigorate our moribund academic life, our lethargic political life, our decadent cultural life, and our chaotic personal lives for the flowering of many-sided personalities and the flourishing of more democracy and freedom" (1989, p. 4). There are three reasons, according to West, for the renascence of pragmatism at this moment in our cultural history:

1. Widespread disenchantment with the traditional role of philosophy as the bastion of "disembodied reason" and thought divorced from action in the world.
2. Scholarly preoccupation with the relationships between forms of knowledge, power, and social control.
3. Emphasis on human agency in the face of constraints based on race, class, gender, and sexual orientation.

The appeal of pragmatism in relation to the above conditions is its distinctly moral emphasis and its impulse to change the world in the direction of more social equality, social justice, creativity, participation, and human freedom. As West so eloquently states, "In this world-weary period of pervasive cynicisms, nihilisms, terrorisms, and possible extermination, there is a longing for norms and values that can make a difference, a yearning for principled resistance and struggle that can change our desperate plight" (1989, p. 4). West regards American pragmatism as "a component of a new and novel form of indigenous American oppositional thought and action" that "may be a first step toward fundamental change and transformation in America and the world" (p. 8).

Who were these early philosophers and what were some of their moral commitments? West himself, a noted contemporary public intellectual, was profoundly influenced by Ralph Waldo Emerson, a forerunner of the better known pragmatists such as Charles Peirce, William James, and John Dewey. We usually associate Emerson with the mid-nineteenth century literary scene and with that group of social and intellectual reformers called the Transcendentalists. He was actually friends with the father of William James and was said to have "blessed the infant William in his cradle" (Menand, 2001, p. 82). West places Emerson at the very roots of American pragmatism, with his emphasis on (a) the dynamic character of personalities and social structures, (b) the flexibility of custom and tradition, especially in an emerging nation; and (c) the transformative possibilities in human history. West notes Emerson's preoccupation with "contingency, flux, unpredictability, and variability"—themes that would emerge in the literatures of the "new science" in the late twentieth century as postmodern descriptors of an evolving universe. Emerson was especially concerned with the development of the individual and with human powers, to the point of conceptualizing human agency as potentially "heroic."

Especially important to the development of pragmatism as a distinct philosophical form was Emerson's rejection of philosophy's quest for certainty, its hope for professional (i.e., scientific) respectability, and its search for intellectual foundations. These anti-foundational commitments would come to characterize the sensibilities of future American pragmatists. These radical (at the time) philosophers used these ideas to reveal the affiliation of traditional philosophical knowledge with structures of power, as well as to enact forms of cultural criticism designed to unsettle, critique, and transform their culture. West addresses the underside of the Emersonian legacy, the ways in which the expansion of individual powers supported and justified the expansion of market forces and thus the imperial domination over nature and the exploitation of people associated with nature (people of color, immigrants, women). He thus reveals the origin of pragmatism as complicated and problematic, situated as it was in a period of nascent capitalism, a set of unjust social relations, and a mind-set of expansion into an untapped frontier.

Charles Peirce coined the term *pragmatism* in a lecture given in Cambridge in the 1870s, but William James introduced the term to the world (Menand, 2001, p. 350). Peirce is perhaps best known for his work in semiotics and for the insight that all knowledge is social (p. 200). His "pragmatic maxim," boiled down to its essence, simply states that the whole of an object or a concept cannot be known without tracing out in the imagination all of the conceivable practical consequences of such a thought, activity, or object. James is more widely known for his contributions to psychology, which included many ideas only now coming to be generally understood. His theories of the "self" included a more holistic view of human consciousness than the atomism and individualism of his time, a rejection of reductionism and defense of multiple experiential worlds, a stress on relations, and a truly radical process view of the self as unfolding in interaction with historical, social, and cultural conditions (Seigfried, 1996, p. 15). James was especially interested in states of consciousness that seemed to indicate an "extra-sensory" realm and was, until the end of his life, "in pursuit of scientific validation of what he took to be the instinctive belief that the universe has a spiritual dimension" (Menand, 2001, pp. 90–91).

John Dewey, born in Burlington, Vermont, in 1859, is perhaps America's most celebrated pragmatic philosopher. His writings on philosophy, religion, logic, ethics, education, politics, and art profoundly influenced American intellectual and cultural life. Dewey's ideas are important for a number of reasons: for their contribution to pragmatist philosophy, for their substantial contribution to a theory and practice of progressive education, and perhaps most important to this chapter, for what he offered to our understanding of the moral dimension of democracy. In *Logic: The Theory of Inquiry* (1938a), he further developed Peirce's idea that the consequences of actions are necessary tests of the validity of propositions and, further, that consequences must be relevant to specific problems. This set of ideas provided an important basis for understanding the ways in which the "proof" of something is necessarily "in the pudding." Ideas must be tested in action to see if they are worthwhile, and furthermore, they must be tested in specific contexts to assess their worthiness. This idea must surely resonate with every teacher who has been expected to carry out some curricular innovation generated around a policy table or in a university laboratory. "These people have obviously never been in a third grade classroom" is an all too familiar response to top down mandates! Dewey's contribution to pragmatist philosophy demands that ideas be tested in the specific contexts in which they would be applied. Those of you who have incorporated action research into your practice might recognize the seeds of that practical form of inquiry in the pragmatist ideas of both Peirce and Dewey.

In the classic text *Democracy and Education* (1916), Dewey thoroughly broke with traditional beliefs about education, working out a complex set of ideas that brought together his thinking about how the mind works, how society is formed, how cultural knowledge is transmitted, and how the curriculum needs to be organized to facilitate the maximum positive development of citizens in a democratic society. His ideas were widely misunderstood and, from his perspective, misapplied, to the extent that he eventually wrote the short treatise *Experience and Education* (1938b) to try to right the misinterpretations of his work. Although Dewey's ideas about education have been profoundly influential in the development of contemporary educational theory and practice, it is probably safe to say that they are still widely misunderstood.

Dewey had a profound faith in the capacity of the common person to engage in intelligent social action. This faith in human intelligence and his elevation of inquiry to an almost religious status is precisely connected to his faith in democracy as the highest form of social expression and organization. Moreover, his commitment to democracy was not just to a particular form of political process but to a way of life, "a way of personal life and one which provides a moral standard for personal conduct" (Dewey, 1939/1989, pp. 100–101). This last point is particularly important to the purpose of this book, which is to nurture and support curriculum work that treats democratic living as the referent for a meaningful life journey. Dewey's ideas are very much at the center of our interest in democratic inquiry.

The pragmatists were a varied group, with interests in a number of academic disciplines—so varied in fact, that it is fitting to ask what unites them as a group of philosophers.

At its heart, pragmatism is concerned with how people think—"the way they come up with ideas, form beliefs, and reach decisions" (Menand, 2001, p. 351). If we "strain out all the differences" between the early pragmatists, according to Menand, we find that they shared an "idea about ideas... (T)hey all believed that ideas are not 'out there' waiting to be discovered, but are tools—like forks and knives and microchips—that people devise to cope with the world in which they find themselves" (p. xi). They believed that ideas are social, that they are produced by humans interacting with each other and the environment, and they believed that the success of an idea depends not on its immutability but on its adaptability. This all sounds fairly commonsense to us now, grounded as most educators are in constructivist thought. Remember, however, that at the turn of the century philosophy was still an expression of the kind of "absolutist thought" that characterized traditional religious doctrine. Ideas were thought to be fixed and immutable, the mind was thought to be separate from the body and experience, and Truth was not only eternal, but external to the thinker. The pragmatists overturned all of these ideas.

Most of the early pragmatists shared some common assumptions relevant to the historical context of an emerging scientific/industrial society. These included, according to Hollinger (1995), first, the notion that inquiry, as a discipline, could sustain and stabilize a modern, scientific culture in which truth was no longer absolute, but tentative and plural; second, that the social and physical world is responsive to human purpose; and last, that inquiry is an activity open to all members of an educated, democratic society. Early pragmatists were preoccupied with the role of science in modern life. This is understandable if we think back to the early years of the twentieth century, when the interface of science and technology was bringing seemingly wondrous symbols of progress to everyday life: Wireless communication, motorized transportation, and gasoline-powered aircraft all promised remarkable advances in transportation and communication. Progress was being made in the eradication of virulent communicable diseases. In a universe characterized by uncertainty, change, and unpredictability, science offered solutions to old and new problems.

Despite their interest in science, most pragmatists did not reject God in favor of science. Some of them, such as William James, spent much of their intellectual energy dealing with questions of religion and spirituality. Many of the pragmatists, to greater and lesser extents, explored the role of intuition, a suprarational cognitive capacity. Peirce, for example, wondered about our capacity to create hypotheses out of our own experience, and called this faculty "some kind of insight or instinct that flashes the new suggestion before our contemplation" (Roth, 1998, p. 62). James leaned toward the metaphysical and suggested a level of meta-cognition (thinking about thinking) capable of joining ideas and concepts at an abstract level. Dewey, in establishing the condition of equilibrium, or cognitive fulfillment, noted the advent of intuition—the meeting of old and new—owing to the "non-logical" working of the mind and body (ibid p. 63). While all three of these philosophers varied in their acceptance of a divine entity (Peirce believed in God, Dewey accepted the notion of a "religious spirit" that arises through human interaction with the world, and James hypothesized a spiritual dimension that "consisted of a kind of extrapersonal consciousness with which individual minds are subliminally connected" [Menand, 2001, p. 91]), all attributed this vaguely defined intuitional capacity to the evolution of the human organism. In other words, the capacity to conceptualize beyond the limits of sensory data arises out of a series of adaptations and accommodations to the environment. It is with this enhanced conceptual capacity, the reaching beyond mere sense perception and immediate experience, that humans become engaged with questions of meaning, or criteria that make experiences worthwhile. Experience thus takes on a transcendent quality, as questions of meaning are linked to the notions of purpose, direction, and the intelligibility of the universe. What separates the pragmatists from the idealists, however, is that this transcendent function is linked not to some sort of absolute truth, or form of existence, but is itself contingent upon the choices that humans make. Pragmatism thus represents a turning point in human history, a point at which *human agency* becomes an explicit factor in the ongoing creation of the world.

CONTEMPORARY CRITIQUES OF PRAGMATISM

Although pragmatism is enjoying a renaissance, its revival is not without critics. Whereas a comprehensive survey of these criticisms is beyond the scope of this chapter, we would at least like to explore what we believe are some of the more compelling challenges to its fundamental assumptions. We do this in the interest of retaining what is most useful to our notion of democratic inquiry, while working out a version that is more responsive to contemporary social conditions. Some of the criticisms of pragmatism are of interest to philosophers. Others are of more general interest. We will address just three of the latter here.

First, the faith in science as the archetypal story of human progress has come under intense scrutiny. We are no longer so sanguine about the role of science in improving our lives. Rather, every scientific advance seems to bring with it new, seemingly intractable problems. The use of fossil fuels to create a life of speed, comfort, and efficiency has brought us the destruction of ecosystems and air quality. The release of energy in the atom has brought about incredible destruction when used as a weapon and generated deadly waste products that will remain hazardous for thousands of years. Ease of travel has helped promote social mobility and also contributed to the breakdown of communities. Medicines cure, but they also create their own diseases, and resistant strains of virus and bacteria emerge with every advance in medical science. Though we have sent travelers into space, we have not solved the problems of human conflict, poverty, and hunger. The notion of progress seems, at its root, problematic, and scientific problem solving an important but limited approach to the problems of modern society. It has often been said that our technological knowledge has outstripped our capacity to deal ethically with the problems technology has brought. A reconceptualized pragmatism, understanding that any material progress is likely to be offset by countervailing forces, would recognize the limitations of scientific problem solving and acknowledge the necessity for progress in the realms of ethical thinking and moral judgment, aesthetics, human compassion, and consciousness.

Second, the exclusion of the perspectives of women from pragmatism has resulted in a narrow perspective. In her book *Pragmatism and Feminism* (1996), Charlene Seigfried notes both the absence of women and minorities from the early history of pragmatism and the absence of any systematic discussions of sexism or racism in its exemplary texts. She sets about to reconstruct the history of pragmatism by focusing on the women who were important to the development of pragmatist theory, such as Jane Addams, Lucy Sprague Mitchell, Ella Flagg Young, and Dewey's first wife, Alice Chapman Dewey. Although their names have been largely absent from the historical record, these women, many of them educators and social workers, were responsible for working out, in practice, many of the pragmatists' ideas. They also helped shape some of these ideas. Dewey, for example, credited Jane Addams with sharpening and deepening his awareness of the relationship between democracy and education, citing her conviction "that democracy is a way of life, the truly moral and human way of life, not a political institutional device" (ibid p. 58). For Addams and her colleagues at Hull House, the key to radical social reform was in the holistic integration of theory and practice. They successfully tested Dewey's theory of problem solving by identifying social problems, gathering data, forming policies for social action based on the evidence, and then lobbying political and social leaders to alleviate or eliminate the problem. Pragmatism and feminism, then and now, are compatible at their most fundamental level, which is "the recognition of the continuum of experience, knowledge, values, and praxis" (ibid p. 260), but a reconceptualized pragmatism must include an ethic of care and connectedness as well as an ethic of justice and equity to achieve the balance that many feminist pragmatists seek.

The third, and perhaps most elusive, criticism concerns the failure of pragmatists to acknowledge their own embeddedness in a particular cultural form. Pragmatists hold critical thinking and rational problem solving in high esteem, so high in fact, that they assume a sort of "false universalism" for these ways of knowing. [This has delegitimized other ways of knowing and marginalized differing cultural perspectives.] In *Educating for Eco-Justice and Community* (2001), Chet Bowers notes Dewey's habit of denigrating traditional cultures (he refers to Native Americans, for example, as savages in more than one of his publications). This bias, according to Bowers, privileges modern Western ways of knowing over other forms of learning that may take place through ceremony, mythopoetic narratives, intergenerational relationships, and even visions and dreams. This problem becomes especially significant if we consider the possibility raised in the first criticism, that particular ways of knowing (specifically scientific problem solving) have actually helped create some of our modern problems, including the environmental crisis. Our ways of thinking may have gotten us into the mess we are in, environmentally, and it is possible that more of the same thinking is incapable of getting us out of it! A pragmatism informed by radical cultural pluralism would suggest that we open ourselves to other epistemological possibilities and learn some of the principles and practices of sustainability, and the ways of knowing that support these, from cultural groups who have managed to live (in some cases for centuries) without destroying their ecosystems.

Taken together, these three criticisms—the critique of core modernist assumptions such as progress and scientific thinking, the absence of voices of women and other marginalized people in early pragmatism, and the exclusion of other cultural voices in the construction of knowledge—raise questions about pragmatism's relevance to our contemporary situation. Judith Green, in the well-argued book *Deep Democracy* (1999), believes that Dewey's pragmatism, when brought into a conversation with critical theory and compatible strains of feminism and cultural pluralism, holds out hope of movement toward the "universally humane" while celebrating diversity. We believe that the revisions of pragmatism by scholars such as Jim Garrison (1997), who emphasizes the aesthetic and moral dimensions of Dewey's philosophy, and Charlene Seigfried (1996), who calls our attention to the holistic and organicist aspects of Dewey's philosophy, suggest that pragmatism is much more than an instrumental approach to problem solving. It is a dynamic mode of inquiry uniquely well suited to a developmental conception of democracy: that is, democracy that is not just a political form, but a way of life, a moral way of life that emphasizes the quality of interpersonal relationships and the full development of individuals in the context of community. So, it is to the challenges facing democracy and the signs of hope for its future that we now turn.

CURRENT CHALLENGES FACING DEMOCRACY

In a somewhat prophetic article in *The Atlantic Monthly*, Benjamin Barber (1992) noted two major global challenges facing the expansion of democracy. He calls these two tendencies "the forces of Jihad" and "the forces of McWorld," representing the opposing tendencies of tribalism and globalism. These tendencies operate with equal strength in opposite directions, one driven by parochial hatreds, the other by universalizing markets. Jihad, with its association in Americans' mind with fanaticism and terrorism, seems related to the breakdown of nation states (as in Yugoslavia and the former Soviet Union), shifting national boundaries, the rise of fundamentalisms, and the assertion of parochial identities. The globalization of the economy, with its tendencies toward opening new markets, shifting capital and production to low-wage countries and regions, fostering cultural homogeneity (McWorld), and overriding local democratic decision making in the interest of "free trade," threatens localism of all sorts, from the violent localism that finds expression in the sentiment of Jihad to the efforts of traditional cultures across the globe to sustain their languages and cultural identities. Many people associate the expansion of markets with the spread of freedom, but as Barber (1992) notes, there is nothing in this high-tech commercial world that looks particularly democratic:

> It lends itself to surveillance as well as liberty, to new forms of manipulation and covert control as well as new kinds of participation, to skewed, unjust market outcomes as well as greater productivity. The consumer society and the open society are not quite synonymous. (p. 59)

Technological developments such as the Internet embody some of these same contradictions, presenting their own challenges to the development of democracy. On the one hand, the proliferation of the World Wide Web provides for virtually unlimited freedom of expression, wide dispersion of information, and effective political organizing. On the other hand, it supports a sophisticated centralized information system with enhanced possibilities for surveillance of the most private details of our lives as well as new forms of economic imperialism (Giroux, 1991). The democratic possibilities of the Internet also contrast with the increasing consolidation of ownership of media companies as well as the creeping commercialism and consolidation of the computerized information technologies themselves (McChesney, 1999).

While internationally we note the "concentration of economic relations across sovereign borders" (Trend, 1996, p. 16) and powerful multinational corporations consolidate their grip over the fragile economies of the postcolonial world, the growth of these entities has also affected our own economic lives in a variety of ways. Despite a highly trumpeted "growth economy," downsizing and the shifting of the manufacturing base to less-developed countries has created domestic dislocation, joblessness, underemployment, and the fracturing of communities. There is a growing gap between rich and poor, characterized domestically by low employment in certain inner city and rural areas and by the withdrawal of the few benefits and protections that have historically constituted a safety net for poor families. Democracy cannot thrive when the distance between the haves and the have-nots, either globally or locally, becomes too great.

One of the most difficult challenges facing our democratic society is finding ways to deal successfully with cultural and religious pluralism. The very forces that create such vibrant diversity in America also cause conflicts because of the incommensurability of beliefs, values, and perspectives. The results of not resolving these conflicts are immense: scapegoating, exclusion, hate crimes, and genocide. After the attacks on the World Trade Center, we witnessed a rise in hate crimes against Arab-Americans, as well as against non-Arab people such as Sikhs, who to some Americans, looked like Arabs. This was a disturbing indicator of just how close beneath the surface of tolerance and civility lurk racism, ethnocentrism, and bias. One characteristic of a healthy democracy, according to Dewey (1916), is the expansion of associations and connections between different people and groups, a movement to embrace differences while we seek to discover commonalities.

One of the hallmarks of a democratic society is the right of citizens to gather to express dissenting opinions. In this past decade, thousands of citizens from all walks of life—students, trade union workers, women's groups, and environmentalists—have gathered to protest the policies of globalization. It was perhaps surprising to television viewers of these demonstrations to witness the incredible police power brought to bear to crush citizen dissent perceived as threatening to order, stability, or the interests of ruling elites. Undoubtedly, the national security state, with vastly expanded police powers, will become an even more visible presence in our lives as we respond to the threat of terrorists and the specter of unending war. This raises many troubling issues for people concerned with the preservation of our basic constitutional liberties. Already, one of the fastest growing sectors of our economy is the prison-industrial complex, and we have the largest per capita number of imprisoned citizens of any nation. Democracy cannot thrive in a police state. The question of how to balance the need for security and domestic stability with the preservation of our historic liberties is likely to occupy democratic thinkers everywhere for the foreseeable future.

Another, more subtle, challenge to democracy is represented by the commodification of most aspects of our lives. This, we believe, has resulted in a narrowing of our conception of what it means to be human. Our species has come to be known by more than one satirical observer as "homo-economicus." Think about the aspects of life that once were dealt with in the context of family or community (healing the sick, childcare, caring for the elderly, food production, clothing making, shelter construction, etc.) that are now part of the market. The trend towards privatization is exemplified by political efforts to shift the control of schools, once considered a community responsibility, to the private sector through the institution of vouchers. The commercialization of formerly public services, such as schooling and prisons, diminishes the opportunities for public discourse over the ethics and procedures of such institutions. Institutions and services thus are reduced to "bottom line" considerations of profit and loss, rather than considerations of value and public worth.

The crisis of democracy is connected to a well-documented sense that our communities are losing their coherence and meaning. Bellah, Madsen, Sullivan, Swidler, and Tipton (1985) point to individualism, isolation and fragmentation as root causes of the turn away from participation in public life. Robert Putnam, noted researcher on civil society and social capital, claims that "there is striking evidence that the vibrancy of American civil society has notably declined over the past several decades" (1995, p. 65). Civil society includes the network of institutions that mediate between the individual and the state: schools, volunteer organizations such as the PTA, nongovernmental organizations, political action groups, churches, charities, and social clubs. The "sleeping giant" of civil society was certainly awakened when our country found itself under attack. Outpourings of assistance and consolation showed us the potential power of civil society to provide unity, mutual aid, and a sense of common purpose, at least in a time of crisis. Whether this spirit will be sustained as the country returns to more stable times remains to be seen.

Indicators of the interlocking crises of democracy, community, and civil society are paralleled by troubling studies showing that student knowledge of the responsibilities of citizenship and of political processes is alarmingly low (Hart Research Associates, 1989). Studies have found that students

> do not see community participation as necessary for good citizenship, that they speak of their personal rights but not of the common good, that their notions of democracy are vague at best and often border on advertising slogans, that nationalism and authoritarian values are often preferable to democratic values, and that the only way they plan on participating in public decision-making is through voting. (Berman, 1997, p. 5)

If student apathy and cynicism about the political process continues unabated, our democracy is indeed at risk.

These and many other indicators suggest that in terms of the expansion of democracy, we are at a crisis point, in the sense that the Chinese character for crisis—*wei-ji*—indicates both danger and opportunity. In terms of our project, that of developing an approach to curriculum work that foregrounds a moral understanding of democratic living, these developments and challenges form a crucial sociopolitical-historical context for our thinking. If, as Richard Brosio (1994) suggests, public schooling in the United States can be read as a history of contradictory imperatives, (a) the growth and expansion of capitalism and (b) the expansion of democracy-egalitarianism, then the current historical moment offers a cogent illustration of that contradiction.

One of the key elements of pragmatism, as we noted above, is the notion of human agency—that we, as decision-making creatures, have the collective capacity to choose and enact the direction of our society and our culture. Educators committed to the democratic-egalitarian purposes of education need to understand the complex intersection of democratic theory, philosophical frameworks for enacting democratic commitments, the role of democratic social movements in history, and the ways in which schooling has the potential to either enhance or diminish the development of active democratic citizens. In one recent study upper-division college students were asked to list the most important citizenship skills they learned throughout their educational experiences. They invariably listed the five same skills: vote, obey the law, pay taxes, salute the flag, and say the Pledge of Allegiance (Andrzejewski & Alessio, 1999, p. 3). We would suggest that this narrow version of citizenship education is inadequate to prepare students for a complex, turbulent, and pluralistic democracy, especially one characterized by "a crisis of meaning" (Trend, 1996), and further that such a weak approach to citizenship education evidences a lack of attention to the democratic-egalitarian imperative in the professional education of educators.

Barber (1992) believes there is a solution to the antidemocratic tendencies of both tribalism (Jihad) and of globalism (McWorld). The solution, which he hopes can save them both from their defects and make them more tolerant and participatory, is "decentralized participatory democracy." In the next section we look at new developments in democratic theorizing that can point the way toward such a strong democracy and examine the ways in which professional educators can participate in and contribute to this movement through the cultivation of the arts of democratic inquiry.

DEMOCRATIC RENEWAL: TOWARD STRONG DEMOCRACY

Democracy, according to Robert Hoffert (2001), encompasses a "chaos of meanings." "When we embrace 'democracy,' we do not make our lives easier or clearer; we take on an engagement of demanding responsibilities, perplexing possibilities, and paradoxical choices" (p. 39). We want to elaborate briefly on this complexity in order to develop our argument for more sustained attention to the development of curriculum workers' capacity to engage in democratic inquiry.

Though most democratic ideas are subject to debate, one that is generally accepted is the concept of individual human worth.[1] Two value commitments emerge from this principal orientation to the value of every human being. The first is the concept of freedom: The primary responsibility of government in a democratic state is to "establish and maintain a fair and secure order in which individuals can maximally pursue their self-defining activities" (Hoffert, 2001, p. 34). The second value is the commitment to the fundamental equality of all human beings. The tension between liberty and equality is the source of much of our political conflict. One example of this tension is the Civil Rights movement of the 1950s and 1960s. During this time the freedom of southern whites to maintain a system of apartheid, protected under local statutes and states' rights, conflicted with the demand by American blacks and white sympathizers for equal rights. Although equality eventually won the day in the form of legislation granting rights to black Americans, this tension is still apparent in policy debates over issues such as affirmative action. Claiming the universality of human worth does not mean that we have always lived up to this value; rather, it is "a high and demanding standard by which [modern democracy] can be legitimately challenged and disciplined and to which it must be unrelentingly educated" (Hoffert, 2001, p. 29).

In addition to the tensions between deeply held values in democracy, there are differing conceptions of what it means to be a democratic citizen. To some people it means the

---

[1]A major exception to this value might come from the "deep ecologists" who question the anthropocentrism of liberal humanistic values. They might argue that the human-centeredness of the value of individual worth is responsible for ecological destruction and argue instead for a greater appreciation for the inherent value, worth, and rights of **all** species. In some ways, however, this commitment could be considered consistent with a general trend in democracy toward the extension of rights to ever-widening spheres.

Private Democracy	Public Democracy
A tradition stemming from the philosophy of John Locke and, later, James Madison. Emphasizes property rights and "possessive individualism" (Sehr, 1997)	A minority strand in American democratic thought associated with Thomas Jefferson. Emphasizes an engaged public involved in the affairs of government (Sehr, 1997)
Procedural Democracy	Deliberative Democracy
Emphasizes the basic principles usually taught in civics classes: majority rule, due process, etc.	Emphasizes free inquiry and debate over issues, aims at consensus
Formal Democracy	Deep Democracy
Emphasizes voting and participation in government through elected representatives	Emphasizes democracy as a way of life characterized by empathy, equity, commitment, and connection (Green, 1999)
Weak Democracy	Strong Democracy
Citizens as consumers of government services, voters, and passive watchdogs to whom representatives are minimally accountable	Citizens as active, responsible, engaged members of groups and communities who participate in public affairs (Barber, 1998b)

FIGURE 2.1

Contrasting Conceptions of Democracy

right to vote periodically in elections. To others it signifies a more active and direct participation in the many decisions that affect our lives. These differing conceptions of democracy are contrasted in Figure 2.1.

As you can see, the conceptions of democracy on the left-hand side of the figure represent a "minimalist" approach to democracy. Those on the right emphasize more active, engaged participation. According to David Sehr (1997), current dominant conceptions of democracy are "oriented chiefly toward individual, private economic activity as the fulfillment of the promise of democracy... [and favor] low levels of popular democratic participation and a withering of the public sphere" (p. 18). We believe that in order to fulfill the promise of democracy, we must move consistently toward increased citizen participation in public affairs.

Benjamin Barber is one of America's strongest advocates for "more democracy." In an article titled "More Democracy, More Revolution" (1998a), he writes about how contemporary revolutionary movements (in the United States) are not necessarily about overturning our system of government, but rather represent a clamor for inclusion in the system. He decries the lack of involvement in public affairs but finds hope in a revitalized civil society. His advocacy for increased citizen participation in public affairs echoes the claim of democrats from Thomas Jefferson to John Dewey, to current theorists such as Judith Green and Cornell West, that **the remedy for all the defects of democracy is more democracy!**

Mouffe (1996) calls this movement "radical democracy" and defines it as "the radicalization and deepening of the democratic revolution—as the extension of the democratic ideals of liberty and equality to more and more areas of social life" (p. 20). Barbara Epstein (1996) differentiates radical democracy from earlier progressive commitments to socialism:

> The term "radical democracy" has a set of positive connotations: it is associated with the social movements of the seventies and eighties, in particular feminism, gay and lesbian rights, environmentalism, and multiculturalism; it suggests a politics oriented more toward cultural than toward political or economic struggles; and it is associated with decentralization and has vaguely anarchistic, or at least anti-bureaucratic overtones. It suggests grassroots politics, diversity, a playful political practice that is not bound by rigid structures but is continually in the process of transformation. (p. 128)

Moving from the currently dominant forms of private, procedural, formal, and weak democracy to the more robust participation suggested by public, deliberative, deep, and strong democracy implies an extension of rights and responsibilities to more and more citizens, many of whom have been marginalized or excluded in the past. A "decentralized participatory democracy" would extend democratic practices to other cultural sites (from the voting booth into the workplace, the community, the school, the home). Strong democracy requires a much higher level of participation and a deeper level of engagement with public issues. Those who have read Dewey's *Democracy and Education* (1916) will recall that this extension of democracy into ever-widening spheres was at the heart of his ideas about democratic living.

The shift toward a strong democracy will require a deep understanding of the moral dimension of democracy. Here is where the work of the early pragmatists such as Dewey and Addams can inform our thinking. With them, we want to advocate for a democracy that is "more than a government structure; it is a way of life that is extensively varied, communicative, and participatory" (Snauwaert, 1993, p. 53). Or as Judith Green (1999) puts it,

> Deep democracy would equip people to expect, to understand, and to value diversity and change while preserving and projecting both democratically humane cultural values and interactively sustainable environmental values in a dynamic, responsive way. Existentially, deep democracy *would reconnect people in satisfying ways.* (p. xiv, emphasis added)

The moral dimension of democracy emphasizes the public interest over the private good and requires a commitment to democracy that is strong, deliberative, deep, and participatory. What do all these conditions have in common? They all signify empowerment: citizens assuming democratic control over aspects of their lives previously deferred to experts and elected representatives. They also signify a democracy that is developmental, that is, devoted to the growth and development of *each and every one* of its members. John Dewey believed that the importance of democratic social institutions lay in their capacity to support and promote the full and free development of human powers. Influenced by Darwin, Dewey defined growth as successful adaptation to a changing environment. This adaptation requires a certain kind of reflective intelligence in a context of human association. Snauwaert (1993) reminds us of the importance of sociability in Dewey's philosophy:

> We are born and live our lives in association with others. Thus, human associations form our primary environments. Being primary, the quality of human association is the fundamental determining factor in our development. The quality and nature of social arrangements determine the moral and intellectual development of the individual. (p. 51)

This quality of sociability and human association lies at the heart of Habermas' (1987) conception of the *lifeworld*, the domain where speakers and listeners meet in a shared context of social and cultural norms to solve problems and resolve conflicts. In contrast, the *systemsworld* is the rule-based domain governed by procedure, technique, efficiency, and outcomes, rather than shared norms. Educators, caught in the prerogatives of the latter domain, often suffer internal conflicts or cognitive dissonance as the values of their lifeworld clash with the values of the systemsworld. The notion of education as a sacred trust asks that we be more than mere functionaries in a bureaucratic system. It calls upon us to exercise wise professional judgment informed by a pragmatic, democratic inquiry that both creates and sustains a utopian social vision and supports the face to face work of deep democracy. Only with such an expanded sense of democratic curriculum wisdom will it be possible to nurture the development of democratic character in our students. At a time when our democratic system faces so many internal and external challenges, there may be no higher calling than to engage in this form of public service.

The debate about whether schools have the capacity to transform society is a long and ongoing one. Pragmatists and progressive educators such as Dewey and Counts (1932) had this conversation in the early decades of the twentieth century, and scholars are still having it. Tyack and Cuban (1995) note that "the belief that schools make a better society—the deeply engrained utopian conviction about the importance of schooling—is alive and well" (p. 14). We believe that schools cannot by themselves make a better society. They are only part of an interconnected social network of values, ideals, beliefs, and practices. We do, however, believe that education is essential to the cultivation of democratic character, all the more so in an era of extreme individualism, consumption, and privatized interests. We also believe that the cultivation of democratic character is the foundation of a strong democracy. A strong democracy does not take shape automatically, nor does it sustain itself naturally. If we lived in a society that was just and compassionate, fair and equitable, and dedicated to the development of the full human potential of its members, we might have no need of an education designed to develop democratic character. All of the institutions of society would carry out this responsibility implicitly. The cultivation of democratic character would be the "hidden curriculum" of our culture. However, given the scope of the crisis in democracy, the antidemocratic forces at work in our own society, and the more complete definition of citizenship that we are developing in this chapter, the times demand a more intentional approach:

> Democratic citizenship without democratic character cannot meet the requirements of a healthy democracy. Once this is understood, the purpose of education in a democratic society becomes clear: to prepare an informed, thoughtful, and creative citizenry for active and critical participation in a democracy, while simultaneously creating and sustaining a just and caring social environment, and ensuring that the very best educational offerings are available fully and equally to all members of that society. (Goodlad, 2001, pp. 84–85)

We think this articulation of the purpose of education in a democratic society captures the essential elements of our argument. It is a strong statement that calls upon educators to clarify their purposes in these challenging times. It also calls upon them to become "public intellectuals"—to participate in and facilitate public dialogue and debate about the moral direction of our country. The task ahead is great, but we believe the intellectual tools are available to support this important work. It is to this "wisdom challenge" that we turn in our next chapter, and following that, to narratives of practice in specific contexts that demonstrate, in concrete ways, the exercise of professional judgment through the deepening of democratic understanding.

References

Andrzejewski, J., & Alessio, J. (1999, Spring). Education for global citizenship and social responsibility. In Kesson, K. (Ed.), *Progressive perspectives, 1*(2). University of Vermont: The John Dewey Project on Progressive Education. Available online at www.uvm.edu/~dewey.

Barber, B. (1992, March). Jihad vs. McWorld. *The Atlantic Monthly, 269*(3), 53–65.

Barber, B. (1998a, Oct. 26). More democracy! More revolution. *The Nation,* pp. 11–14.

Barber, B. (1998b). *A place for us: How to make society civil and democracy strong.* New York: Hill and Wang.

Bellah, R., Madsen, R., Sullivan, W., Swidler, A., & Tipton, S. (1985). *Habits of the heart: Individualism and commitment in American life.* New York: Harper and Row.

Berman, S. (1997). *Children's social consciousness and the development of social responsibility.* New York: State University of New York Press.

Bowers, C. A. (2001). *Educating for eco-justice and community.* Athens: University of Georgia Press.

Brosio, R. (1994). *A radical democratic critique of capitalist education.* New York: Peter Lang.

Cherryholmes, C. (1999). *Reading pragmatism.* New York: Teachers College Press.

Counts, G. (1932). *Dare the school build a new social order?* New York: John Day.

Dewey, J. (1916). *Democracy and education.* New York: Free Press.

Dewey, J. (1938a). *Logic: The theory of inquiry.* New York: Henry Holt.

Dewey, J. (1938b). *Experience and education.* New York: Collier.

Dewey, J. (1939/1989). *Freedom and culture.* Buffalo: Prometheus.

Epstein, B. (1996). *Radical democracy: Identity, citizenship, and the state.* New York: Routledge.

Freire, P. (1995). *Pedagogy of hope.* New York: Continuum Press.

Garrison, J. (1997). *Dewey and eros: Wisdom and desire in the art of teaching.* New York: Teachers College Press.

Giroux, H. (1991). *Postmodernism, feminism, and cultural politics: Redrawing educational boundaries.* New York: State University of New York Press.

Goodlad, S. J. (2001). Making democracy real by educating for an ecocentric worldview. In R. Soder, J. I. Goodlad, & T. J. McMannon (Eds.), *Developing democratic character in the young* (pp. 69–92). San Francisco: Jossey-Bass.

Green, J. M. (1999). *Deep democracy.* Lanham, MD: Rowman & Littlefield.

Habermas, J. (1987). *The theory of communicative action.* Volume 2: *Lifeworld and system: A critique of functional reason.* T. McCarthy, Trans. Boston: Beacon Press.

Hart Research Associates. (1989). *Democracy's next generation: A study of youth and teachers.* Washington, DC: People for the American Way.

Hoffert, R. W. (2001). Education in a political democracy. In R. Soder, J. I. Goodlad, & T. J. McMannon (Eds.), *Developing democratic character in the young,* (pp. 26–44). San Francisco: Jossey-Bass.

Hollinger, D.A. (1995). The problem of pragmatism in American history: A look back and a look ahead. In R. Hollinger & D. Depew (Eds.), *Pragmatism: From progressivism to postmodernism,* (pp. 19–37). Westport, CT: Praeger.

McChesney, R. W. (1999). *Rich media, poor democracy: Communication politics in dubious times.* New York: New Press.

Menand, L. (2001). *The metaphysical club: A story of ideas in America.* New York: Farrar, Straus and Giroux.

Mouffe, C. (1996). *Radical democracy: Identity, citizenship, and the state.* New York: Routledge.

Putnam, R. (1995). Bowling alone: America's declining social capital. *Journal of Democracy, 6*(1), 65.

Roth, R. J. (1998). *Radical pragmatism: An alternative.* New York: Fordham University Press.

Sehr, D. T. (1997). *Education for public democracy.* New York: State University of New York Press.

Seigfried, C. H. (1996). *Pragmatism and feminism: Reweaving the social fabric.* Chicago: University of Chicago Press.

Snauwaert, D. T. (1993). *Democracy, education, and governance: A developmental conception.* New York: State University of New York Press.

Trend, D (Ed.). (1996). *Radical democracy: Identity, citizenship, and the state.* New York: Routledge.

Tyack, D., & Cuban, L. (1995). *Tinkering toward utopia: A century of public school reform.* Cambridge, MA: Harvard University Press.

West, C. (1989). *The American evasion of philosophy: A genealogy of pragmatism.* Madison: University of Wisconsin Press.

Chapter 3

The Arts of Inquiry:
Toward Holographic Thinking

INTRODUCTION

In your professional preparation to be a teacher, you have probably encountered models and maps of thinking or inquiry. Perhaps you are familiar with Bloom's Taxonomy of Learning (1956) (Figure 3.1), which denotes increasing levels of conceptual abstraction, especially as it relates to educational questions such as those found on tests. Starting at the most concrete level, with knowledge or facts, Bloom's Taxonomy maps a continuum of cognition, moving upward through comprehension, application, analysis, synthesis, and evaluation. This is an example of a model of thinking that is linear and sequential; it moves stage by stage from simple to complex. David Kolb's (1984) Experiential Learning Cycle (ELC) (Figure 3.2) represents a more cyclical mapping of an inquiry process, moving from concrete experience to observation and reflection, then to the formation of abstract concepts, and on to testing knowledge gained in new situations. Although Kolb's ELC model is somewhat less linear and hierarchical than Bloom's Taxonomy, it still suffers from the implication that learning has a particular sequence to it and that we move through steps or stages in our thinking and our learning. Most models of inquiry are formulaic and mechanistic, and they seldom represent how we actually think.

When we sought a visual representation of the arts of inquiry for this chapter, the problem we faced was how to capture the spirit of our inquiry guidance without reducing it to a formula or a rigid model. As we thought about visual metaphors for what we are proposing, we came up with the metaphor of the hologram. A hologram is a special type of photographic slide that has a unique way of storing information about objects that are photographed. Each piece of a hologram stores information about the whole image, but from its own unique angle. A hologram is created using laser beams that capture three-dimensional images on the surface of light waves.

Ken Wilber describes a hologram like this:

[E]ach individual part of the picture contains the whole picture in condensed form. The part is in the whole and the whole is in each part—a type of unity-in-diversity

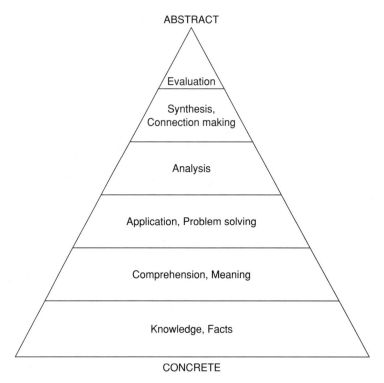

FIGURE 3.1
Bloom's Taxonomy

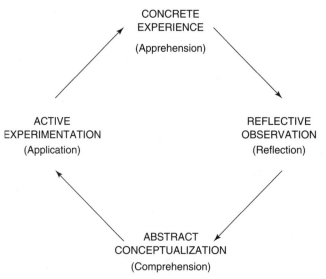

FIGURE 3.2
David Kolb's Experiential Learning Cycle

and diversity-in-unity. The key point is simply that the *part* has access to the whole. (1982, p. 2)

In this chapter we introduce seven interrelated modes of curriculum inquiry in a multifaceted holographic map (Figure 3.3). Keep in mind that each inquiry mode in the hologram is simply one element of a larger, ever-expanding whole, and just as the whole consists of its parts, so each part contains the whole. If we examine any one of the elements deeply, we begin to see the connections and relationships to all the others that are implicit in each. This will become clearer as you acquaint yourself with our seven modes

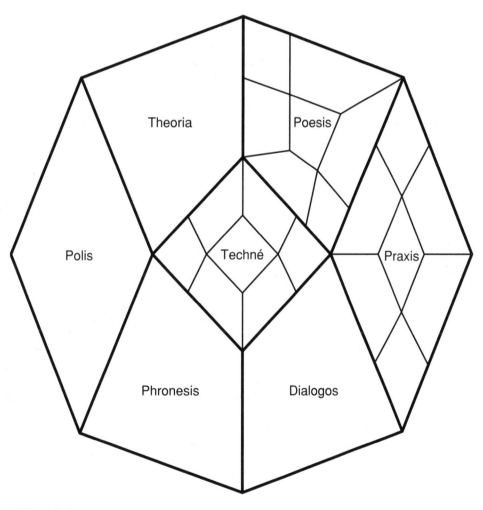

FIGURE 3.3
Seven Modes of Inquiry

of inquiry, and even more apparent as the ideas become part of the conceptual framework you bring to making wise curriculum judgments.

THE PROCESS OF MAKING JUDGMENTS

The process of thinking and decision making is *not* neat, efficient, linear, or mechanistic, as most models would have us believe. It is not always even rational! Our perceptions of the world around us are colored by our prior experiences—our social conditioning. We respond emotionally, even viscerally, to what we perceive and often for subconscious reasons. Sometimes we think things through, but most often we act on the basis of habit. Sometimes we feel forced to act in certain ways, as if we had no real choice in the matter. Occasionally we make rational hypotheses about the imagined consequences of our actions and weigh the potential costs and benefits. We may try things out and then process the results of those actions in our thoughts. Such experiences create conceptual frameworks for future thinking and action. Next time you are faced with making an informed judgment, even a seemingly trivial one, make note of your thought processes. How do you decide between possible courses of action? What in your past experience influences your decision? Do you compare potential consequences? Are you making a choice on the basis of self-interest or for the larger good? If the latter, how do you decide what constitutes the larger good? What values or beliefs are at the core of your decision?

The previous chapter discussed the philosophy of pragmatism and its importance to the preservation and expansion of our democratic way of living. Recall that it was the pragmatists who stressed the importance of testing ideas in the real world and assessing their consequences. Dewey (1936) in particular believed that human affairs are best conducted through intelligence rather than through either habit or force. He writes, "There are ultimately but three forces that control society—habit, coercive and violent force, and action directed by intelligence. In fairly normal times, habit and custom are by far the strongest force" (p. 166, quoted in Henderson, 2001, p. 5).

Many educational judgments are made on the basis of habit or custom. Separating children into grades by age is a custom. Dividing the high school day into 50 minute learning sessions is a custom. Exploring ideas in the context of separate academic disciplines such as math, history, and English is a custom. The reality that educational decisions are rooted in habit and custom is one explanation of why, despite years of reform efforts and millions of dollars poured into educational research, schools remain—in structure, form, and content—quite similar to the way they have been throughout much of the twentieth century. In addition to the pervasiveness of habit, some educational judgments are made under a sense of "coercive force"; teachers, for example, who understand high stakes standardized tests as counterproductive, even harmful to their students, are virtually forced to administer such tests. To be a "refusenik" is to risk censure or termination of employment.

We believe that habit and custom as a basis for educational judgments will not suffice in times of rapid and complex change, and the application of coercive force on professional decision making has no place in a democratic society. To adequately respond to the vast changes occurring in our society, in terms of shifting demographics, new technologies, changing work and family patterns, serious ecological issues, foreign and domestic policy, and the crisis in democracy discussed in the beginning of Chapter 2, educators and students alike are called upon to exercise ever more sophisticated forms of intelligence. If educators do not take on the responsibility of making informed judgments directed by intelligence, the profession will increasingly find itself subject to the decisions of others. Already, teachers' decision making is constrained by a number of factors: administration; school boards; local, state, and federal policy; limited budgets; textbook companies; and testing programs, to mention just a few. We will address some of these challenges to professional judgment in Chapter 4. If educators hope to preserve what purview they have over the content, processes and structures of schooling, or in our more poetic terms, "the envisioning and enacting of a good educational journey," then the cultivation of curriculum wisdom and the capacity to communicate that wisdom to a pluralistic public is essential.

The question that guided the development of our arts of inquiry map was this: What are the habits of mind, ways of thinking, and the professional knowledge base essential for the exercise of wise curriculum judgment that is grounded in moral insight and oriented toward the expansion of deep democracy? Pragmatism, as developed by Dewey and others, offers us an excellent foundation for making intelligent curriculum judgments that address the lifelong consequences of educational activities. Pragmatism and democracy, according to Cherryholmes (1999) "are allies because pragmatism requires the openness that democracy provides and pragmatism encourages the experimentation that constitutes democracy" (p. 40). However, pragmatism, for reasons noted in Chapter 2, is a necessary but not sufficient basis for the development of curriculum wisdom.

In his instructive book *Reading Pragmatism* (1999), Cherryholmes notes that pragmatism is "fallibilistic," contextual, contingent, and holistic. Let's examine these related characteristics one at a time, beginning with "fallibilism," or our propensity to make errors. Discourse on thinking and experience, says Cherryholmes, "continually moves from where we are to where we are not, from what is known to what is unknown" (p. 40). We make this conceptual movement through inductive reasoning, by imagining the consequences of our actions. Given the inherent complexity and uncertainty of the world, our predictions are just as likely to be flawed as they are to be correct. Unlike positivists (who believe in the possibility of positive knowledge) or metaphysicians (who believe there is an Absolute Truth that we can arrive at), pragmatists are intellectually honest in their admission that human nature being what it is, our judgments are susceptible to error and their outcomes are unpredictable.

Most teachers understand the importance of "contextualism." If you have ever tried to repeat a curriculum unit from one year to the next, you have probably discovered that differences in the chemistry of the group of children, in your expanding knowledge base and understanding, in the world outside the school, and even in the season and the weather, all affect the outcomes of the best laid plans. In part, this explains why even the soundest educational research, generated in specific settings, is seldom seamlessly applicable to other settings. In real estate they stress the importance of "location, location, location." In education we might say "context, context, context." Different situations are, as Cherryholmes (1999) says, "by definition, different" (p. 42).

Contingency has two related meanings. First, it can suggest an event or problem that might arise unexpectedly, and which we must be prepared for. Second, it can be something that occurs as a result of some other occurrence. Despite decades of research and policy oriented toward creating orderly and predictable learning environments, in which students spend maximum time on task, carry out instructions methodically, learn what is taught, and behave in courteous and respectful ways, most practitioners would probably say that contingency characterizes their classrooms. The actions of one student can easily disrupt the proceedings, as can circumstances outside the classroom, on the streets, or in the news. Each day is a surprise, and what happens is intricately linked to everything else that is happening.

Holism has many different meanings, but we will focus on Cherryholmes' criticism of "dualisms"—binary thinking codes that characterize much of modern Western analytical/scientific thought. Dualisms such as rational/irrational, theory/practice, fact/value not only place things in opposition but also establish hierarchies of value by placing one characteristic over and above another. Feminist scholars, for example, point out the ways that such dualisms as male/female, spirit/matter, reason/emotion privilege the characteristics of masculinity, detachment, and rational thinking over embodied, feminine ways of knowing. To think holistically is to think beyond such fragmentary oppositions and to perceive the wholes constituted by the parts. It is to understand, in a Taoist sense, the nature of complementary forces that express the interdependence of opposites.

In summary, to be pragmatically wise, one must adopt an approach to decision making and problem solving that recognizes the inherent unpredictability of situations, admits the possibility of error, understands that each moment is different from the one preceding it, is carefully attentive to the present circumstances, and works to transcend fragmentary thinking. We must be careful observers of the consequences of our actions, and we must be alert to the implications of these consequences for our democratic way of life. Central to this notion is the importance of not allowing the ends to dictate the means: How we arrive at a destination is as important as the fact that we do arrive. We can coerce students into memorizing facts for a standardized test and we can offer extrinsic rewards for achievement. Students may indeed raise their test scores, but if in the process they have lost their intellectual curiosity, become passive learners, and internalized the lesson of submission to an external authority, what have we done for the cause of democracy? Pragmatic wisdom calls for congruence between the means and the ends, and the ends-in-view must be consistent with the criteria of deep democracy. All of this requires the cultivation of a very sophisticated form of intelligence.

THE MAP AND THE TERRITORY

We invite you to think of the process of becoming pragmatically wise as a journey. To assist you in this journey, we have outlined in this chapter an "inquiry map" that draws upon the thinking of many scholars and educators from the field of curriculum studies. Although we believe this map promises to enhance and extend the ends-in-view decision-making capabilities outlined by the pragmatists, we are not so naïve as to confuse the map with the journey:

> In one of his early essays, John Dewey compared the studying of a discipline with the studying of a map. After wandering through some new terrain, an explorer produces a map; it is not intended to replace the thrill of the journey, the experience that other people will

have if they explore the territory for themselves, but it does show the relationships among the main features they will encounter. The map gives future travelers a preliminary set of conceptions, and they can prepare for the dangers, but they can also integrate the various things that happen to them as they move about. (Phillips & Soltis, 1998, p. 66)

We share this map in the hope that in the future a pragmatically informed curriculum wisdom tradition might be established. Although our ideas are drawn from the contemporary field of curriculum studies, we have chosen to give our modes of inquiry archaic Greek names. In part, this is to remind ourselves that the liberal democratic tradition that has brought us many of the rights and privileges we currently enjoy is very much rooted in a historical tradition with ancient roots. Also, we wanted to convey an archetypal sense of the modes of inquiry that we will present. C. G. Jung, who posited a complex psychoanalytical theory of the nature of the unconscious, popularized the notion of an archetype. Jung discovered, upon investigating thousands of dreams, that universal images popped up fairly regularly. He called these images *archetypes*. Archetypes are similar to Plato's *eidos* or "forms" in that they represent essential elements or characteristics that are somewhat universal in nature. To Plato, for example, "treeness" is a specific form, without which the constituent matter that makes up trees would be unintelligible. Similarly, archetypes provide a kind of structuring energy for images that exist in what Jung called our "collective unconscious." Stories and myths contain archetypal elements: Hermes, for example, of the Greek pantheon, is an archetypal character:

> Versatility and mutability are Hermes' most prominent characteristics. His specialties are eloquence and invention (he invented the lyre). He is the god of travel and the protector of sacrifices; he is also god of commerce and good luck. The common quality in all of these is again consciousness, the agile movement of mind that goes to and fro, joining humans and gods, assisting the exchange of ideas and commercial goods. (Hoeller, 1996)

The golden-sandaled Hermes, in his role as messenger between gods and humans, is the perfect overall archetypal image for our inquiry map. Hermes is the root of *hermeneutics*, a method of philosophical inquiry that moves between the whole and the part, the enchanted and the mundane. It is the space **between** the spirit and the letter of some matter. Our inquiry map represents a hermeneutic approach that is practiced in the playful dialogical space between the holistic truth of curriculum work and any particular interpretation.

Curriculum wisdom, in this holistic, holographic, archetypal sense, is a quality of consciousness that moves fluidly and freely between the sacred and the profane, or the world of the gods and the world of mortals. The process of "envisioning" involves insight and imagination (the world of the gods). The process of "enacting" involves social criticism and informed practicality (the world of mortals).

Envisioning and enacting are incomplete without each other. When in play together, they constitute "the Tao of curriculum wisdom." To meet this curriculum wisdom challenge of envisioning and enacting, we have identified seven inquiry domains that have archetypal dimensions. These seven modes of inquiry are *techné* (craft reflection), *poesis* (soulful attunement to the creative process), *praxis* (critical inquiry); *dialogos* (multiperspectival inquiry); *phronesis* (practical, deliberative wisdom), *polis* (public moral inquiry); and *theoria* (contemplative wisdom). An archetype can be both a guide on a journey and a stage within the journey.

While one archetype may be the dominating force in a person's life at a particular time, one can experience multiple archetypes in a nonlinear, nonchronological way. Most curriculum scholars focus on one or another of these inquiry domains. We contend that educators who want to build their capacity to educate for democratic living need to cultivate their intellectual and spiritual capacities in all of these domains, for as you will see, they are interdependent, dynamically balanced, and synergetic, much like a healthy ecosystem.

Unlike other models of inquiry, we do not claim that our inquiry map mirrors actual thinking. Nor is it in any way sequential, linear, formulaic, or mechanistic. We like to think of it as a curriculum "conversation" (Pinar, Reynolds, Slattery, & Taubman, 1995), which is both serious and playful: serious because the world faces problems of enormous proportion and educators have a sacred responsibility to the future; playful in the way of the trickster, who lies in wait to trip us when we become rigidly attached to our assumptions and thinking patterns. Playful seriousness, or serious playfulness, may seem like too much of a paradox. Many of the ancient wisdom traditions, however, value paradox and understand it as an important aspect of spiritual development. To dwell comfortably with contradictions, to rest content with not knowing, to move ahead, mindfully, in the face of chaos, confusion, and uncertainty is to be spiritually awake and wise like a fool.

THE SEVEN MODES OF INQUIRY

You will notice that we have chosen to organize each of these domains around hypothetical problems common to many educators. Following the statement of a problem situation, we outline the contours of the mode of inquiry, including representative concepts and exemplary scholars. We suggest the kinds of questions that might be addressed in relation to the problem posed to introduce the domain, and we note the limitations of the form of inquiry. In this way, we hope to demonstrate the problem-solving potential of these forms of inquiry interacting in playful synergy with each other. Curriculum wisdom requires a multidimensional mindfulness, and it is to these multiple dimensions that we now turn.

Techné

After three years of work by various panels and commissions, your state has finally adopted a new Framework for Curriculum and Assessment. The Framework includes learning standards, drawn mostly from national standards in the disciplines, ethical guidelines for the creation of opportunities to learn, and sample performance-based assessments that are linked to the standards. You have been asked to serve on a school committee that will determine how to best implement the new standards. Your task is to come up with a professional development plan that will assist the teachers in your school in learning new curriculum design skills that will bring your school curriculum into alignment with the new educational policy document. How will techné, as a form of inquiry, assist you in making good decisions about this issue?

We begin with techné, usually defined as skill or craft, especially as it relates to the creation of a product, for it is the mode of inquiry that best characterizes the work of educators. Techné is the material matrix and the practical activity in and by which we carry out our craft, be it teaching, pottery-making, or auto mechanics. Artists and artisans all must attain a high level of technique in order to produce products that are appreciated by others. Techné is also used to denote applied science that is concerned with production, in contrast to *episteme*, which denotes pure scientific knowledge for its own sake (Aristotle, 1962). In this sense, the work of a surgeon or an engineer also requires techné.

Teaching involves a lot of craft knowledge about techniques, strategies, and methods. Teachers must think about how to design a classroom to facilitate learning activities. They need to know how to organize subject matter in ways that connect with what students already know and how they learn. They need to have a repertoire of instructional methods at their disposal and a working knowledge of the effectiveness of different approaches such as direct instruction, cooperative learning, and individualized learning plans. They need to understand how to design appropriate assessments that actually reveal student learning. They need to know how to adapt and modify lessons so that students with varied learning styles and "intelligences" can be reached. Perhaps hardest of all for many beginning teachers, they need to know something about group dynamics and how to manage a classroom full of active young people.

Techné is most associated with instrumental, how-to thinking. As a form of inquiry, it identifies problems to be solved, hypothesizes solutions, makes plans based on these hypotheses, implements solutions, and reflects upon the outcome. In *Reflective Teaching*, Henderson (2001) defines craft reflection as "a teacher's thinking during recurring cycles of instructional study, application, observation, and reflection" (p. 17). You will recognize the basic components of educational action-research, a form of classroom-based inquiry that many teachers now practice.

Ralph Tyler's 1949 text, *Basic Principles of Curriculum and Instruction*, which we described in Chapter 1, is an exemplary text in this genre. It specifies, in a systematic way, how to go about planning and evaluating learning experiences. In more contemporary curriculum work techné is exemplified by Wiggins and McTighe's *Understanding by Design* (1998), a blueprint for the craft of designing standards-based curriculum. In the field of leadership studies, techné is represented by the skills-oriented work of Carl Glickman in his book *Leadership for Learning* (2002), in which he elaborates on structures for classroom assistance such as peer coaching and critical friends, and on prescribed forms for assisting teachers in the classroom. There are hundreds of texts available on the techné of teaching, learning, and leadership; in fact, the greater part of the professional literature deals with technique and method. The Association for Supervision and Curriculum Development (ASCD) is a prime source for such literature.

Questions addressed in this mode of inquiry are usually "how" questions. In the case of the problem posed in the beginning of this section, some of the questions you might ask include, How can we best design curriculum to integrate the new learning standards? Should we maintain a separate subjects approach or should we try to implement an interdisciplinary, problem-based approach? Should we create teams of teachers who will work with block schedules? How can we create learning experiences that promote the higher-order thinking indicated by the new standards?

Educators are often so caught up in the refinement of craft knowledge, the day-to-day business of teaching, and the pressures of the profession that we often fail to continuously ask the more meaningful "why" questions. Concern with techné—with the details of method, process, and technique—can cause us to fail to see the forest for the trees. We may forget to continuously reexamine the fundamental aims of education or our own values and beliefs about how children learn and what is worth knowing. We may neglect to step back and view the larger picture; to step aside, shift our perspective, and try to see things from a different angle; or to gaze inward toward a more profound source of knowledge. These concerns highlight the limitations of techné and point us toward other archetypal ways of knowing in our inquiry map.

If educators are only interested in teaching their subject matter well, then acquaintance with techné may provide an adequate framework for their continuous professional development. Such educators may be fine technicians, but they are not likely to lead their students toward an appreciation of democracy as a moral way of living. Without the interplay of other modes of inquiry, such educators are not likely to meet our curriculum wisdom challenge. So we turn to poesis, a more personalized, aesthetic dimension of the craft of teaching.

Poesis

For many years the teachers in the elementary wing of your school have worked to develop a literature-based approach to reading instruction. You have attended conferences together, carried out action research on your experiments, and continued to build your literature collections. Now, pressured by new federal mandates to implement "scientifically-based" reading instruction for all children, your principal has asked you to reconsider your commitment to whole language instruction and to adopt a federally sanctioned phonics instruction program. This structured program, along with the basal reading series that accompanies it, will standardize reading instruction in the school and promises to ensure that all children will have the same skill sets when they leave elementary school.

Like techné, poesis is also concerned with making, but in this case it is the soulful, expressive aspect of creation rather than mere skill or technique. Poesis suggests an aesthetic process (poesis//poetry), the bringing together of structure, content, and form to create beauty and meaning. The aesthetic is receptive, loving, passionate, and holistic; it involves surrender, cares deeply, includes immediately felt relations of order and fulfillment, and is concerned with the integration of the parts. Through such "making," the expressive self, in all of its complexity, is revealed. In Dewey's *Art as Experience* (1934), he brilliantly explores the nature of ordinary experience as a profoundly aesthetic event, and perception, creation, activity, discrimination, reflection, and culmination as interrelated and interactive components of holistic, gestalt-like experiences. An engagement with poesis is an engagement with the tacit dimensions of experience: the emotional, the perceptive, the intuitive, and the creative.

Decisions informed by poesis are made by considering not just the instrumental solving of a problem, but the multifaceted effects of a solution as well. Does the solution add beauty and depth to the situation? Has the experience culminated in a sense of profound order, harmony, or well being for the participants? Asking aesthetic questions can generate a deeper involvement with questions of meaning and enable the conceptual movement from perceived part to imaginative whole. Poesis transforms teaching from a role or a function into a calling.

Dewey, as Barone (2000) notes, "was the primary tiller of the soil in which latter-day theorists would plant their ideas about the place of one particular kind of art form in the lives of ordinary human beings" (p. 122)—the art of storytelling. Discourse about stories, according to Barone, has "become a virtual cottage industry" in the field of education. Pioneered by William Pinar and Madeline Grumet (1976), autobiography as a form of curriculum theorizing attests to the importance of narrating our lived experience and identity and of the construction of identity and the self as an educational actor (Pinar, 1994). Michael Connelly and Jean Clandinin (1988) highlight the importance of teachers' lived experience in curriculum planning and educational inquiry.

Pat Carini (2001), drawing upon years of experience observing how children learn at the Prospect School in Putney, Vermont, illustrates the importance of children's expressive activity in their construction of knowledge about the world. She is concerned that the instrumental language of standards, scores, and classifications so common now in educational discourse diminishes us and our students:

> There is an accompanying neutering and flattening of who we are humanly—to ourselves, toward others, and of others toward us. Transparent, we lose our faces. The children lose theirs. We erase them. The power to animate leaks away. (p. 69)

Poesis is the enemy of standardization, to the extent that standardization dehumanizes us. Stories (and paintings and songs and dances) add texture and richness and depth to our humanity. Poesis reminds us of the centrality of humanness/humaneness in the educational experience, as opposed to a focus on test scores and narrow, predictable learning outcomes.

Faced with the dilemma of exchanging your whole language program for a reading program that promises standardized, consistent results, you might ask the following questions with poesis in mind: Will the more simplified skills-based approach to reading engender the sense of wonder, pleasure, and awe that children experience when they read fine literature? Will the basal readers foster the multilayered, complex meaning-making that the literature does? Will I be as personally invested in the pedagogical encounter as when I have chosen books that I love with specific children in mind? Will these new workbooks and skill sheets foster the kinds of expressive extension activities (mural making, journal writing, drawing, painting, poetry writing, and creative dramatics) that the holistic use of literature stimulates?

Making wise judgments about curricular issues such as these is an important aspect of professional growth. "A judgment," says Dewey (1934), "as an act of controlled inquiry demands a rich background and a disciplined insight" (p. 300). Coming to know the self of a student and coming to know one's own self—developing insight—is at the very core of developing wise curriculum judgments. Poetic insight alone, however, cannot complete the pedagogical picture. Without understanding the social context of students' lives, we may not have the tools we need to foster the level of equity and social justice necessary for a truly deep democracy. So we turn to praxis to enhance our understanding of the importance of critique in educational inquiry.

Praxis

It is close to election time, and influential political leaders (and candidates) in your state have called for stricter accountability on the part of public schools. The best way to ensure quality education, they have stated, is to institute high-stakes testing, eliminate "social promotion," and establish a voucher system so parents with children in low-performing schools can obtain education elsewhere. You are a member of a district-wide assessment team that has been charged with the task of developing an accountability system that assesses student performance fairly and equitably and meets the public's need to know that their local schools are worth investing in. How will praxis as a form of inquiry assist you in making sound educational judgments about this complicated issue?

The concept of praxis has a long history in philosophy. Definitions range from "the human activity through which man changes the world and himself" to more elaborate definitions involving "notions of freedom, creativity, universality, history, the future, revolution, etc." (Bottomore, 1991, p. 440). Praxis is almost always identified with doing, especially the "doing" involved in human social activity. The term is not used, however, to denote unreflective action or craft (as in techné) but rather a unity of knowing and doing or theory and practice.

In education the word *praxis* is usually used to signify the integration of critical inquiry into teachers' reflective practices. Critical inquiry involves looking at the big picture, the social, economic, and political context of issues. Not to be confused with critical thinking, which deals primarily with cognitive strategies such as recognizing faulty arguments, weighing truth claims and evidence, and the skills of formal and informal logic (Burbules & Berk, 1999), critical inquiry involves a consideration of the "overt, tacit, and covert power relations between people" (Henderson, 2001, p. 22). Related to critical inquiry is critical pedagogy, an educational movement concerned with social injustice that seeks to "transform inequitable, undemocratic, or oppressive institutions and social relations" (Burbules & Berk, 1999, p. 47). We are using the term *praxis* to signify action that is grounded in a serious examination of the root causes of injustice and that is oriented toward human liberation and equity.

There are a number of important concepts germane to this mode of inquiry that illuminate the dynamics of power, domination, and oppression. The concept of hegemony, for example, helps us understand how certain sets of ideas, values, and beliefs come to dominate the consciousness of a society. The concept of resistance demonstrates ways that people resist dominant forms of knowledge and control, overcome oppression, and construct alternative social meanings. For example, patriarchy was largely taken for granted in the United States until a revitalized women's movement in the 1960s engaged in resistance in the form of consciousness raising and political action. Similarly, the civil rights movement of the same era represented resistance to the hegemony of while privilege. Now, although we are still a ways from genuine gender and racial equality, the hegemonies of patriarchy and white privilege are, if not completely overcome, subjects of public discourse, remedial legislation, and social change.

In education, concepts such as "cultural capital" (signifying the physical and mental resources that children gain by being members of privileged groups) and the "hidden curriculum" ("the unexpressed perpetuation of dominant culture through institutional practices" [Wink, 2000, p. 54]) help us understand why schooling tends to *reproduce* (another concept from critical pedagogy) existing social class structures and power arrangements.

With praxis in mind, we cannot take the "objectives conditions" of a situation at face value but must begin to dig into the root causes of any perceived problem. Writers from the critical pedagogy tradition such as Paulo Freire (1990/2000), Carmen Luke and Jennifer Gore (1992), Peter McLaren (2002), Barry Kanpol (1994), Jean Anyon (1997), and Michael Apple (1999) best address the forms of analysis and action embodied in praxis. They remind educators of the importance of continuously examining the structural constraints embedded in our work and inspire us to diligently pursue personal and social justice.

Approaching the topic of high stakes, standardized testing from a praxis perspective raises a number of important issues that are seldom addressed in public discourse. First, a critical theorist would point out that there is nothing natural or God-given about testing as a way to assess student learning. They would point out that testing is a human-devised activity, designed to achieve specific ends. Tests are not, as Alfie Kohn (2000) points out, "a force of nature, but a force of politics, and political decisions can be questioned, challenged, and ultimately reversed" (p. 50).

Educators grounded in the ideas of critical pedagogy might ask the following questions that have to do with the social, political, and economic consequences of tests: What ends are served by testing? Will it move our social world toward more equity and social justice? What are some of the potential unintended consequences of high-stakes testing? Is the creation of a competitive classroom atmosphere most conducive to learning? Should schools be in the business of sifting, sorting, and classifying children? What kinds of knowledge do tests measure, and are these truly the best indicators of genuine learning? Why do test scores so often correlate with family income? What sector of society stands to benefit the most from increasing the numbers of tests taken in a district? What sector of society stands to gain the most from privatizing education? (If your answers to the last two questions was "the corporate sector," then you are beginning to understand the links that critical theorists draw between economics and education).

Many of the limitations of critical theory and critical pedagogy have been addressed internally through a dialectic critique and the assimilation of new ideas. From its early Marxist roots, for example, when there was a simple correlation drawn between schooling and the economy (see, for example, Bowles and Gintis, 1976), to the later work by Giroux (1997) and others on resistance and empowerment, critical theory has attempted to grow and change in response to internal criticism. The language of critical theory tends to be highly specialized, a problem that has been mitigated somewhat by "translations" of its theoretical perspectives into everyday language (see Wink, 2000). The voices of women have been less audible in critical pedagogy than those of (especially white) men, although there has been important work done to develop a feminist critical pedagogy (Luke & Gore, 1992). Another critique of critical pedagogy comes from C.A. Bowers (2001), who claims that critical pedagogy is so rooted in its own modernist assumptions about progress and rationality that it fails to take issues of the environment and eco-justice into account. These claims—that critical pedagogy does not adequately account for difference and that it is not self-critical enough of its own modernist assumptions—are addressed more fully by the mode of inquiry we turn to next, dialogos.

Dialogos

You are a fourth grade teacher in a school characterized by its diversity. Students in your class come from a variety of cultural backgrounds, including, but not limited to, African-American,

Caribbean, European-American, Latina/Latino, and Native North American/Alaskan. It is the beginning of the school year, and you are thinking ahead to October, when the usual Columbus Day celebrations take place. Over the summer you have read and studied alternative narratives about Christopher Columbus and this traditional American holiday and you are troubled by the unproblematic way it is usually celebrated in your school. How can dialogos enrich your understanding of this curriculum problem and point you toward a solution that will deepen and enhance democracy?

The spirit of *dialogos* (Gr: *dia*: through, across; *logos*: idea, word, speech, reason, study) embodies a commitment to multiperspectival inquiry, literally reaching across differences and dialoguing with diverse others to construct knowledge. Dialogos reminds us that, while people might engage in shared experiences, their perceptions of their experiences are shaped differently by their perspectives and constructed out of their racial, class, ethnic, sexual, gendered, age, and ability-related identities. Understanding such socially constructed differences can lead to the "disposition to honor diversity" and the recognition that in a pluralistic society no one cultural element is the norm, and every perspective must be considered important and treated with honor and respect. With the ability to play with differing, even contradictory intellectual perspectives, intelligence is sharpened and made subtler.

In the academic arena many new interpretative frameworks have been developed to address the theoretical complexities of culture, difference, and "otherness," including postmodernism, poststructuralism, multiculturalism, deconstruction, cultural studies, and postcolonialism (see Dimitriadis & McCarthy, 2001). All of these frameworks have been brought to bear on educational problems to be solved. Pinar et al.'s synoptic text *Understanding Curriculum* (1995) perhaps best represents the multiple conversations that compose dialogical understanding in the field of curriculum studies. In the political realm issues of difference find expression in what some people call identity politics. In popular culture aesthetic forms such as "world music" attest to the circulation of cultural forms around the globe and their encounter, interface, and interpenetration.

Beneath the surface of appreciation for difference is an even more profound critique of society than that generated by critical theory. While critical theory and critical pedagogy are radical, even revolutionary, they still embrace many modernist concepts such as the superiority of reason as a way of thinking, the notion of progress, and the idea of the existence of truth as something that might be revealed when the layers of "false consciousness" are stripped away through "conscientization" (Freire, 1990). The postmodern sensibility embodied in dialogos, however, shatters such modernist illusions as reason, progress, and truth by demonstrating how knowledge and power, operating under the auspices of these icons of modernism, have acted in concert to privilege certain ways of knowing over others. In the modern, Western, industrialized world, we have come to value reason, technology, progress, materialism, and science as constitutive of a superior worldview. Stepping outside that worldview, however, from an indigenous perspective or even from the point of view of a modern environmentalist, it is easy to see how technology, progress, materialism, and Western science are in large part responsible for the rapacious destruction of the earth's biosystems and for diminishing the possibilities for a sustainable, livable future. The ability to shift perspective in this way makes it difficult to accept that one worldview is superior to others. Totalizing stories, or worldviews that pretend to a false universalism, are increasingly suspect:

> The nineteenth and twentieth centuries have given us as much terror as we can take. We have paid a high enough price for the nostalgia of the whole and the one, for the reconciliation of the concept and the sensible, of the transparent and the communicable experience…let us wage war on totality. (Lyotard, quoted in Pinar et al., 1995, p. 470)

Returning to our problem statement, the issue of how to deal with Columbus Day becomes quite complex when approached from a postmodern, dialogos sensibility. Clearly, the Columbus myth is a totalizing narrative, a story that masks brutality, torture, genocide, and the initiation of the slave trade (Bigelow & Peterson, 1998). Putting aside, for the moment, questions of developmentally appropriate curriculum (wise judgment is clearly important when considering how to approach sensitive topics with young children), a dialogos-inspired set of questions might begin with these: Why is Columbus portrayed as heroic rather than brutal and barbaric? How did the indigenous people whose land, wealth, and labor were stolen by Columbus experience this historic cultural encounter? How are the men who sailed under the leadership of Columbus portrayed in children's books? Why do our textbooks mostly fail to mention the forced labor system that Columbus installed in Hispaniola? Highlighting the way that differing perspectives reveal different realities, Loewen, in *Lies My Teacher Told Me* (1995), notes that, "Columbus's conquest of Haiti can be seen as an amazing feat of courage and imagination by the first of many brave empire builders. It can also be understood as a bloody atrocity that left a legacy of genocide and slavery that endures in some degree to this day" (p. 70). We would be better off, says Loewen, and more honest historically, if we were to treat the heroic stories of explorers and settlers as a meeting of three cultures (Europe, Africa, Native America) rather than as a discovery by one.

The issues raised here demonstrate what an enormous task it will be to move beyond colonized history and Eurocentric language. Understanding the importance of dialogos, we move toward an embrace of radical difference—interpersonally, epistemologically, and culturally. We suspend our tendencies to judge, to confer meaning, and to bring closure to uncomfortable ideas and situations. Dialogos requires that we keep our personal and professional beliefs "bracketed" through multiperspectival dialogue and critical self-examination and that we remain open to new possibilities, to reconstructions of meaning, and to dynamic transformations.

While deep democracy is well served by the cultivation of dialogical sensibilities, other skills and capacities need to be brought into play to move the democratic project forward. When exercising wise judgment in a democratic society, we must negotiate the differences uncovered by dialogos in public spaces, come to some sort of consensus about what constitutes the good life, and bring both knowledge and virtue to bear on decisions about what action to take in a given situation. One limitation of dialogos is that the focus on identity, whether in academe or in politics, while vital, can make it difficult to come to some shared vision of the good life or a common sense of purpose and value. So we turn to phronesis, a mode of inquiry that brings us closer to the problem of how we collaboratively arrive at wise educational judgments.

Phronesis

You are part of a team of three upper level elementary teachers who share teaching responsibilities for 65 fourth and fifth graders. Classroom management has become increasingly difficult throughout the school year. A group of boys has been acting physically and verbally aggressive to each other and to other children; they use foul and inappropriate language and they seem intent on disrupting the classroom at every opportunity. All of you agree that you are losing control of the classes, but you have not been able to agree on a solution. Your proposals vary widely: One of your colleagues wants to bring in the principal, a male authority figure, to "get tough" with these boys. The other wants to institute a system of assertive discipline, with clear and inevitable consequences for infractions of the class rules. You have your doubts about the ultimate effectiveness of these methods and are convinced there must be a better way. How can phronesis help you understand this situation and act effectively?

The dualistic nature of knowledge and action has a long history in Western thought. Articulated most forcefully by Plato, who conceived of philosopher-kings who spent their lives in contemplation and directed the actions of others, this dualism finds current expression in the separation of theory and practice. In education, knowledge is produced in universities and think tanks and implemented in classrooms by teachers. This is very apparent in new federal mandates for teachers to use scientifically-based methods of instruction, which are to be developed by experts using large-scale clinical trials as in medicine.[1] The idea of phronesis attempts to unpack this theory/practice distinction and move toward a reintegration of knowledge and practice. It is sometimes translated as practical wisdom or practical judgment.

Coulter and Wiens (2002) argue that phronesis is best understood as "embodied judgment linking knowledge, virtue, and reason ... the emphasis of phronesis is mostly on perceiving more in a particular situation and finding a helpful course of action on the basis of strengthened awareness" (p. 15). There is an intuitive dimension to phronesis, the cultivation of responsiveness to people's needs, desires, and interests: For Dewey, "all inquiry, not just moral inquiry, begins and ends with an affective intuition that involves a distinct feeling for the quality of a situation" (Garrison, 1997, p. 33). Our concern, however, as noted in the Preface, is for a phronesis that is more than simply practical judgment; we argue for a more robust phronesis that is deepened and extended through its interactions with the other six inquiry modes.

The topic of moral choice in a complex and pluralistic democracy is a difficult one. The United States is a society composed of thousands of religious groups, a large nonreligious sector, citizens from hundreds of countries of origin, and multiple subcultures with distinct languages, customs, and worldviews. All of the competing values and beliefs come together in the public school, one of the few remaining public spaces in our increasingly privatized and commodified culture. It is no wonder that schools are sites of intense political struggle over questions of meaning and value. The difficulty inherent in this situation, however, does not absolve educators from making moral choices. Moral choices are present in virtually every educational decision, small and large: whether to divide children into ability groups, how to present controversial curriculum content, what form of discipline to institute, and to what extent you encourage freedom of thought in your classroom.

While individuals are certainly faced with private moral choices on a daily basis, in a democracy we are faced with the necessity of making collective moral choices as well. Will

---

[1]For the complete document, "No Child Left Behind," see http://www.ed.gov/pubs/stratplan2002-07/stratplan2002-07.pdf.

we vote to provide enough money for our local schools? Will we provide a safety net for everybody in our society? Will we choose economic gain over environmental protection? All of our collective political decisions are essentially moral choices. Dewey (1916) writes,

> Democracy is more than a form of government, it is primarily a mode of associated living, of conjoint communicated experience. The extension in space of the number of individuals who participate in an interest so that each has to refer his own action to that of others, and to consider the action of others to give point and direction to his own, is equivalent to the breaking down of those barriers of class, race, and national territory which kept men from perceiving the full import of their activity. (p. 87)

We are social beings, and intelligence is a social characteristic. The more we interact with diverse others, the more varied stimuli we are required to respond to, the more our intelligence grows. We construct ourselves in relation to others and we grow in self-understanding as we reflect upon our relationships with others. We make moral choices not as isolated individuals but as members of communities. Our actions affect others and spread out from our lives like ripples in a pond; similarly the judgments and decisions of others impact our lives.

Phronesis involves deliberative, collaborative inquiry into problem definitions and solutions. One of the qualities of a democratic frame of mind is a commitment to shared decision making and to processes of consultation, discussion, negotiation, and the democratic sharing of power. True democracy must proceed from a democratic psychological disposition from which all motives of power (in the sense of domination) are excluded, or at least held in check. Writing about the moral philosophy of Hannah Arendt, Coulter and Wiens (2002) note that good judgment for Arendt "is not a matter of objective knowledge or of subjective opinion *(another dualism)*, but a result of intersubjectivity; becoming a good judge depends largely on one's capacity to consider other viewpoints of the same experience" (p. 17).

Maxine Greene (1988), a student of Hannah Arendt's and a celebrated educational philosopher, writes eloquently about the dialectic of freedom. She is concerned about the way we create our realities and ourselves in public spaces through encounters with others:

> Each time he/she is with others—in dialogue, in teaching-learning situations, in mutual pursuit of a project—additional new perspectives open; language opens possibilities of seeing, hearing, understanding. Multiple interpretations constitute multiple realities; the "common" itself becomes multiplex, and endlessly challenging, as each person reaches out from his/her own ground toward what might be, should be, is not yet. (p. 21)

Here we are making an argument for inclusivity in the process of making wise judgments. The more perspectives included in deliberations, the more intelligence will be brought to bear on the issue. Of course, it is not always possible to involve everyone in decision making, so it is necessary to cultivate the imagination: "Judging actors can attempt to imagine the various relevant perspectives on a matter based on their own past experiences and their access to other experiences through, for example, reading literature and watching films" (Coulter & Wiens, 2002, p. 18). Making wise judgments calls us to account for engaging all relevant viewpoints, especially those that might be invisible or marginalized. This is the responsibility of those who would engage in phronesis.

Drawing on the work of Joseph Schwab, who was influenced by Dewey, Gail Mc-Cutcheon (1999) has written extensively about the art of deliberation in teacher decision making. She defines deliberation as "a process of socially constructing knowledge about the curriculum to resolve a practical problem" (p. 36). She provides a practical guide, based on case studies, to the deliberative process, detailing how groups can work together to solve educational problems through collaborative practical reasoning. Through the practice of phronesis, teachers reclaim their roles as knowledge constructers, collaborative inquirers, and researchers. They learn to exercise wise curriculum judgment.

The problem situation outlined here is a classic one, having to do with the disruptions caused in classrooms by a small group of children, usually, but not always, a group of hyperenergetic boys. The problem, and its relation to phronesis, is multilayered. If we think about the emphasis in phronesis on re-integrating knowledge and practice, then we might ask a question such as, "How can we study the situation and respond to it based on knowledge that we generate in our particular context?" If we consider the emphasis on becoming more aware, in order to take responsible action, then we might ask questions such as, "What are these boys telling us by their actions about their needs and desires?" "What are their underlying motivations?" "What is my role and how might I change my participation?" And if we think about the importance of inclusivity in the deliberative process, we might certainly ask, "How can we collaborate to solve these problems, setting aside our preconceptions and assumptions?" "Who else needs to be brought into these conversations? Parents? The rest of the children in the classroom?"

If we think about the moral dimensions of phronesis, we must face the fact that the behaviors of these "bad boys" are likely to become sedimented, "disrupting and changing the adaptive patterns of many other children in the classroom, sometimes for years" (Gallas, 1994, p. 56). Their opportunities to become functional citizens in a democracy will be severely compromised. We have a moral obligation to observe these children and the classroom dynamics carefully and objectively, looking for the unrecognized potential strengths of these children, and to intervene in a way that is designed to foster their genuine empowerment, so that they can loosen up their needs to assert dominance over each other, the teachers, the other children, and the classroom situation.[2] Phronesis can remind us to become more aware of the many dimensions of situations, to respect the knowledge generated in practical settings, to examine the moral dimensions of our teaching, and to work together cooperatively to solve problems.

Polis

You are a principal at a large middle school in a district governed by a school board that has recently become dominated by a majority of religious conservatives. They have expressed the concerns of a small but active and vocal sector of the community about declining morals and objectionable behavior on the part of the students. The board has moved to institute a character education program in the middle school, preferably one based on the value system of the majority members, which will reflect a Christian orientation. They wish

---

[2]This problem situation was inspired by Karen Gallas' (1994) chapter "'Bad' Boys in the Classroom", in *The Languages of Learning*.

to display the Ten Commandments in a visible place in the school and believe the curriculum should reflect traditional family values. They have given you a month to come up with a plan. How can immersion in the inquiry mode of polis inform your thinking and action?

> A "public" is, in part, defined by the relationship between its *ethical* commitments and its *political* associations. The ancient Greeks had a word for this connection. They called an ethical-political association a *polis*. (Henderson, 2001, p. 41)

Philosophers since Plato, Socrates, and Aristotle in the western intellectual tradition from which much of our political philosophy is derived have concerned themselves with the relationship between ethics and politics. If we understand ethics as the study of how moral standards influence our behavior, and politics as the methods by which we govern our individual and collective behavior, the intimate connection between these concepts should be clear. Issues of right and wrong, just and unjust, fair and unfair, underlie much of the legislation that we live by, at least theoretically. Public moral inquiry, the central topic of the inquiry domain that we have named polis, has to do with the essential questions of what constitutes a good citizen and how we come to collectively define what philosophers call the good life.

Although there are intense conflicts over ethical/political issues because we live in a pluralistic society with many conflicting values, people at many different points on the political spectrum agree that democracy has at its core one central ethical theme: the uniqueness and worth of every individual. Claiming the universality of human worth does not mean we have always lived up to this value; rather, it is "a high and demanding standard by which [modern democracy] can be legitimately challenged and disciplined and to which it must be unrelentingly educated" (Hoffert, 2001, p. 29).

The polis of the United States, just like the polis of the ancient Greeks, falls far short of its utopian democratic ideals. This country as a political entity originated at a time in which the very land of the Republic was being stolen from the indigenous people who lived upon it, at a time when the fathers of the democracy themselves owned slaves, and at a time when women were second-class citizens without access to the public sphere. One way to read the history of the United States, suggests Elizabeth Minnich (1997), is as a history of "aspirational democracy." The struggles for basic human rights, and the struggles for recognition, have characterized the development of this country. Even today, the struggle continues in many different forms: Immigrants struggle for basic housing, health, and workplace rights; gay and lesbian citizens struggle for equal partnership rights; and workers struggle for rights to workplace safety and job security. We might thus characterize our polis as hierarchical in its origin, with white, male, heterosexual, Christian, property owning citizens at the source, and the ongoing narrative one of struggle for inclusion, recognition, affirmation, and rights by women, people of color, working class people, gays and lesbians, minority religious groups, and other politically marginalized entities. In other words, democracy is a work in progress.

Our schools, too, reflect these struggles, and educational history can, in part, be read as a similar story of the struggle for inclusion, recognition, affirmation, and rights. Think of such progressive educational advances as multicultural curricula, the development of women's history, and the disability rights movement. Minnich (1997) is worth quoting at length here:

> I want to say, then, that progressive education, pragmatism, feminism, and multicultural/diversity critiques all have at their animating core a conviction, inspired by democratic ideals and agitated by consistent failures of those ideals, that old, deeply entrenched, hierarchically ranked divisions among human "kinds", lives, and abilities must be critiqued and dismantled. That is a task that moves us into all spheres, from the philosophical through the educational to the political and into the moral. In all these areas—and perhaps especially in epistemology, which in some cases provides a pivot point for or a common thread among them—such critique aims to reveal the mutual implications of legitimated knowledge and ways of knowing and of injustices systemically as well as interpersonally inflicted on categorically defined and devalued groups. It does so because, as many progressives have said, it is unjust divisions of humans that subvert not "only" democracy's aspirational ideals but also the possibility of the unbiased, open inquiry that human betterment and the education upon which it depends requires. (p. 188)

Minnich captures one of Dewey's fundamental premises: that there is an inextricable link between the ends-in-view of a strong democracy, the construction and legitimation of knowledge, and the prevalent forms of education and inquiry in a society.

In Chapter 2, we discussed the disappearance of the public sphere in the context of challenges facing our democracy. The privatization of our lives means that fewer and fewer people are engaged in the face to face work of sustaining a democracy. If we are interested in the possibility of a strong democracy, we must be willing to do the work. In an earlier work (Henderson & Kesson, 2001) we challenged educators to the task of "public intellectual leadership." A public intellectual, we noted, "cultivates an open, inclusive public around a compelling moral purpose and then establishes an informative, expansive, and reciprocal working relationship with this public" (p. 4). This work is perhaps the culmination of our curriculum wisdom challenge, a "challenging undertaking requiring the [educator's] best social, intellectual, and creative abilities" (p. 4).

Educators and writers such as Ann Lieberman (Lieberman & Grolnick, 1997), Debbie Meier (2000), Carl Glickman (1998), and Alfie Kohn (2000) exemplify the public nature of educational leadership. They address multiple, connected themes: the development of leadership abilities in teachers (Lieberman), establishing "covenants," or agreed upon principles, between schools and communities (Glickman), public advocacy for democratic schools and classrooms (Meier), and public consciousness raising about high-stakes testing (Kohn). All of their concerns revolve around the core issues of democracy: equity, community, liberty, and fairness. They all meet the three challenges we set out for public intellectual leadership: They have identified and nurtured a public for their work; they inspire this public, moving them to experience the compelling public moral nature of the democratic problem under consideration; and they have found ways to work collaboratively with this public on the resolution of the problem under study (Henderson & Kesson, 2001, p. 10).

In this inquiry domain of ethical/political considerations, we understand that the study of social and educational problems necessarily evokes in-depth consideration of the values and ethical considerations inherent in a situation. Educational leaders need to become skilled facilitators of ethical conversations, with the intention of helping develop the disposition to question and clarify one's values and value hierarchy as an ongoing process. In a complex, pluralist democracy competing interests must be weighed against each other. Citizens who lack the skills to examine their own values and beliefs will be predisposed to making habitual dogmatic decisions rather than rational, compassionate ones. Polis recognizes that there are values common to a democratic society that transcend individual and group identity interests.

The problem situation in this section represents a fairly common situation in contemporary schooling. A vocal minority, who are worried about the secular influences on their children, have become politically active in local school politics and hope to influence the selection of the character education curriculum. You have been called upon to exercise wise curriculum judgment about a topic that is morally complex. A deep understanding of the ethos of polis might spark the following sorts of questions as you engage in deliberations: What deeply held beliefs underlie the desires of the vocal minority? What are some of the contrasting beliefs in the community? What are some of the strengths and weaknesses of the various positions? If I were to draw a Venn diagram, what would the overlapping areas of interest look like? How can I build consensus around these? How do I distinguish between private and public morality with reference to all members of society? How might I define and support, for example, "family values" without marginalizing or condemning any social group? Is my understanding of this issue informed by the Constitution and by state law? How can I foster reciprocal dialogue between all members of the community and allow for the play of diverse perspectives? What does a review of the educational literature on character development reveal about most effective practices in this area? Of these, which practices seem best suited to lead students toward an engagement with deep democracy, characterized by respect, honesty, collaboration, and solidarity? Is there a way to align the interests of my community as a whole with the best professional judgment of the teaching staff and myself?

Solving problems fraught with value conflicts is no easy task in a pluralistic society. Leadership in an age of crisis is a daunting challenge. It is not surprising that the turnover rate is so high for principals and other school leaders and that there is a growing shortage of qualified candidates for these positions. Engaging in the work of public moral inquiry requires a high level of empathy, interpersonal skill, courage, and principled action. It requires a sophisticated form of intelligence, and a grounded sense of ethics. We believe these characteristics are enhanced and extended by engagement with our final mode of inquiry, theoria.

Theoria

You have been invited to chair a committee that will respond to the wishes of your community to design and create a charter school. This is an exhilarating and challenging assignment. You have been invited to "think outside the box" and, with your chosen staff, design a school that is learner centered, future oriented, and community based. Your colleagues possess an enormous amount of "practical wisdom"; they are skilled and thoughtful teachers who understand the world from a critical perspective and have developed a high level of collaborative skill. Your group clearly possesses a sense of the polis, who have placed their trust in you. How can you benefit from an engagement with our remaining mode of inquiry, theoria?

Theoria is obviously related to the word *theory*, which has a complicated relationship to education. As Thomas (1997) notes, there is no consensus on either the meaning or the value of theory in education, and readers of educational texts are usually obliged to guess what the writer means when they use the word. Thomas proposes a continuum of usage for the word *theory*, with practice at one end and "elegant" statements of truth at the other. In between these extremes are progressively more formal usages, beginning with personal theory and moving on to critical reflection on craft, the development of hunches and hypotheses (or their reverse, grounded theory), the notion of theory as explanation (e.g., multiple intelligences theory), and formal scientific theory (e.g., $E = MC^2$). Graduate students are required to carry out their research within the context of a theoretical perspective; teachers are expected to have a theoretical justification for their practices. Theory can be a useful guide in the construction of knowledge and it can provide a "container" for data, helping us understand and interpret information and observations. As Thomas points out, however, drawing upon Feyerabend and Foucault, it can also limit and constrain thought by forcing the user to "cleave to the structure of established and respectable methodologies, literatures, rules, and procedures" (p. 87). He points out the real harm such dependency can do, using cogent examples of how educators continue to rely upon Piagetian development theories long after they have been found to be mistaken. Theory is powerful and resilient and easily becomes what Foucault (1980) calls a "totalizing discourse."

We acknowledge the dangers of an over-reliance on theory and concur with Dewey, who Thomas (1997) interprets as saying that "investigations should be specific. They should not derive from theory, nor should they be aimed at establishing theory" (p. 98). Indeed, as Thomas notes, Dewey was far ahead of his time in this thinking, perhaps even a postmodernist, for his perspective is currently operative not just in the philosophy of science, but in scientific research itself. Given this trend in the "respectable disciplines," we educators should not be too worried about loosening our attachment to the "orderliness of theory" (p. 99).

Given what we have just said, why do we include theoria in our inquiry map? Why not just advocate for the local, the particular, and the contextual—an anarchistic approach to the construction of knowledge? We want to recapture the Aristotelian sense of the archetypal dimension of theoria as a contemplative mode of inquiry, one that brings to bear the power of the intellect on all situations. We believe there is a role for such a visionary intelligence, characterized by the presence of both reason and intuition. Mindful of the various aspects of a situation, but unconstrained by conventional wisdom or habitual thinking, theoria allows us to speculate, to imagine, and to envision possibilities. An independent epistemological stance that questions all assumptions and approaches problem solving and the evaluation of evidence with an open mind disciplined in scientifically sound methods is essential to a democratic frame of mind.

Theoria is well represented in curriculum work by Jim Macdonald's (1996) essay, "Theory as a Prayerful Act" and in educational philosophy by Maxine Greene's (1998) *Dialectic of Freedom*. In leadership studies Sergiovanni (1992) offers a visionary approach to moral leadership. Theoria engages the question of ends-in-view carried out by professional educators involved in public moral inquiry in a democratic society. Democracy, in this framework, is a spiritual pursuit, embodying as it does people's deepest desires for freedom and self-determination. At work here is a kind of metaphysical stance, an epistemology that recognizes both what is and what might be—the unrealized human potential.

Theoria is important because we need to dream about possibilities, even in the midst of despair. We need to cultivate the capacity to envision a peaceful world, even when those who rule prefer force and violence to diplomacy and negotiation. We need to imagine a sustainable world in which people care enough about the health and well being of future generations to not poison the earth. We need to believe in the possibility of a just world in which no one goes hungry or dies of preventable diseases or fails to get an education just because they had the misfortune to be born in poverty. We need to imagine a future in which our desires are not circumscribed by the narrow demands of a consumer society in which the primary values are monetary and the highest goals of humanity merely material-ist ones, a future in which human beings are no longer ranked hierarchically on the basis of the color of their skin, the country of their birth, or the wealth of their parents. Without the capacity to imagine things otherwise, how will we transform our world into a more just, caring, healthy, sustainable, peaceful place? If you think about it, democracy itself is mere-ly a dream someone had, a product of someone's imagination at some point in history not so long ago. The idea that people could govern themselves, without the help of kings and queens, must have seemed as remote then as does the possibility that we might someday live without violence and war. Theoria, then, supports us in this work of envisioning, so that the work of enacting might be informed by open-ended possibilities for a better future.

Theoria may be the most difficult mode of inquiry to sustain in this fast-paced world of data, outcomes, accountability, and the bottom line. Very little in our workaholic, con-sumer culture fosters contemplation, the quiet and sustained reflection on thinking itself. How often do you find time to sit in silence in a lovely place and allow your mind to wan-der or perhaps to focus intently? When do you allow yourself the luxury of creative, diver-gent, imaginative thought that has no purpose but itself? If your answer to these questions is seldom or never we encourage you to explore this contemplative mode of inquiry.

We hope your charter school committee has agreed to give itself time to engage in the contemplative act of theoria. If so, you might be moved to ask questions such as these: What are the most important aims of education? Should we focus only on high test scores and workplace skills or are there other equally important outcomes? What constitutes the good life? What kind of world do we want to create? In such a world, what knowledge is worth having? What is the relationship between learning and human development? Can we design a school that will foster care, compassion, and creativity? Can we rethink the mean-ing of school? What are the best qualities in human "being"? How will our curriculum nur-ture those qualities?

CONCLUSION

Perhaps while reading this chapter, there were moments when you questioned the value of examining these aspects of inquiry separately. Maybe the distinctions between them seemed artificial, even unnecessary. At times, they may have seemed to dissolve into each other. We think it is useful to have a deep understanding of the parts to better understand the whole, but now that we have separated these modes of inquiry out for analytical pur-poses, it is time to put them back together again.

Let's return to our organizing metaphor of a hologram. The relationships between our inquiry domains are part/whole relationships. Although the domains can be considered in isolation from each other, the model's effectiveness is enhanced by thinking of them in terms of relational factors such as interdependence, dynamic balance, feedback loops, and synergy.

Interdependence.   Each of our inquiry modes is dependent upon the others for elaboration and amplification. Praxis, for example, would not have the critical strength it does without the well-developed theoria that provides much of its explanatory power. When we discussed praxis, we mentioned the work of Bowles and Gintis (1976), who utilized Marxist economic theory to explain the persistent ways that social class tends to reproduce itself through social institutions such as the school. Without this theoretical support, critical pedagogy would lack a powerful analytical tool. Similarly, the arts of polis, or the capacity to facilitate public ethical conversations, are enhanced by phronesis, or the arts of collaborative, deliberative inquiry.

Dynamic Balance.   The modes of inquiry exist in a sort of creative tension; the very nature of the inquiry map as conversation ensures that no one perspective gains dominance. Techné, for example, tends to overpower the work of teachers because of the pressures of the profession, but if it is in conversation with poesis, techné's tendency toward proceduralism will be modified by the continuous reflection upon meaning. The propensity of people who engage in theoria to universalize their ideas is similarly mitigated by the demands of phronesis, or the act of collaborative inquiry in specific contexts.

Feedback Loops.   All systems have control processes—ways that information feeds back into systems to maintain equilibrium. Feedback loops are a result of the dynamic balance in our model; when one part of the system is terribly out of balance, information gets fed back into the system that works to reestablish balance. When conflict arises in the polis, for example, one may need to look to dialogos to tease out what is at the core of radically different understandings of a situation. When differences are revealed in this way, however, the art of phronesis may become an important way to resolve differences and come to consensus.

Synergy.   Synergy is the way in which parts acting together achieve an effect of which they as individuals are incapable. It should be apparent by now that when all of these modes of inquiry—the parts—are operative in an individual (epistemologically) or in a system or an organization (socially), the value of the whole is enhanced. Interestingly, there is a theological definition of synergy that is less well known, the doctrine that "regeneration" is effected by a combination of human will and divine grace. Given our hermeneutic approach, in which we value the movement between insight/imagination and practical wisdom, or, metaphorically speaking, the world of the gods and the world of mortals, this theological notion of synergy seems illustrative. In the remainder of this text you will have an opportunity to read narratives of practice of educators and educational leaders who have discovered the synergy of working in this playful, interactive mode.

    An exercise in synergistic thinking that you might find helpful is to narrate a problem situation from your own practice and then approach it from each of the seven modes of inquiry. Ask yourself the kinds of questions that are relevant to each perspective. Try to have a conversation with someone you know who holds a perspective related to one of the domains that you do not feel well grounded in. When you converse with diverse others about your problem situation, try to see the strength in their perspective and the flaws in your own (Nash, 1997). See if you can bracket your habits and customs, suspend your taken-for-granted assumptions, and entertain multiple possible solutions. Then judge for yourself whether your understanding of the situation has been enhanced by the process of engagement with our holographic inquiry/artistry map. If you feel that it has, then you have begun to experience and cocreate a curriculum wisdom tradition.

References

Anyon, J. (1997). *Ghetto schooling: A political economy of urban educational reform.* New York: Teachers College Press.

Apple, M. (1999). *Power, meaning, and identity: Essays in critical educational studies.* New York: Peter Lang.

Aristotle. (1962). (Ostwald, M. Trans.) *Nicomachean Ethics.* Indianapolis, IN: Bobbs-Merrill Educational Publishing.

Barone, T. (2000). *Aesthetics, politics, and educational inquiry.* New York: Peter Lang.

Bigelow, B., & Peterson, B. (Eds.). (1998). *Rethinking Columbus: The next 500 years.* Milwaukee, WI: Rethinking Schools.

Bloom, B. S. (Ed.) (1956). *Taxonomy of educational objectives: The classification of educational goals: Handbook I, cognitive domain.* New York/Toronto: Longmans, Green.

Bottomore, T. (1991). *A dictionary of Marxist thought.* Oxford: Blackwell.

Bowers, C. A. (2001). *Educating for eco-justice and community.* Athens, GA: University of Georgia Press.

Bowles, S., & Gintis, H. (1976). *Schooling in capitalist America.* New York: Basic Books.

Burbules, N. C., & Berk, R. (1999). Critical thinking and critical pedagogy: Relations, differences, and limits. In T. S. Popkewitz & L. Fendler (Eds.), *Critical theories in education: Changing terrains of knowledge and politics* (pp. 45–65). New York: Routledge.

Carini, P. F. (2001). *Starting strong: A different look at children, schools, and standards.* New York: Teachers College Press.

Cherryholmes, C. H. (1999). *Reading pragmatism.* New York: Teachers College Press.

Connelly, F. M., & Clandinin, D. J. (1988). *Teachers as curriculum planners: Narratives of experience.* New York: Teachers College Press.

Coulter, D., & Wiens, J. R. (2002, May). Educational judgment: Linking the actor and the spectator. *Educational Researcher, 31*(4), 15–25.

Dewey, J. (1916). *Democracy and education.* New York: Free Press.

Dewey, J. (1934). *Art as experience.* New York: Perigee Books.

Dewey, J. (1936). The social significance of academic freedom. *The Social Frontier, 2*(6), 165–166.

Dimitriadis, G., & McCarthy, C. (2001). *Reading and teaching the postcolonial: From Baldwin to Basquiat and beyond.* New York: Teachers College Press.

Foucault, M. (Colin Gordon, ed.) (1980). *Power/knowledge: Selected interviews and other writings 1972–1977.* New York: Pantheon Books.

Freire, P. (1990, 2000). *Pedagogy of the oppressed.* New York: Continuum.

Gallas, K. (1994). *The languages of learning: How children talk, write, dance, draw, and sing their understanding of the world.* New York: Teachers College Press.

Garrison, J. (1997). *Dewey and Eros: Wisdom and desire in the art of teaching.* New York: Teachers College Press.

Giroux, H. (1997). *Pedagogy and the politics of hope: Theory, culture and schooling: A critical reader.* Boulder, CO: Westview Press.

Glickman, C. D. (1998). *Renewing America's schools: A guide for school-based action.* San Francisco: Jossey-Bass.

Glickman, C. D. (2002). *Leadership for learning: How to help teachers succeed.* Alexandria, VA:

Association for Supervision and Curriculum Development.

Greene, M. (1988). *Dialectic of freedom.* New York: Teachers College Press.

Henderson, J., & Kesson, K. (2001). Curriculum work as public intellectual leadership. In K. Sloan & J. T. Sears (Eds.), *Democratic curriculum theory and practice: Retrieving public spaces* (pp. 1–23). Troy, NY: Educator's International Press.

Henderson, J. G. (2001). *Reflective teaching: Professional artistry through inquiry.* Upper Saddle River, NJ: Merrill/Prentice Hall.

Hoeller, S. A. (1996, summer). On the trail of the winged god: Hermes and hermeticism throughout the ages. *Gnosis: A Journal of Western Inner Traditions, 40.* (reproduced by permission of the author at http://www.webcom.com/~gnosis/hermes.htm)

Hoffert, R. W. (2001). Education in a political democracy. In R. Soder, J. I. Goodlad & T. J. McMannon (Eds.), *Developing democratic character in the young* (pp. 26–44). San Francisco: Jossey-Bass.

Kanpol, B. (1994). *Critical pedagogy: An introduction.* Westport, CT: Bergin & Garvey.

Kohn, A. (2000). *The case against standardized testing.* Portsmouth, NH: Heinemann.

Kolb, D. A. (1984). *Experiential learning.* Upper Saddle River, NJ: Prentice Hall.

Lieberman, A., & Grolnick, M. (1997). *Networks and reform in American education.* New York: NCREST.

Loewen, J. W. (1995). *Lies my teacher told me: Everything your American history textbook got wrong.* New York: Simon & Schuster.

Luke, C., & Gore, J. (1992). *Feminisms and critical pedagogy.* New York: Routledge.

Macdonald, J. (1996). Theory as a prayerful act. In B. Macdonald (Ed.), *Theory as a prayerful act: The collected works of James Macdonald.* New York: Peter Lang.

McCutcheon, G. (1999). Deliberation to develop school curricula. In J. G. Henderson & K. R. Kesson (Eds.), *Understanding democratic curriculum leadership* (pp. 33–46). New York: Teachers College Press.

McLaren, P. (2003). *Life in schools: An introduction to critical pedagogy in the foundations of education.* Boston, MA: Allyn & Bacon/Longman.

Meier, D. (2000). *Will standards save public education?* Boston: Beacon Press.

Minnich, E. K. (1997). The American tradition of aspirational democracy. In R. Orrill (Ed.), *Education and democracy: Reimagining liberal learning in America* (pp. 175–205). New York: College Entrance Examination Board.

Nash, R. J. (1997). *Answering the virtuecrats: A moral conversation on character education.* New York: Teachers College Press.

Phillips, D. C., & Soltis, J. F. (1998). *Perspectives on learning* (3rd ed.). New York: Teachers College Press.

Pinar, W. F. (1994). *Autobiography, politics, and sexuality.* New York: Peter Lang.

Pinar, W. F., & Grumet, M. R. (1976). *Toward a poor curriculum.* Dubuque, IA: Kendall-Hunt.

Pinar, W. F., Reynolds, W. M., Slattery, P., & Taubman, P. M. (1995). *Understanding curriculum.* New York: Peter Lang.

Sergiovanni, T. J. (1992). *Moral leadership: Getting to the heart of school improvement.* San Francisco: Jossey-Bass.

Thomas, G. (1997, Spring). What's the use of theory? *Harvard Educational Review, 67,* 1.

Tyler, R. W. (1949). *Basic principles of curriculum and instruction.* Chicago: University of Chicago Press.

Wiggins, G. & McTighe, J. (1998). *Understanding by design.* Alexandria, VA: Association for Supervision and Curriculum Development.

Wilber, K. (1982). *The holographic paradigm and other paradoxes.* London: Shambala Press.

Wink, J. (2000). *Critical pedagogy: Notes from the real world.* New York: Addison-Wesley/Longman.

Personal and Structural Challenges

Introduction

At this point in the book, you may be feeling a range of emotions from hope about the possibilities of practicing curriculum wisdom to exhaustion at the prospect of enacting decision making that places a burden of professional responsibility squarely on your shoulders.[1] The notions presented in this book may feel compelling, but your entire professional experience may be based on implementing others' curriculum decisions. Success in your school may have been predicated on your ability to follow the rules, cover the content, and help kids pass proficiency tests. You may be feeling a sense of confusion or even overwhelmed at the prospect of undertaking the challenge of curriculum wisdom.

For others of you, these concepts are giving you pause, evoking a sense of wonder and curiosity about the possibilities of developing your ability to exercise wise curriculum judgments. You are less overwhelmed, and the ideas in the first three chapters have articulated and awakened a vision that makes intuitive sense. You may have found yourself nodding your head saying, "Yes, this makes sense. I have seen evidence of this in my professional experiences, but I have never articulated it before."

For some of you, this curriculum wisdom challenge is an affirmation of what you already know. It is balm for a wound that may have developed as a result of being in a profession that does not nurture what you intuitively know about teaching and learning. "Finally," you may be thinking, "I'm receiving guidance on exercising wise curriculum judgments for the students in my care!" You feel this way because your work is centered on the academic, personal, and social needs of each student. You already envision and enact the democratic good life in accordance with your own professional understanding.

Regardless of your feelings and thoughts, it is also very likely that depending on the day, the time of year, the status of your life, and the level of your energy or fatigue,

---

[1]The principal author for the discussion of personal challenges in this chapter is Rosemary Gornik. She wrote this part of the chapter in close collaboration with James Henderson.

you could place yourself in one, both, or all three of these work-life categories! Practicing the arts of curriculum inquiry in this book is not easy, for both personal and institutional reasons. This chapter addresses the challenges of practicing curriculum wisdom. We will be examining complex and difficult psychological and political problems, and in the pragmatic spirit of this text, we will treat these problems as "challenges." We recognize that curriculum wisdom is a demanding professional ideal and way of working, but it is not an impossible dream. We firmly believe that, despite complex and persistent obstacles, educators can "deepen" their curriculum judgments, but they must choose to do so. To return to our concluding comments in Chapter 1, we have a deep and abiding confidence in the creative and critical capacities of educators. We feel that while some may be more ready than others, all educators can undertake the inquiry journey that lies at the heart of curriculum wisdom. It is a matter of professional pride and determination. However, we make this affirmation fully recognizing that the practice of curriculum wisdom is deeply embedded in the politics of education.

We begin this chapter by introducing a theory of adult identity development that provides insight into how we make meaning and how that meaning making affects curriculum decision making. We will then psychologically "unpack" several personal challenges associated with the practice of curriculum wisdom. Our focus will be on the interrelated problems of **resistance**, **relevance**, and **readiness**. We will then offer practical suggestions for addressing these problems through applications of the arts of inquiry discussed in Chapter 3. Our attention then turns to institutional challenges. We will examine deep-seated structures that suppress, inhibit, or constrain the practice of curriculum wisdom. We will focus on matters of **time** and **power** and conclude with a set of recommendations.

ADULT IDENTITY DEVELOPMENT

For centuries, the complexities of the human spirit have been pondered in attempts to understand our nature, our selves, and others. A variety of human developmental theories abound, focusing on behavior in order to determine the stage, phase, type, style, or voice of the individual. Moreover, human development has often been characterized as proceeding in a more or less linear and uniform fashion from initial stages of incompetence in grasping reality to final competence, in which we come to respond to the world "as it is" (Hermans & Kempen, 1993).

More recent theories of human development posit that development occurs within the context of the interaction between individuals and the cultural dynamics and forces in their environment (Josselson, 1994; Kegan, 1994). You are probably familiar with the notion of "constructivism" as a theory of learning and development, which derives from the Latin *construere*, translated as "to interpret" or "to analyze." The emphasis is on active construction of a particular meaning or significance. Although Dewey (1916/1966) did not use the term constructivism, he argued that students created knowledge through personally directed and teacher-supported inquiries. He believed that the development of the self into a personally and socially responsible and reasoning human being was the essence of education. Education is not preparation for life; education is life. Many teachers know that interpretations of constructivism are the basis for many "best practice" ideas in education. For example, the National Science Teachers Association (NSTA) promotes "real-life application" of scientific principles, and the National Council of Teachers of Mathematics (NCTM) advocates "hands-on" math activities that stress active meaning making.

Kegan (1982, 1994) presents a "constructive developmental" theory of adult development that focuses on identity construction and explains the growth or transformation of how we construct meaning. In his view the development of the human mind continues beyond adolescence and "adulthood itself is not an end state, but a vast evolutionary expanse encompassing a variety of capacities of mind" (Kegan, 1994, p. 5). Accordingly, we all possess different ways of making sense of our experiences and our environment. This is probably not news to you. You have daily reminders of the myriad ways you and your colleagues make sense of the same experience. Think back for a moment to an Individualized Educational Plan (I.E.P.) meeting peppered with intense emotion. In the rapid-fire exchange, each person at the table is organizing the experience through his/her own lens. You discover in the debriefing after the meeting just how many different interpretations there were of the same experience. Each person used his/her own unique lens to filter what was understood, organized, and analyzed.

The language we use connects experience to understanding, and the meaning of that experience is generated as each person tells the story in an effort to grapple with the complexities of the situation (Josselson, 1995). As we tell our story and transform our experiences into personal understanding, our identities as human beings are actually being shaped. Just as knowledge is socially constructed, the self is socially constructed through language and maintained in the narratives and the stories we tell every day (Gergen, 1991). Human development in this view is an interactive process between you, the educator, and your work environment; and this interaction is, in turn, embedded in a larger social-cultural context.

PERSONAL CHALLENGES: RESISTANCE, RELEVANCE, AND READINESS

Your identity as a teacher is often maintained by being in alignment with the values created by the school environment. The expression "don't rock the boat" may come to mind. It seems that once an educator has been socialized and learns to function within the school's bureaucracy, this organizational ideology becomes a habit of mind (Eisner, 1994). Dissonance is created when that ideology is called into question. In this case, practicing the modes of inquiry to deepen your curriculum judgments may create dissonance, which then places a demand on your mind. You are changing your expectations about a "quality" work life; therefore, you are challenging your personal identity.

A problem exists when we as educators are trained to accept realities defined by those in authority and expected to acquire whatever skills are demanded to meet world-class standards and predetermined outcomes and then also expected to cultivate a deeper sense of social awareness through inquiry into the democratic good life. School cultures that foster a quest for certainty encourage habits of mind that are antithetical to intellectual life and the inclination to see things from more than one angle (Eisner, 1994). Many educators are not able to "construct a system of meaning that alerts us to the workings of power and the ways in which it shapes our consciousness" (Kincheloe, 1999, p. 78).

Many of us may not possess the capacity to engage in critical self-study and to judge what is in the pedagogical interest of students in democratic societies (van Manen, 1992). Many of us may not be aware of our deeply held educational beliefs that inform practice. Some of us may even lack a conscious moral compass for our work and may not be able to clearly articulate why we do what we do (Henderson & Hawthorne, 2000).

This is not an attack on those of us who may resist practicing curriculum decision making in a deeply critical and visionary manner. Some of us may resist because we cannot see its relevance. In our personal way of making sense of our lives, if we were asked to function in this manner, we would feel out of balance. Nor is this an indictment of those of us who may see its relevance, but find it difficult to fully embrace inquiry practices in our daily work lives. Even though some of us find this book's wisdom challenge very compelling and inspiring because it summons us to place the needs of the child at the center of every decision we make, we may be like the moth drawn to the flame and might be heard to say, "The vision looks great, but I am out of my comfort zone and at risk of crashing and burning if I get too close." We make these two general points to acknowledge the fact that questions of "personal readiness" lie at the heart of this book's call to wisdom. Educators who attempt to understand and practice the arts of inquiry as discussed in Chapter 3 may face enormous adult developmental challenges.

KEGAN'S DEVELOPMENTAL THEORY: MAINTAINING A BALANCE

Kegan's developmental theory is an important source for understanding our capacity to practice curriculum wisdom because his research focuses not on what we know about teaching and learning but how we know it. This "epistemological" shift (from the what to the how of knowing) highlights a critically important question for this book: **How have we constructed our professional identities**?

Kegan's (1982) "constructive developmental" theory of adult development describes five orders of consciousness and is based on the work of Piaget (1954). According to Kegan, each of us strives to maintain a stable order of consciousness as a way of maintaining coherent understanding and to make meaning out of the experiences we have every day with students, colleagues, and parents. Through a process of equilibration (Piaget, 1954), this coherence (balance) is maintained for cognitive, affective, and social functioning as new experiences are assimilated into our existing framework.

When your efforts to maintain an understanding of a perplexing problem at school become overwhelmed by an experience that is not readily incorporated into your existing meaning-making structure, the balance cannot hold. Your knowing shifts toward a new balance and growth occurs. Your meaning-making structures have now expanded to accommodate something new, and we could say that the complexity of your mind has increased. Kegan (1982) emphasizes the fact that adults are in a constant state of motion from one order of consciousness to the next. We oscillate between personal discomfort and self-insight as we attempt to construct our reality.

How and why each of us maintains our own unique equilibrium helps us understand why some educators may resist this book's wisdom challenge because they may not see its relevance, why some may see the relevance but proceed with caution and will resist if asked to go too far, and why some may be ready for the wisdom challenge and embrace it as a way of life. The next section will psychologically unpack several personal challenges associated with the practice of curriculum wisdom with reference to the interrelated problems of resistance, relevance, and readiness. Using a hypothetical vignette, the story of three fictional teachers will be told to reflect three different orders of consciousness. These portraits are based on data gathered in interviews with practicing teachers (Gornik, 2002; Roth, 1996; Silver, 2001). The portraits also combine Kegan's (1994) descriptions of the emotions, ideas, behaviors, and concerns of adults who have been identified as exhibiting a particular "order" of consciousness.

The reader is asked to keep in mind that while the characters are fictional, the portraits have been painted based on behaviors and attitudes of actual adults in real-life settings. The reader is also reminded that these portraits form a composite for the purposes of comparison. Kegan's cognitive-developmental theory has informed the creation of an assessment tool called the subject-object interview (Lahey, Souvaine, Kegan, Goodman, & Felix, 1988). This tool identifies 5 gradations between each of the 5 orders of consciousness, so over 20 subtle developmental distinctions are made. However, this level of detail is beyond the scope of this chapter. We will examine the 3 orders of consciousness that are most relevant for the adult developmental task of practicing curriculum wisdom.[2]

RESISTANCE WITHOUT RELEVANCE

Let us imagine that a new teacher is hired in your grade level. Kelly has several years of experience in another district and was placed in your school because of her unusual success in educating students with gifted and remedial needs in the regular classroom. Kelly is respected in highly regarded professional circles as a master teacher who creates a community of learners where all students learn to take personal responsibility for their own learning. In her classroom students are encouraged to think for themselves, to care deeply about the needs of others, and to embrace life imaginatively as life-long learners (Henderson & Hawthorne, 2000). Kelly works hard to meet the needs of students in a democratic society.

In a meeting after school at the request of the principal, Kelly shares her experiences with you and your other grade-level colleagues. She invites all of you to visit her classroom and encourages you to think about and enact some of these practices with your students. You observe with interest that one of your colleagues, John, is under great internal stress because he makes meaning from a more traditional frame of reference. John, like most teachers in your school, likes stability and predictability. He works hard to take care of his students by providing a classroom environment where they know exactly what he expects and he communicates that expectation every day. John is known for his nurturing

---

[2]Kegan's first order of consciousness, characterized as the "impulsive" self, generally emerges between the ages of 2 and 5. Children distinguish between internal and external sensations but will not experience their thoughts and feelings as separate from others' thoughts and feelings. The second order of consciousness, called the "imperial" self, generally emerges between the ages of 5 and 12. Perceptions and impulses are now reorganized from the perspective of a separate mind with separate intentions existing with other separate minds.

style and his desire to serve the needs of others, often at the expense of his own needs. John has a tendency to suffocate students with his attentions and often worries that he might be perceived as deficient if he lets students do more on their own. He agrees with Kelly that a classroom should be like a community and defines this as adhering to the rules of authority. Engaging with others in mutual reciprocity makes sense to John, but he does not understand what Kelly does in her classroom and cannot see its importance.

John may be unable to value Kelly's classroom curriculum because his role as a teacher is so clearly defined by the authority of others. In his view he was hired to follow the rules, and he wonders how could he possibly let go of his classroom structure and neatly organized lesson plans. John takes great pride in following the rules, and now the rules have changed. He feels as though he has grown as a teacher but will often lament the days when his entire curriculum fit neatly in five subject-area books located in the center of his desk and lesson plans consisted of page numbers from the textbook and topics of content. He cannot imagine a classroom in which children think for themselves and believes that the best thing he can do for his students is to have them memorize subject-matter content to prepare them to pass the proficiency tests.

John feels stressed by the messiness of it all and worries that he may not meet the principal's expectations and, worse yet, not even know exactly what the principal's expectations are! He is bound by tradition and feels most confident when his opinions reflect the opinions of significant others, in this case his principal. His meaning making is embedded in the environment, and now the environment is changing and unclear. He does not know how to make sense of the classroom environment Kelly is advocating, which is distressing for him because his work environment defines his identity both as a teacher and a person. He is out of balance, does not like it, and is not sure how to proceed.

To further complicate things for John, some of the other teachers are refusing to even entertain the notion of a classroom as an inquiry-based community of learners. In private meetings after school these teachers gather to discuss strategies for overcoming the pressure to make the change. Now John is in a double bind because of a conflict of loyalties. John's grade-level colleagues are also significant others in his formulation of his teaching identity, and he has always felt most confident when his opinions reflected the opinions and practices of his grade level colleagues. John feels out of balance. He wants to please his principal and plans to do so, as soon as he can figure out what she wants. He is a good soldier and will follow the expected mandates, even if his first inclination is to resist a classroom like this. If he is forced to do this, he wants to know the method, the formulae, and the recipe so he can get it right. On the other hand, John has an allegiance to his colleagues, and the pressure on the grade-level team is overwhelming. As he attempts to keep everyone happy, he is in a bind because sustaining one relationship injures the other.

Recall that Kegan (1982, 1994) described five main orders of consciousness that he also calls "epistemologies" or "ways of knowing." Kegan would say that John is operating out of a third, or traditional, order of consciousness. In this order of consciousness, meaning making involves the subordination of self-interest to the needs and values of a relationship. John focuses on the interpersonal relationships, which fulfills his needs and becomes the context for supporting himself. Marked by mutuality and meaningfulness of shared agreements, John is aware of his own needs as well as those of others. According to Kegan (1994), people in this "balance" are capable of reasoning abstractly and thinking hypothetically, internalizing and distinguishing between the views of others and their own views, and constructing "obligations and expectations to maintain interpersonal relationships" (p. 30). Kegan (1994) explains,

> The third order of consciousness amounts to the psychological threshold for what sociologists call "socialization": we become truly a part of society (rather than its ward or charge) when society has truly become a part of us. Our capacity to internalize, and identify with, the values and beliefs of our social "surround"—as these may be communicated by family, peer group, state, religion, ethnic clan, geographic region, or social position—makes us inductable into the commonweal. (p. 76)

John is able to hold other's points of view, but other's differing points of view get constructed in John's mind as a "problem." The source of John's professional beliefs is not internal. It comes from his principal and his grade-level colleagues. These individuals must continuously make their points of view known to John; they must remain "psychologically present" in order for John to feel whole (Lahey et al., 1988). He is incapable of evaluating others' views without placing his own sense of stability at risk. His identity is negotiated by constantly internalizing others' perceptions of him. Since John constructs his worldview from the traditional frame of reference, he resists this reform effort. He does not see its relevance.

We now turn to some of the personal challenges for those of us who may see the relevance of this wisdom challenge but find ourselves uncertain about fully embracing this vision and therefore resist it as a personal and professional way of life.

RESISTANCE WITH RELEVANCE

Unlike John, you see the relevance of creating an inquiry-based community of learners in the classroom. This concept gives you pause, evoking a sense of curiosity and excitement about further developing your teaching. You are less overwhelmed than John, and the ideas Kelly shared have awakened in you a vision that makes intuitive sense. She has stimulated and affirmed within you an understanding of how students flourish when given opportunities for authentic learning experiences.

You have empathy for John. You see in him a former version of yourself. You recall a time in the not too distant past when you thrived in a web of well-defined social relationships, just like John. You can see that John assumes, as you once did, that his personal issues and experiences are the context within which all reality is constructed. You recall feeling happiest when your entire grade level was working in harmony, which often required that you remain passive in your interactions with others. You did this to keep the peace and avoid conflict.

During the meeting with Kelly, however, you found yourself nodding your head in agreement about much of what she said. Long before she joined the grade-level team, you had become aware of a shift in your thinking. You felt a sense of "emergence," perhaps a feeling of urgency to free yourself from the confines of being defined by other's opinions and the traditional educational paradigm that has been become the hallmark of your school. Your role and identity as a teacher has been changing. You still value and cultivate many interactions with others but no longer cooperate out of fear of losing their respect.

Kegan (1982, 1994) would say that you are in transition between a traditional and a modern order of consciousness. Now you focus on mutual understanding and are able to stand apart from the group. Your referent now is your own professional accomplishments and achievements. You want to stretch yourself and learn more about a classroom environment as a community of learners. While you do not fully understand it, you are intrigued by curriculum work as a wisdom challenge.

With a combination of excitement and a twinge of dread, you agree to serve on the committee to explore these practices with others in the school. Unsettled by all the accountability mandates that seem to be making your classroom much too regimented, you are designing lessons that will prepare students for the tests, but you do it in a manner that honors each child's needs. Privately, you are fed up with your colleagues and their need to cover the content—only rarely taking into account the individual needs of their students. Recently, you found yourself somewhat uncharacteristically sparring with other teachers in the lunchroom about making these changes, even though you cannot imagine a wholesale shift in your classroom environment.

Psychologically, you are able to separate yourself from the views of your grade-level colleagues. Your self is not defined by the opinions of others, and you are motivated to work with others to achieve something greater together. You know you have a lot to learn and remain open to suggestions. You can take suggestions from others and read the literature because your internal coherence or balance is not upset when you expose a potential vulnerability. As a result, you become a better problem solver because you can take a more comprehensive view and remain more tolerant of others' perspectives. Because you organize your reality in accordance with your own educational ideology, you have the capacity to internally mediate your own and others' points of view. Not as bound by the rules as John, you have learned that conflicts arise when you hold a value too tightly and are not able to understand the opinions of others. You see this in John and remember when you did the same thing.

You value two-way communication and are willing to observe in Kelly's classroom in order to learn more. You sometimes feel the need to ask Kelly for the formulae or the technique to make this all happen. You still need and like to know the expectations of the principal and will need her support if you are to continue to push yourself. Sometimes you feel like expressing yourself more independently; other times it is too confusing, undefined, and ambiguous, and all this uncertainty makes you scared that your very job will be at risk if you do not comply. It makes sense to stretch, but only to a point. You can relate to John's struggle because if pushed too far you too will retreat to the familiar and the known. As the moth to the flame, the appeal is there, but the risks are all too real. Kegan's (1982, 1994) research indicates that at any given moment, one-half to two-thirds of the adult population appear to be functioning in the transition between a "third" and a "fourth" order of consciousness.

READINESS

Let's assume you observe Kelly's teaching and feel in awe of what she is able to do with the students. Kelly seems to have such a sense of herself. She possesses a personal authority for learning and unabashedly allows herself to be vulnerable in order to learn and stay open to new ideas. She seems to have a theory about most everything and maintains a curiosity about all that is going on in the classroom and the school. You are amazed at the abundance of her imagination when she problem solves. She does not seem to mind admitting that she does not know everything and actually relishes the not knowing because she finds inquiry fun and playful.

Kegan would say that Kelly is stabilized in the modern order of consciousness and is making the transition to the postideological, or postmodern, order. Kelly has the capacity to differentiate and integrate two potentially competing experiences and to consider her needs and the needs of others independently. She uses her theories to interpret her experiences while continually strengthening and revising them. She has a sense of self-authorship. Kelly demonstrates such leadership on the team that her colleagues wonder why she does not want to become a principal. Kelly tells you that she does not want to leave the classroom and believes that she can make the biggest difference working directly with students.

Kelly will tirelessly research new ideas from educational journals, which support what she believes to be in the best interest of students in democratic societies. She also operates like a self-employed entrepreneur who is willing to try new ideas and learn from experience. She seems to be a master at what appears to be an unending cycle of asking questions, seeking information, taking action, and weighing the consequences of her decisions. You marvel that she has the *chutzpah* to try these ideas and then share them with the principal without seeking approval before she tries it.

From a constructive-developmental point of view, Kelly has the capacity to construct an overarching system of beliefs but remains open to other conflicting ideologies. You watched in amazement when another teacher confronted Kelly in the teachers' lounge. The conflict arose around the alleged lack of progress a student was making. The student in question was in Kelly's language arts class, and Kelly was being blamed for not providing the structure needed for this student to succeed. The other teacher was very critical of Kelly, and it was common knowledge that she felt threatened by Kelly's independence and teaching style. Kelly, rather than fighting back, asked a series of questions in a sincere effort to deepen her understanding of the problem. Kelly confidently entertained the possibility that the environment in her classroom may need to be altered for this student. Kelly probed deeper and deeper, reflected broadly, and honored the other teacher's point of view. Because Kelly's identity as a teacher was not wrapped up in what the other teacher thought of her, she was able to engage in creative, even playful, problem solving and used the knowledge of the other teacher to benefit the student. Kelly was actually excited about the possibilities of finding new ways to meet the needs of this student and did not feel defensive over the confrontation. Kelly used the conflict to gain information and to forge a new relationship with this teacher by stepping outside the conflict. She seemed able to "resist the tendency to privilege what is familiar and judge critically what is different" (Kegan, 1994, p. 204).

Kelly went to work immediately to gather more information about this child's needs and was ready, if necessary, to make adjustments in the student's activities. Still upholding her belief that students need to make their own meaning for authentic learning, Kelly ultimately provided the student with some limited opportunities for memorization and drill techniques, which are a part of her teaching repertoire. However, she did not view these "approaches as ends in themselves, but rather as means to the goal of encouraging students' active meaning making" (Henderson & Hawthorne, 2000, p. 10).

You are amazed by the manner in which Kelly handled this situation. Kelly seems to respect and appreciate each teacher's unique view and considers her needs and the needs of others independently. She intuitively knew that the problem was between herself and the child, not between herself and the other teacher.

Think back to our earlier discussion about adult identity development and the notion that each of us possesses our own lens for interpreting experience. Kelly has the capacity to interpret experience through a lens that explores and challenges assumptions about reality (Silver, 2001). Sometimes Kelly forgets that others do not have the same capacity to manage their emotions in this manner. Kelly reframes emotions as valuable "feedback" and then uses the information to permeate the wall that was erected between the angry teacher and herself (Silver, 2001). You think to yourself that in a similar situation, you would have backed off or, perhaps, fought back, thus making it a personal rather than a professional issue concerning a student's needs. Simultaneously, you feel a little sorry for Kelly because as a master teacher with a well-developed sense of self-control, competence, and independence, she is isolated from the team. You are not surprised when you hear through the grapevine that the principal had to remind Kelly that she has different needs than the rest of us. You aspire to be like Kelly and at the same time you are so glad that you are not Kelly! This affirms your conclusion that embracing the wisdom challenge is perhaps too risky and costly.

DEVELOPMENTAL RESOLUTIONS—UNDERSTANDING THE FIT

We hope you have begun to see the interplay between an ordering of your consciousness and your "psycho/logical" capacity for envisioning and enacting an enduring educational journey with your students. At this point, however, we need to attempt to understand the developmental demands of this book's wisdom challenge. Although you may have identified with one or more of the teachers in the illustrative stories, the very nature of these personal identity challenges belies the use of specific techniques. What we need to understand is that the demand of this work requires not a new set of skills but a new "threshold of consciousness." Remember what Kegan (1994) says about adulthood: **It is not an end state, but a vast evolutionary expanse encompassing a variety of capacities of the mind.** The complexity of our minds and the manner in which we construct our realities can change, and this change is made possible by the emergence of a qualitatively new order of consciousness. This book's wisdom challenge raises a number of questions concerning our unique professional developmental paths:

- What do I need in order to honestly and authentically confront the personal demands of this wisdom challenge?
- How well does my current order of consciousness match the demand?
- What order of consciousness can I cultivate?
- How good is the fit between the professional challenges raised in this book and my personal capacities?

Teaching, like most human activities "emerges from ones' inwardness, for better or worse" (Palmer, 1998, p. 2). Therefore, answers to these four questions are individual and must be addressed in accordance with how each of us constructs our personal and professional identity. This recognition poses two additional questions:

- How can educational institutions be designed to nurture each teacher's inner life?
- And should they?

A working premise of this book is that, indeed, organizational life must be designed to nurture professional identities. Palmer (1998) turns this premise into a pressing question: "How can schools educate students if they fail to support the teacher's inner life?" (p. 6). We strongly believe that schools cannot perform their public mission in societies with democratic ideals unless teachers are encouraged to understand themselves. To do this, teachers may need to rethink their basic views of education, as well as the nature of their working relationships with colleagues, students, parents, and other curriculum stakeholders.

DEVELOPING YOUR CAPACITY TO MEET THE DEMAND

Perhaps you have determined that the practice of curriculum wisdom is a worthy challenge, but without the necessary support to cultivate your inquiry capacities, you will be in over your head. You might stay afloat for a while, treading water in an attempt to keep everyone happy, but you may not succeed and would be at risk of burnout. You may feel that you make meaning in accordance with Kegan's traditional order of consciousness but are now being asked to make meaning at a modern order or beyond.

Those of us who make meaning from a traditional order of consciousness and find ourselves in a school environment that asks us to aspire to this book's wisdom challenge could be at risk. We could be at risk of being seen as lacking ambition, fearful, or perhaps even lazy or stubbornly resistant, when the very expression of our internal integrity, which is from a traditional framework, is taken as evidence of maladjustment (Kegan, 1994). This is very difficult, and we may be wondering if we are able to survive the disillusionment and set aside our "truth" that good educators follow the rules and remain compliant to the wishes of the principal. Much of the literature on progressive educational leadership would describe those of us who construct the world from the traditional order of consciousness as fearful, dependent, overly concerned with the opinions of others, and somehow learning deficient and in need of some sort of remediation (Kegan, 1994). The central premise of this section is, however, that our inquiry capacities may be greater than we think they are. What we may be lacking is, simply, an adequate conception of the changes we need to make in order to meet this book's wisdom challenge.

What exactly is this psychological capacity that allows educators to meet the demand to assume an "inquiry ownership" of their work? Those of us in the transition between the traditional and the modern orders of consciousness must understand that we must shift our frame of reference from an adherence to the external values of the "social surround" to the creation of internal values (Kegan, 1994). If we can begin to shift our frame of reference in this way, we will be personally positioned to work on the arts of inquiry as described in Chapter 3. The rest is simply a matter of practice! Fourth-order thinking and beyond, is by definition "guided by its own vision, that is by its own internal way of authoring; the capacity to organize our way of knowing in a way that can originate value," not adhere to an external authority (Kegan, 1994, pp. 172–173).

Kegan (1994) notes that an informational stance to professional development leaves the form as it is and focuses on changing **what** educators know. This could be characterized as an "in-service training" model that focuses on a set of skills to be learned. Kegan contrasts this professional development strategy with a transformational approach that changes the form by focusing on developing **how** teachers know: "Training increases the fund of knowledge, while education leads us out of or liberates us from one construction or organization of mind in favor of a larger one" (p. 164).

Recall that you were asked in Chapter 3 to notice your thought process as you decided between two courses of action, to notice what influenced your decisions, and to notice the values at the core of your decision making. The core of your thought process is the way you make meaning—the *way* you construct reality. The quality of your judgments in the classroom will depend upon how you frame the problem. How you frame the problem is in large part determined by the manner in which you make sense of your professional reality. Keep in mind the next time you are faced with making an informed curriculum judgment that the quality of your decisions is, psychologically speaking, dependent upon your order of consciousness—the way in which you make meaning. Recognizing that you choose the reality you live is the first and perhaps the most important step in developing your capacity to meet this book's wisdom challenge.

Personal insights, according to Kegan (1994) cannot be taught, learned, or memorized but the consciousness that gives rise to insights can be developed (p. 128). So let us now look at the seven modes of inquiry that serve as a map for curriculum judgments. These seven modes will guide your thinking in a manner that will help you take the first step to develop not just what you know about curriculum and instruction but how you know it. You are reminded that the modes of inquiry found in Chapter 3 are interdependent and may be experienced singularly or in a multiple, nonlinear, nonchronological way. What follows is one way, but certainly not the only way, to think about understanding the arts of curriculum inquiry.

MODES OF INQUIRY AS WISDOM GUIDANCE

The Traditional Way of Knowing

As stated above, educators operating from a traditional way of knowing are often the keepers of the rules, very role consciousness, and focus much energy on mutual reciprocity with others. Others are experienced as sources of internal validation and orientation, and authority and ideas about self and other are reflected in the social surround. Power dynamics are related to authority (Kegan, 1994).

From a developmental perspective, educators functioning at this order of consciousness will most readily use two modes of inquiry to make pragmatically wise judgments: techné, interpreted as craft inquiry, and phronesis, interpreted as simplified deliberative inquiry. There is a powerful ethic of care embedded in each of these forms of inquiry, and solutions are negotiated, shared, and designed to culminate in a sense of order and harmony. Curriculum work designed to reproduce prevailing educational practices makes a great deal of sense to the traditional knower. Educators who work with this inquiry gestalt may facilitate student-centered learning, but they are quite concerned about using good techniques to maintain the order and harmony of their classroom. They view schools as human institutions based on values that reside in the local community and the larger society.

Traditional knowers also comfortably engage in a simplified phronesis because of its focus on defining problems and possible solutions. Shared decision making, consultation, discussion, and negotiation are key here and support the need for the mutuality and reciprocity so necessary for maintaining a proper social balance. For these reasons, the techné and phronesis modes of inquiry are, in general, accessible to traditional educators.

The Modern Way of Knowing

Educators operating from the modern way of knowing are guided by their own vision, their own internal way of authoring the world. They have the capacity to enact ways of knowing that originate values without adhering to external authorities. Known for their self-authorship, self-regulation, and strong sense of personal autonomy, they can function in multiple roles. They have the capacity to construct an overarching belief system or ideology and the capacity to differentiate two competing experiences. Their meaning making is focused on personal theory testing rather than on subjective experience, and they have the capacity to consider their own needs and the needs of others independently. They construct a personalized educational philosophy and possess the capacity to act upon or set aside the values of the psychosocial surround. The old status quo is replaced by something new.

From a developmental perspective, educators functioning at this order of consciousness should be ready to expand their inquiry repertoire from techné and phronesis to incorporte poesis, the poetic, soul-searching mode of inquiry; praxis, the critical mode of inquiry; polis, the ethical-political mode of inquiry; and theoria, the public moral mode of inquiry. Through these multiple inquiry lenses, curriculum work is understood as the facilitation of human liberation. Educators enacting this inquiry gestalt have the ability to look at the big picture while understanding and addressing hegemonic forces in education. They are able to step outside the power and political relations that tacitly shape the culture of schools because they have cultivated an overarching social philosophy that is attuned to the overt, tacit, and covert power relations between people. These educators take action less on habit/custom and more on critical intellect by asking penetrating, unsettling questions and thinking deeply about the possible consequences of their actions.

These educators will challenge existing knowledge/practices and ethically ground their actions to create classrooms that embody democratic living. They understand that the study of social and educational problems necessarily evokes in-depth considerations of values and ethical issues embedded in a situation, and they can manage the ambiguity of competing forces. They develop a disposition to question and clarify their values and weigh competing interests. They summarily reject habitual and/or dogmatic decision making and they are concerned that their curriculum judgments are personally and culturally responsive.

The Postmodern Way of Knowing

Educators operating from a postmodern way of knowing are rare. They are so rare that the description below relies heavily on characteristics found in people in Kegan's (1994) research.

These educators readily embrace paradox and contradiction. They celebrate difference and embrace the plurality of the world. They regularly and courageously hold their own views up for skepticism and scrutiny. They remain purposefully vulnerable to discovering another world or way of being within the self. Educators at this order of consciousness take seriously the integrity of a worldview different from their own. They resist the tendency to canonize the familiar and actually "suspend the tendency to evaluate the others 'culture' through the lens of their own, and seek rather to discover the terms by which the other is shaping meaning and or creating value" (p. 311). Conflict, in their view, reminds them that their worldview is insufficiently subtle, and so they explore conflict as a means of deepening their perceptions of reality. In effect, they seek ways to continuously refine their worldview through dialogue with others.

From a developmental perspective, educators functioning at this order of consciousness will readily engage in all seven modes of inquiry, including dialogos, the multiperspective mode of inquiry. They see curriculum work as an exercise in visionary intelligence and they enthusiastically speculate, imagine, and envision educational possibilities through multifaceted curriculum conversations (Pinar, Reynolds, Slattery, & Taubman, 1995). Inquiry is seen as an intervention that focuses on the realm of possibilities. Problems are viewed as opportunities to clarify values for the entire school community.

Comfortable with ambiguity and uncertainty, the postmodern knower possesses facilitation and communication skills that are honed to develop a vision and clarify values for action. These educators have a sensitivity to unique perceptions, tolerance for complexity, and openness to intellectual play. Their rich inner and outer dialogue recognizes a multiple and diversified self that is immersed in a continuous process of "becoming." A high value is placed on shared experiences and reciprocal transactions. Open-ended, animated, and multilayered inquiry that explores the uniqueness and complexity of human perceptions occurs on a regular basis. These educators carefully explore diverse viewpoints, confront basic beliefs/dogma, and challenge their own and others' egocentric tendencies.

Two final points before we leave the topic of personal challenges: First, Kegan writes that, no matter how any of us are developmentally positioned, we all are doing the best we can. His purpose is not to make us feel deficient but to increase our sensitivity to the current challenges of continuing adult development. We share this focus. We ask you to not feel diminished if you fall within the one-half to two-thirds of the population that is embedded in Kegan's traditional order of consciousness. If this is how you are psycho/logically positioned (and only you can make such a developmental assessment), it is not surprising. Most of us are living in cultures that are caught in a swirl of traditional, modern, and postmodern forces; given this historical circumstance (a social phenomenon that is rapidly spreading around the planet in this information age), we collectively face the problem that the traditional ways of "constructing" reality are no longer working. Kegan (1994) calls this the "hidden curriculum" of modern life. We must become wiser in how we understand ourselves, value others, and appreciate our world; this, of course, is the developmental message of this book. Kegan's theory is helpful because it provides psychological guidelines for our necessary growth. Kegan (1994) writes,

> Constructions beyond the complexity of the [modern] order of consciousness are prized above those embedded in the [modern] order, and [postmodern] constructions are [even more] prized…, *but not because complexity is a virtue.* They assume an advantaged position

because with each, the next way of constructing reality provides *even more protection from the captivation and dominance of other reality constructions.* (p. 333) (emphasis added)

This is indeed what lies at the psychological core of this book's wisdom challenge: **We must not become captivated and dominated by our own constructions of reality**. As long as we remain embedded in our own worldview, our searching, imagination, problem solving, boldness, bravery, caring, vision, collaboration, generosity, compassion, and judgments will be limited. Every one of the modes of inquiry asks us to step outside of our own meaning constructions. We are morally compelled to do this because the overarching purpose of education in societies with democratic ideals is to liberate minds, strengthen critical powers, engage human sympathies, and practice personal and social responsibility (Scheffler, 1985). For this reason, educators have an enormous responsibility to continuously cultivate their inquiry capacities.

The second point that needs to be made in this section reinforces the pragmatic foundations of this text. As discussed in Chapter 3, the seven inquiry modes are designed to serve as a practical guide or map for a certain professional journey. They should not be confused with the actual practice of wise curriculum judgments. They are a practical tool and should be used accordingly. This is also true of Kegan's cognitive-developmental theory. His description of different orders of consciousness has been included in this book as a guide for professional growth. If his theory serves that purpose, it should be used. If it does not, it should either be deconstructed, modified, or discarded. Because we are writing this book in a spirit of pragmatic inquiry, we don't assume that Kegan is correct in his analysis and explanation of adult development, but we think his ideas may be helpful.

STRUCTURAL CHALLENGES TO THE PRACTICE OF CURRICULUM WISDOM

Many educators with whom we have worked are intuitively and affectively drawn to curriculum wisdom. They resonate with the modes of inquiry presented in Chapter 3. They see the relevance of this professional artistry and feel ready to work in this way. However, despite their receptiveness, they still feel reservations. We have talked to many such educators, and their reticence is often expressed along these lines:

All of this sounds great, but it's very idealistic (i.e., not practical) because

- There's just not enough time to learn all these ways of thinking and also learn subject-matter content and teaching techniques; my plate is already too full.
- It sounds good, but what I do in the classroom is prescribed for me by (the district, my principal, the standardized test, etc.). I don't have the decision-making power to implement any of it.

These issues are important ones. In some ways, as outlined in the first part of this chapter, they are human developmental issues. In other ways, they reflect the reality that there really are sociological and political circumstances beyond the direct personal control of educators that constrain professional development that is intellectually demanding and grounded in arts of curriculum inquiry. We call these constraints "structural challenges" because they exist at an institutional level, involving specific political, social, economic, and organizational contexts.

Structural challenges emerge in many subtle ways and at many different sites: within the school; between the school and the community; in the educational bureaucracy; in the unions; in the larger political economy; at the levels of local, state, and federal governments; and in university teacher and administrator preparation programs. They represent constraints (either real or perceived) on curriculum decision making. Our premise is that whether constraints are real (existing as written policy and/or procedures) or perceived (assumed on the basis of conventional wisdom or past experience), they are still susceptible to transformation through the persistent and steady exercise of wise curriculum judgments, particularly when there is collaboration and solidarity among practitioners.

As we have noted throughout this text, the cultivation of curriculum wisdom involves arts of inquiry that challenge one's professional identity. Education is a complex endeavor, and teachers and administrators work within a complicated network of what Sarason (1990), a leading scholar of educational reform, calls "power relations." These power relations are operative in all structural challenges. Sarason, writing about the "predictable failure of school reform" makes it clear that unless the fundamental power relationships of the educational system are altered, all of our reform efforts will continue to replicate the mistakes of the past. Think about a number of questions central to the education project:

- Who makes curriculum decisions?
- How are instructional tasks assigned?
- How is knowledge generated/chosen?
- How is the workplace organized?
- How is time allocated?
- Who decides how limited financial resources will be spent?

These and many other questions highlight issues of power relations. Along with Dewey and the other pragmatists in Chapter 2, we believe in the importance of expanding curriculum decision making in appropriate ways to increasing numbers of people and sites. This reflects our belief that the people most affected by decisions should have a significant say in the formation of them. Expanding decision making in historically undemocratic, hierarchical institutions such as schools will require, as Sarason says, the transformation of existing power relations. We believe the development of curriculum wisdom is closely tied to the transformation of existing power relations. In other words, changing the basic structure of power relations is a central factor in the cultivation of curriculum wisdom.

Our arts of inquiry model is grounded in the idea that meaningful educational change is most effective when it comes "from the inside out." Transformation that is rooted in substantive adult developmental change has a better chance of resisting the flux and flow of shallow special interest politics and educational bandwagons that sometimes characterize educational reform. When reform is undertaken for superficial reasons, such as peer group pressure, coercion from administration, or conformity to prevailing politics and conventional wisdom, it does not endure. This is why we spent a substantial amount of time articulating the personal challenges aspects of this work. However, the best intentions and personal efforts of transformative educators may be less than successful or even frustrated in a context of unsupportive and inhibiting structures. We want to highlight some of these structural problems and suggest ways that educators can collectively bring the arts of inquiry to bear on resolving them.

At the macro level of educational policy and decision making, two conflicting conditions currently exist. On the one hand, there are many efforts to upgrade the autonomy and qualifications of the teaching profession, represented by such initiatives as the creation of professional standards boards comprised of teachers who are increasingly responsible for setting criteria for certification and recertification, peer coaching, peer mentoring, and experimentation with "site-based" management systems that redistribute power laterally rather than hierarchically.

On the other hand, there is the effort to regulate teacher decision making and "de-skill" teachers through such processes as externally developed curricula and standards, scripted teaching, the implementation of compulsory standardized testing schemes at more and more levels of schooling and the resultant pressure to "teach to the test" or align the curriculum with externally mandated purposes. Examples of this tendency can be found in the Bush administration's federal policy document, *No Child Left Behind* (2001), which is a massive tome that asserts among other things that instructional methods must be "scientifically based and proven" through large-scale clinical trials such as those preceding the approval of new drugs, before being adopted in classrooms. Although it is reasonable to expect that teachers should know how to read and interpret research and to develop teaching strategies based on studying data about how students learn and what instructional techniques prove effective over time, this new policy initiative largely ignores the wisdom of teachers, gained over time through working in particular sites with particular groups of children in accordance with the enduring values of democratic living.

In Chapter 3 we developed a number of hypothetical problem situations. On close examination you will see that each narrative involved an implicit or explicit set of power relations. For example, under poesis we wrote about the problem of de-skilling through the imposition of a particular instructional methodology. Indeed, the Bush administration's policy on education represents an unprecedented involvement by the federal government in educational decision making (some people might even call it micro-managing). The federal government has played a historic role in educational policy and is responsible for such positive accomplishments as desegregation, school breakfast and lunch programs, and the Head Start initiative. In these respects it has carried out its most appropriate mandate to ensure equality and access to all students, regardless of their social class or economic status. However, mandating instructional methodologies and specific subject-matter content from afar removes decision making from the people who best know the backgrounds, interests, and skills of the students in their care.

In this case the problem situation is rooted in specific historical circumstances. In the 1980s dissatisfaction with simplistic texts, basal readers, decontextualized phonics instruction, and worksheets led many elementary teachers to experiment with diverse approaches to literacy that involved the use of richer and more complex literature, contextualized approaches to teaching literacy skills, and an emphasis on reading for meaning (Routman, 1991). This grassroots movement, later supported by extensive research, became known as "whole language" and soon came to characterize literacy instruction in many classrooms, although there has been continuing and highly politicized debate about its efficacy.

With the advent of *No Child Left Behind*, certain phonics instructional methods are being touted as "scientifically proven" (despite critical claims to the contrary by experts). The grassroots curriculum work of specific teachers in specific sites is being overridden by politically motivated policy decisions. It is worth mentioning that powerful corporate interest groups, with phonics instruction products to sell, stand to benefit financially from a policy that is political, rather than educational. The policy reinforces hierarchical power relations, in that carefully chosen professional researchers generate knowledge that teachers are expected to implement. It thus separates the envisioning and enacting components of curriculum wisdom. This example demonstrates how government policy can act as a structural constraint on knowledge generated by specific teachers in specific contexts and work against the enactment of wise curriculum judgments.

We agree with Fullan and Hargreaves (1996) that the exercise of professional judgments in the context of a complex and uncertain environment such as the classroom or the school "defines the teacher's professionalism" (p. 19). Lasting and meaningful school reform, they say, should be

> ...aligned with approaches to leadership, administration and professional development which respect, support and build upon teachers' capacity to make informed discretionary judgements [*sic*] in the classroom with the students they know best. By contrast, approaches which seek to regiment and regulate the teacher's actions; to constrain and contract their opportunities for discretionary judgement [*sic*] and to standardize the process and the products of learning, undermine teachers' professionalism and the moral principles on which it is based. (p. 19)

Change that is imposed from the outside in often aims for quick solutions and focuses on curricular revisions, testing and accountability schemes. These interventions often have shallow and unsustainable effects and do not, as Fullan and Hargreaves (1996) say, "get at underlying issues of instruction and teacher development" (p. 13). They do sometimes provide short-term political gain, but they do not contribute to the long-term positive development of our democracy.

Fullan and Hargreaves (1996) also describe other structural reasons that most attempts at educational reform fail. These include a lack of resources available to solve complex problems, unrealistic time lines, tendencies toward "faddism," and a lack of follow-up and adequate support for new initiatives. Additionally, they suggest, "many strategies not only fail to motivate teachers to implement improvements but also alienate them further from participating in reform" (p. 13). Why is it, we might ask, that when it comes to meaningful educational change, "the more things change, the more they stay the same?" Sarason (1990) notes that, in response to this dilemma, "the most frequently articulated answer revolved around the process of decision-making" (p. 51). Admittedly, educators will never be solely responsible for decision making. Education is a complex social enterprise, and parents, community members, business people, and politicians share responsibility for the success of the endeavor. It is teachers and school administrators, though, who are closest to the situation, who are held accountable for student learning, and who have the professional knowledge (as compared to experiential, common sense understandings) needed to support learning in a time of rapid social change.

The development of curriculum wisdom is consistent with approaches to school reform that value the intellectual capacities of teachers, that take account of accumulated knowledge that is gained from experience, and that acknowledge the "moral and social purposes [teachers] want to fulfill through their teaching" (Fullan & Hargreaves, 1996, p. 17). Such an approach to school reform necessitates the alteration in power relations that Sarason says is essential for meaningful educational change.

Our Chapter 3 illustration of praxis inquiry highlights a similar set of power relations. In that problem situation political leaders, under election pressures, called for strict accountability and demanded to institute high-stakes testing, eliminate social promotion, and establish a voucher system so parents with children in low-performing schools could obtain education elsewhere. In the face of shifting political winds such as these, there may not seem to be much that teachers and school administrators can do other than to button up their windbreakers and hope that the weather changes. Unfortunately, this ducking out of the wind approach has the consequence of reinforcing the isolation that is another of the structural constraints on the development of democratic curriculum wisdom.

Two points are worth noting when dealing with politically motivated policy change. First, the most important politics are probably local politics. If externally imposed mandates are counterproductive to good pedagogy, a teacher can continue to fine-tune her craft (techné), cultivate all the arts of inquiry, and ensure local accountability by engaging in full communication with the parents of her students. Most parents care less about federal and state policy than they do about whether or not their children are engaged and productive learners. Second, and more demanding, educators who are public intellectuals, who take their ethical responsibilities to heart, can take it upon themselves to communicate their knowledge to a wider public. This can happen by writing letters to the editor of your local newspaper about an educational policy, providing radio commentary, speaking to your parent-teacher association, or working through your teachers' union to effect change. It can be uncomfortable to "speak truth to power" and challenge dominant policies and practices, but it is often through heroic individual and collective efforts such as these that harmful practices are changed. Think about such radical educational changes as the elimination of corporal punishment, the passage of laws against child labor, which allowed poor and working class children to attend school, and the provision of hot meals in school so that children who came to school hungry could learn more effectively. All of these school improvements came about because individuals cared enough to speak out about injustices and work for structural changes. In the developmental framework outlined earlier in this chapter, individuals characterized by modern and postmodern ways of knowing are the most likely to take on these public democratic roles.

Both of these hypothetical situations, taken from the discussion of the poesis and praxis modes of inquiry, deal with the removal of decision-making power from the people closest to the situation. In both cases there was an attempt to impose from "on high" a policy that would have a severe impact on students and teachers alike. Current trends toward de-skilling educators ignore Sarason's premise that successful educational reform must draw upon the creativity and experience of people with an obvious stake in improving schools. There is nothing simple, however, about initiatives to increase participation in decision making. All of the personal and interpersonal challenges articulated in the first part of this chapter must be met, and the structural constraints within the micro-context of a professional culture must be overcome.

In the problem situation that was part of the description of phronesis, a team of teachers was finding it hard to agree upon a strategy for dealing with behavior problems. The structural challenges inherent in this situation relate largely to our inexperience with processes of collaboration, negotiation, and collective problem solving. As we have noted, teaching is an isolating profession. Historically, teachers have closed their doors and proceeded to teach, ignoring to greater or lesser degrees school-wide processes or new mandates. Given the current focus on "systemic change," "school/community partnerships," and other whole-system initiatives, this is no longer possible. Nor, from our perspective, is it desirable.

Democracy is a social process and requires that we continue to refine our face-to-face interaction skills. We need to alter the isolating structures of the workplace so that it becomes a place that invites collaboration, the sharing of ideas and activities, and interpersonal relationships. Conflict is inevitable, and it is important to think about conflict as a creative process. The teacher education narrative in Chapter 7 will explore creative approaches to conflict resolution in more detail.

It should be noted that even institutional innovations that are oriented toward positive school improvement can backfire. Fullan and Hargreaves (1996) discuss the ways, for example, that collegiality, often advocated for its potential to transform school culture, can paradoxically "reduce innovation and imaginative solutions to individual situations, as susceptibility to the latest chosen innovation and 'groupthink' carry the day" (p. 7). Here is an example of how one or more elements of our inquiry map can counterbalance the excesses of another: poesis and theoria both remind us to stay in touch with our own feelings, reflective processes, and visionary intelligence, so that the value of individual insight and diverse ways of thinking might be preserved while people learn to work creatively and productively in groups.

In our problem situation that illustrated the value of polis, we narrated a story of how community members who were committed to a particular religious orientation gained positions of power on a governing board. In a hierarchically structured governance system, school boards sit atop educators in terms of decision-making power. In this case some important components of democracy can be seen to be in conflict. On one hand, the community democratically elected the board (the fact that the board was elected by a small number of voters is a testimony to the power of political organizing!). On the other, a prescriptive approach to character development based on religious dogma conflicted with the pragmatist approach to free inquiry and the exploration of differing points of view (dialogos). In a case like this, overcoming structural power challenges involves moral persuasion, consensus building, and the patience and skill to engage in sustained public ethical conversations.

So far, we have discussed structural challenges as though power were located merely in relationships, in roles that people play, and in the ways that institutions are organized. We have not addressed the more subtle ways that power flows throughout society: in the ways that knowledge is organized, generated, and selected; in the ways that consciousness is shaped toward particular ends (for example, by advertising and other forms of media); and in the ways that consent is "manufactured" to dominant ideologies (see Achbar & Wintonick, 1992). Critical theorists, who engage in praxis, name this power/knowledge complex *hegemony*, and critical pedagogy is dedicated to revealing such subtle structural issues.

In the book, *A Radical Democratic Critique of Capitalist Education*, Richard Brosio (1994) argues convincingly that schools are trapped in a perpetual tension between two

conflicting dynamics: the demands of capitalism and a consumer society and the imperatives of democracy. Although popular wisdom would have it that capitalism is the highest
form of democracy, with its free markets and unlimited choices, other thinkers note the
structural inequalities that inevitably result from a competitive economic system that virtually requires winners and losers. These scholars, including Brosio, assert that "the forces of
capitalism and democracy are structurally opposed to one another, and this creates conflict—
and 'internal incompatibilities' within the school itself" (Brosio, 1994, p. 8).

Public schools have historically served cross purposes: to sift and sort students for
roles in a competitive economic system and to ameliorate the worst of the injustices through
interventions that promote greater equity and social justice. Brosio cites such historic educational interventions as school integration, ethnic studies, and bilingual education as instances of democratically oriented reforms. In contrast, reforms such as the privatization of
schools; standardized, high-stakes testing; and current initiatives such as the return to the
traditional history curriculum (read: pre-multiculturalism) with an emphasis on patriotism
are efforts to reinforce the corporate economy and the power of dominant, conservative
elites. When we analyze the many problems of education through this critical lens, it is
both illuminating and overwhelming: illuminating because the theory sheds light on conditions that have seemed inexplicable and intractable; overwhelming because we are no
longer thinking in terms of changing relationships, processes, or procedures, but of
changing a pervasive mindset, a taken-for-granted worldview. We are talking about social
transformation.

In the opening paragraphs of this section, we raised some general concerns about issues of time and power. We hope we have shown that there is nothing natural about limit-
ing educational conditions; they are the results of innumerable decisions situated within
complex networks of power. All conditions can be transformed, although deep change requires genuine struggle. The struggle is a positive one—a struggle for greater equity, justice, creativity, care, and passion in education. It is also a negative one, not just against
rigid power structures and hierarchies, but also against the social, cultural, and institutional inertia that prevails. Habits, as Dewey (1936) reminds us, are hard to break. Cultural patterns, in particular, are slow to change.

We are at a crossroads in the field of education. A complex set of social conditions
point in different possible directions. Will teachers become mere functionaries in an increasingly bureaucratic system, plugged into teaching scripts developed by experts far
from their classrooms? Will their lesson plans be reduced to pages in a textbook and
their instruction to prefabricated questions in a study guide? Will they abdicate curriculum decision making to the makers of standardized tests and return to the old "skill and
drill" methods of instruction for fear that students will not score well on tests? Or will
they engage in the demanding practical and intellectual task of becoming democratically wise, with its implied promise of greater respect, autonomy, and professional status?
Will educators opt to take a quantum leap and move forward into modern and postmodern ways of knowing, with all that implies? Fullan and Hargreaves (1996) lay out the
choice well:

> This is a time in the evolution of schools and teaching when the future of the teaching profes-
> sion is "up for grabs." Most people have come to the realization that an improved status quo
> will not do the job. It is a time for teachers as *impassioned moral agents* to fight for the positive

preconditions that will shape the profession for the next era: an era in which the learning of teachers will become inextricably bound to the learning of those they teach. (p. xiii)

Merely altering the power relationships in schools will not do the job. However, the transformation of power relationships, coupled with practicing the arts of inquiry, might put us on the road to establishing a sustainable curriculum wisdom tradition with deep democracy as its inspiration.

All of the challenges of education will never be overcome. As old challenges are met, and conditions transformed, new ones surely will arise. It is a mistake to think of school re-form as something that we can put into place and have done with. Our democratic utopia will necessarily remain on the horizon, something to work toward, not something to be fi-nally attained. The map of the arts of inquiry in Chapter 3 is a work in progress, a concep-tual organizer that can lend both focus and substance to our practice. It is not an end point, but always a beginning.

Recall that this chapter was written to address the challenges of practicing curriculum wisdom. We examined very complex and difficult psychological and structural challenges. We recognize that curriculum wisdom is a very demanding professional ideal and way of work-ing, but it is not an impossible dream. We hope this chapter has made this wisdom challenge a little more understandable and possible. We continue to have a deep and abiding confidence in the creative and critical capacities of educators and fully believe that committed teachers will take responsibility for developing that capacity. Yes, some may be more ready than others, but all educators can undertake the inquiry journey that lies at the heart of curriculum wisdom.

Not surprisingly, this wisdom challenge cannot be reduced to a few techniques or sound bytes. If however, after reading this chapter you yearn for a few points to ponder that might make this task more "digestible," we end this section with a few nuggets—points to ponder that may make this book's wisdom challenge more accessible.

POINTS TO PONDER

- Develop an attitude of curiosity about your own growth in this process.
- Think about this one challenge at a time rather than embracing the complexities of the entire challenge.
- Be patient about all that is unresolved in your heart and try to love the questions themselves (Palmer, 1998).
- Learn to enjoy the tension of opposites or be at risk of premature resolution.
- Upend your tendency to canonize the familiar (Kegan, 1994, pp. 231).
- Find yourself in a place that will provide the right blend of challenge and support.
- Keep in mind that **every one of us** is trying to satisfy the expectations of love and work.
- Listen to your own and others' stories. They mark the path to understanding how meaning is made and identities are shaped.
- The next time you begin to state an opinion, pause first and reframe it as a question.
- The forms of inquiry are not a target or a method, but a framework (Henderson, 2001).

- Regularly look for diverse meaning making—for ways in which the same experience could have a different meaning for someone else (Kegan, 1994).
- Be aware of the values and beliefs that direct your behavior.
- Adopt an attitude of curiosity as a way to manage the discomfort of the stretch.
- Persevere in the attempt to understand, in spite of difficulties.
- Forgive yourself for past behaviors that may have been less conscious or enlightened and celebrate the growth you experience today.
- Give yourself permission to know more today than you did yesterday.
- Give others permission to know more today than they did yesterday.
- Speak truth to power.
- Remain humbled each day by how much you have to learn.
- Embrace the transcendent power of love.

References

Achbar, M., & Wintonick, P. (Directors). (1992). *Manufacturing consent: Noam Chomsky and the media.* (Film)

Brosio, R. (1994). *A radical democratic critique of capitalist education.* New York: Peter Lang.

Dewey, J. (1936). The social significance of academic freedom. *The Social Frontier, 2*(6), 165–166.

Dewey, J. (1966). *Democracy and education.* New York: Free Press. (Original work published 1916)

Eisner, E. W. (1994). *Cognition and curriculum reconsidered* (2nd ed.). New York: Teachers College Press.

Fullan, M., & Hargreaves, A. (1996). *What's worth fighting for in your school?* New York: Teachers College Press.

Gergen, K. (1991). *The saturated self: Dilemmas of identity in contemporary life.* New York: Basic Books.

Gornik, R. (2002). *Teacher inquiry capacity: A case study.* Unpublished doctoral dissertation, Kent State University.

Henderson, J. G. (2001). *Reflective teaching. Professional artistry through inquiry* (3rd ed.). Upper Saddle River, NJ: Merrill/Prentice Hall.

Henderson, J. G., & Hawthorne, R. D. (2000). *Transformative curriculum leadership* (2nd ed.). Upper Saddle River, NJ: Merrill/Prentice Hall.

Hermans, H. J. M., & Kempen, H. J. G. (1993). *The dialogical self: Meaning as movement.* San Diego, CA: Academic Press.

Josselson, R. (1994). Identity and relatedness in the life cycle. In H. A. Bosma, T. G. Graafsma, H. D. Grotevant, & D. J. de Levita (Eds.), *Identity and development* (pp. 81–102). Thousand Oaks, CA: Sage.

Josselson, R. (1995). Imagining the real: Empathy, narrative and the dialogic self. In R. Jesselson & A. Lieblich (Eds.), *Interpreting experience: The narrative study of lives* (Vol. 3, pp. 27–44). Thousand Oaks, CA: Sage.

Kegan, R. (1982). *The evolving self: Problem and process in human development.* Cambridge, MA: Harvard University Press.

Kegan, R. (1994). *In over our heads: The mental demands of modern life.* Cambridge, MA: Harvard University Press.

Kincheloe, J. L. (1999). Critical democracy in education. In J. Henderson & K. Kesson (Eds.), *Understanding democratic curriculum leadership* (pp. 70–83). New York: Teachers College Press.

Lahey, L., Souvaine, E., Kegan, R., Goodman, R., & Felix, S. (1988). *A guide to the Subject-Object Interview: Its administration and interpretation.* Unpublished manuscript. Harvard University, Cambridge, MA.

No child left behind. (2001). http:www.ed.gov/legislation/ESEA02

Palmer, P. J. (1998). *The courage to teach. Exploring the inner landscape of a teacher's life.* San Francisco: Jossey-Bass.

Piaget, J. (1954). *The construction of reality in the child*. New York: Basic Books.

Pinar, W. F., Reynolds, W. M., Slattery, P., & Taubman, P. M. (1995). *Understanding curriculum: An introduction to the study of historical and contemporary curriculum discourses*. New York: Peter Lang.

Roth, S. E. (1996). *Exploration of ego development of teachers and principals as it relates to the professional growth of a staff: A case study*. Unpublished doctoral dissertation, Ohio University.

Routman, R. (1991). *Invitations: Changing as teachers and learners K-12*. Portsmouth, NH: Heinemann.

Sarason, S. B. (1990). *The predictable failure of educational reform: Can we change course before it's too late?* San Francisco: Jossey-Bass.

Scheffler, I. (1985). *Of human potential: An essay in the philosophy of education*. Boston: Routledge & Kegan Paul.

Silver, J. (2001). *A constructive developmental approach to Tavistock Group Relations Conference Learning: A narrative study*. Unpublished doctoral dissertation, Fielding Graduate Institute.

van Manen, M. (1992). *On pedagogy as virtue*. Paper presented at the meeting of the American Educational Research Association, San Francisco.

Chapter 5

Implications for Educational Practice

INTRODUCTION

You have now been introduced to the understanding of curriculum work as a **wisdom challenge**. Curriculum wisdom is the practice of sophisticated educational judgments with reference to envisioning and enacting a "democratic good life." It is both a concept and a calling—a professional ideal and an inquiry-based *way* of working. It is multifaceted decision making focusing on solving immediate teaching-learning problems **and** on fostering enduring democratic values; hence, it can be described as "doubled" means/end and means/visionary end problem solving. It requires authentic *curriculum enactments*. Wisdom capacities are, in general, not cultivated in a work environment where educators are only expected to implement the decisions of others—where educators' judgments are not trusted. Chapter 1 introduces this interpretation of curriculum work. Chapter 2 provides a synopsis of the tradition of American pragmatism, with its foundational insights into curriculum wisdom. Chapter 3 presents an inquiry-based map or scaffolding for this curriculum work. Any other type of practical advice would be misleading and foolish. Curriculum wisdom is simply too complex and subtle to allow for a more literal, technical treatment because there is no ultimate definition for *democratic morality*—no final democratic doctrine. At best, there are only informed interpretations. The message of Chapter 3 is that the curriculum wisdom challenge is, necessarily, practiced through arts of inquiry.

Curriculum wisdom is a profoundly personal and political challenge. It is, perhaps, the most difficult and demanding of all the professional virtues, and it requires a fundamental shift in power relations. Chapter 4 discusses the personal and structural obstacles facing curriculum workers who decide to undertake the wisdom challenge. This analysis highlights deep-seated developmental and institutional issues. We now turn to an examination of the implications of practicing curriculum as a wisdom challenge.

PRACTICAL IMPLICATIONS: THREE LENSES

There are at least three ways to picture the practice of curriculum wisdom, and each "lens" provides important insights into this challenging professional endeavor. Curriculum wisdom is, first of all, sophisticated educational decision making. It is the attempt to transform specific courses of study into instances of democratic living. Since this is a matter of professional discretion, the practice of curriculum wisdom involves a **paradigm shift** with reference to the current standardized test-driven educational policy environment. Second, to practice curriculum wisdom is to embrace a certain quality work life. Curriculum wisdom is neither a technique nor a task; it is a **way** of being and knowing. Third, the practice of curriculum wisdom is embedded in a particular curriculum development–professional development–organizational development–community development ecological niche. Therefore, the enactment of curriculum wisdom requires careful attention to a certain **systemic reform**.

Figure 5.1 depicts the three lenses on the practical implications of curriculum wisdom: (i) a paradigm shift, (ii) a way of professional living, and (iii) a systemic reform effort. The

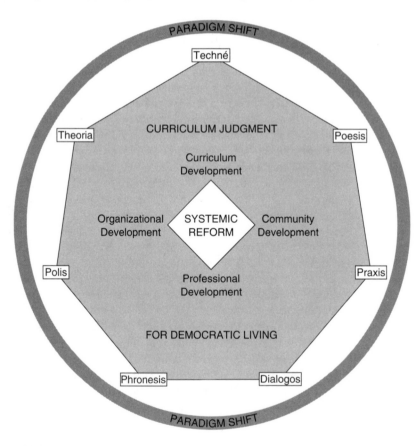

FIGURE 5.1

Three Lenses on the Practice of Curriculum Wisdom

figure shows the interrelationship between curriculum, professional, organizational, and community development activities. The modes of inquiry are dispersed around the figure to call attention to the work life implications. The fact that this work may involve a fundamental shift in orientation is depicted by the phrase: "Curriculum Judgment for Democratic Living." We now turn to a more in-depth examination of each of these perspectives on the practice of curriculum wisdom.

A Paradigm Shift

Curriculum wisdom is the attempt to transform courses of study into instances of democratic living. Not only does this require sophisticated judgment, but it may necessitate a basic change in professional orientation that is often described as a paradigm shift in the educational literature. Educational policies in most states in America, as well as most countries, are generally geared to standardized tests. Educational quality is tied to test score improvement. This may be appealing in its simplicity, but is it wise? Curriculum wisdom is practiced from a different frame of reference. Educational quality is linked to instances of democratic living. The underlying premise of curriculum wisdom can be stated quite simply: **Just because students test well on standardized measures does not mean they are becoming good human beings**.

This fundamental shift in orientation should not imply that curriculum wisdom is an antitesting, antievaluation professional stance. On the contrary, evaluation is a central feature of this curriculum work. However, the evaluative focus is on the enduring values of good living, not on the spurious values of good test taking behavior. If properly designed, standardized tests could possibly support curriculum wisdom practices. For example, Yeh (2001) argues that mandated tests in the United States "should focus on critical thinking, defined as careful argumentation. This could address the primary criticism of such tests—that they drive an instructional focus on rote factual learning" (p. 16). Yeh illustrates how such tests could be constructed; certainly, such tests could be a useful tool for democratically minded educators. The key point, however, is that the tests would inform curriculum judgment, not be used as a substitute for judgment. The master would be the educator, not the state-mandated test. Educators' central evaluative concern would be on how well they are facilitating democratic living in their classrooms.

Facilitating democratic living in the classroom requires subject matter instruction in a context of democratic self and social learning. The relationship between these three dimensions of student learning is depicted in Figure 5.2. This **3S** perspective provides concrete guidance on how to undertake the curriculum wisdom challenge. The framework encourages a balanced approach to traditional subject-centered concerns and progressive student-centered and society-centered advocacies.[1] In fact, this 3S frame of reference offers a general test of how well a course of study is functioning as an instance of democratic living. It serves as a succinct referent for evaluating the quality of a curriculum judgment.

Using 3S student learning as a point of reference, a number of critical questions could be asked of any curriculum. How does the curriculum address subject-matter learning in a

---

[1]For additional information on this balanced ideological approach, see Ackerman (2003) and Walker (2003).

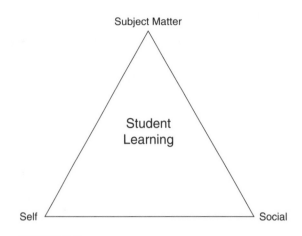

FIGURE 5.2

Three Dimensions of Student Learning

context of democratic self and social learning? If the curriculum lacks this proper 3S balance, why is this the case? Is there a "hidden" curriculum problem? Marsh and Willis (2003) note that this occurs when "parts of the environment that are unplanned or even unplannable (such as all the unacknowledged attitudes, beliefs, codes of conduct, and conventions for social relationships that form the overall, but constantly shifting, milieu of the school) seem to exert a more subtle but far greater influence over what students learn than does the official curriculum itself" (p. 11). Hidden curriculum problems can only come into view when the educational milieu is part of the deliberations, which requires educators to work from the holistic 3S orientation.

Perhaps the lack of a proper 3S balance is due to a "null" curriculum problem. Eisner (1994a) writes:

> If we are concerned with the consequences of school programs and the role of curriculum in shaping those consequences, then it seems to me that we are well advised to consider not only the explicit and implicit curricula of schools but also what schools do *not teach*. It is my thesis that what schools do not teach may be as important as what they do teach. (p. 97, author's emphasis)

Is the lack of a balanced 3S perspective in curriculum work due to an unconsciousness about the nature of the self and social learning embedded in particular subject-matter instruction? For example, as students are being prepared to score well on a standardized literacy test, what are they learning about themselves as lifelong readers? Are they learning to see themselves as lovers of books? What are they learning about social relations? What are they learning about the value of competition and the relevance of cooperation and collaboration?

Dewey's (1963) *Experience and Education* is a good foundational source for understanding this 3S referent for democratic curriculum work. Dewey wrote this short book in response to what he viewed as the excesses of the progressive educational movement in the United States. He was concerned that progressive educators were citing his publications as justification for a narrow "child-centered" education, and he wanted to set the record straight with respect to his own educational philosophy. He acknowledges that he is not a "traditionalist" and that he wants to advance a robust democratic education in a responsible manner. His goal is to substitute democratic responsibility for traditional authority as the referent for educational work.

Dewey (1963) states that traditional approaches to education are, by definition, focused on obedience to past authority: "Since the subject-matter as well as standards of proper conduct are handed down from the past, the attitude of pupils must, upon the whole, be one of docility, receptivity, and obedience" (p. 18). He notes that because progressive educators reject such passive learning, they face an enormous challenge: "When external control is rejected, the problem becomes that of finding the factors of control that are inherent within experience. When external authority is rejected, it does not follow that all authority should be rejected, but rather that there is need to search for a more effective source of authority" (p. 21). From the point of view of the democratic good life, this more "effective" source of authority is cultivated **within** each student through "deep" subject-matter learning that fosters a progressive self and social learning. Facilitating this shift in educational orientation—from an external to an internal source of authority—requires sophisticated, context-specific judgments. Educational decisions must be based on complex "developmentally appropriate" deliberations, and this decision making would parallel the adult developmental considerations in Chapter 4.

Wiggins and McTighe (2001) provide a useful framework for conceptualizing 3S student learning. They call it *"Six Facets of Understanding."* The six facets are

- *Explanation*: sophisticated and apt explanations and theories, which provide knowledgeable and justified accounts of events, actions, and ideas.
- *Interpretation*: interpretations, narrative, and translations that provide meaning.
- *Application*: ability to use knowledge effectively in new situations and diverse contexts.
- *Perspective*: critical and insightful points of view.
- *Empathy*: the ability to get inside another person's feelings and worldview.
- *Self-knowledge:* the wisdom to know one's ignorance and how one's patterns of thought and action inform as well as prejudice understanding (pp. 44–62).

This framework touches on all the 3S bases as educators are asked to consider the relationship between good subject-matter learning and good self and social learning.

Care, however, must be taken in using Wiggins and McTighe's (2001) text as a practical guide for curriculum wisdom. The authors do not explicitly address the transformation of courses of study into instances of democratic living, nor do they advance arts of inquiry as the basis for curriculum decisions. As Wiggins and McTighe repeatedly state throughout their text, their focus is on "deep" subject-matter learning. Nevertheless, their "facets of understanding" framework is a useful point of departure for conceptualizing 3S student learning.

Ultimately, no model can serve as a definitive guide for curriculum wisdom. This guidance must come from deep within each educator through the practice of the arts of inquiry. This is why the topic of curriculum judgment is treated as an inspirational matter, involving a professional way of life, and this consideration serves as our next lens on curriculum wisdom. However, before turning to this matter, there is one additional aspect of curriculum judgment that needs mentioning.

Informed judgment is not only required to transform courses of study into instances of democratic living; it is also necessary in deciding how to enact such curricula in the context of test-driven policy mandates. Standardized test implementation is the political order of the day for most educators, at least in K–12 (kindergarten through twelfth grade) public school settings, and these educators must, therefore, decide how to enact curriculum wisdom **while** implementing standardized-test policies (Snyder, Bolin, and Zumwalt, 1992). The decision on how best to handle this enactment-implementation dilemma requires additional practical, context-specific judgment. Educators must be creative not only about the facilitation of developmentally appropriate, democratic 3S learning but also about how to work in this way while preparing their students for standardized tests.

It should be noted, however, that the enacting and implementing orientations are not mutually exclusive. Returning to the earlier point about the design of standardized tests, it is likely that the facilitation of democratic 3S learning will result in higher standardized-test scores.

A Way of Professional Living

There is no protocol for curriculum wisdom; it cannot be approached through a set of techniques or tasks. Curriculum wisdom must, necessarily, be conceived as a **way** of being and knowing. Eisner (1994a) provides important insight into this lens on curriculum wisdom. He argues for the centrality of educational "criticism" and "connoisseurship" in the exercise of artful educational practice. It is worth quoting him at some length:

> Effective criticism, within the arts or in education, is not an act independent of the powers of perception. The ability to see, to perceive what is subtle, complex, and important, is its first necessary condition. The act of knowledgeable perception is, in the arts, referred to as connoisseurship. To be a connoisseur is to know how to look, to see, and to appreciate. Connoisseurship, generally defined, is the art of perception. It is essential to criticism because without the ability to perceive what is subtle and important, criticism is likely to be superficial or even empty. The major distinction between connoisseurship and criticism is this: connoisseurship is the art of appreciation, criticism is the art of disclosure. …Criticism is the public side of connoisseurship. One can be a connoisseur without the skills of criticism, but one cannot be a critic without the skills of connoisseurship. In using language to make public qualities and meanings that are not themselves discursive, something of a paradox exists. How can words express what words can never express? The successful resolution of this paradox lies at the heart of the critical act. (pp. 215, 219)

The curriculum wisdom challenge requires educators to cultivate their connoisseurship and critical capacities with reference to the democratic good life. In order to transform courses of study into democratic experiences, they must be able to deeply perceive and publicly render the subtle interplay between specific subject-matter learning and democratic self and social learning. The degree to which they do not develop the necessary connoisseurship and critical capacities is the degree to which their curriculum wisdom is limited.

The arts of inquiry support this necessary capacity building; but because these arts are so demanding, it is a very high standard for curriculum and teaching work. To work in this way is, ultimately, to make a quality work decision that emerges out of a deep sense of professional calling. The day that teachers are willing to strike over this "quality of work life" issue will be an important political victory for democratic education. That day will, we hope, dawn for all societies that declare democratic ideals, and the march to this auspicious future begins one dedicated educator at a time. Each time a curriculum worker decides to inquire into the democratic good life, a small step has been taken toward building a mature democratic culture. Each time an educator acquires a deeper understanding of the relationship between democracy and education and then publicly manifests that understanding through curriculum and teaching work, a small victory has been registered for the democratic good life.

Systemic Reform

The practice of curriculum wisdom requires educators to cultivate an "ecological" awareness, aptly described by Eisner (1994b):

> The reform of education not only requires deeper and more comprehensive analysis of schools; it must also attend to the dimensions of schooling that must be collectively addressed to make educational reform educationally real. This attention must go well beyond changes in individual aspects of educational practice. ...Applied to schools, it means that the school as a whole must be addressed: ...the intentions that give direction to the enterprise, the structure that supports it, the curriculum that provides its content, the teaching with which that content is mediated, and the evaluation system that enables us to monitor and improve its operation. ...To approach the reform of schools ecologically or, as others put it, systemically, requires, at the very least, attention to intentions—what aims really matter in the educational enterprise as a whole? (pp. 10–11)

With reference to the practice of curriculum wisdom, this systemic reform is grounded in particular interpretations of "curriculum development," "professional development," "organizational development," and "community development." *Curriculum development* is understood as the design of courses of study that are experienced as instances of democratic living. Wiggins and McTighe (2001) present a "backward design" process that involves three steps: Identify the desired results of "in-depth" student understanding of subject matter, determine the acceptable evidence for inferring that students are progressing toward this understanding, and plan learning experiences and instruction (pp. 9–19). Wiggins and McTighe's first two steps require, in Eisner's (1994a) language, a certain subject-matter connoisseurship and criticism. With the assistance of their six facets of understanding, educators must be able to discern deep subject-matter learning and then must publicly articulate their understandings as a clear and concise rubric of "desired results" and "acceptable evidence."

The curriculum development in this book is based on the same design principle but with a broader focus. Educators go through the same connoisseurship, criticism, and planning process. However, in this case, they are discerning the democratic good life in the context of specific subject-matter learning (that is, they are working from a 3S perspective), creating a rubric for evaluating students' 3S growth, and then planning appropriate learning experiences and instruction.

Wiggins and McTighe (2001) characterize this curriculum development logic as backward design because in their experience most educators begin their curriculum work by planning specific instructional activities before making decisions about appropriate goals and evaluation, and they wish to reverse this curriculum development order:

> Why do we describe the most effective curricular designs as "backward"? We do so because many teachers *begin* with textbooks, favored lessons, and time-honored activities rather than deriving those tools from targeted goals or standards. We are advocating the reverse: One starts with the end—the desired results (goals or standards)—and then derives the curriculum from the evidence of learning (performances) called for by the standard and the teaching needed to equip students to perform. (p. 8)

Curriculum development, as interpreted in this book, is best characterized as **visionary** rather than **backward** design. It is forward thinking and is democratically progressive in its orientation. The educator envisions how a course of study can serve as an instance of democratic living, enacts this vision, and then evaluates the results. To do this, the educator draws on his or her connoisseurship/criticism abilities—his or her understanding of in-depth subject-matter learning in the context of a democratic good life. One of the three practitioner commentators in Chapter 6 provides a concrete illustration of this very sophisticated curriculum development work.

The professional development that is "ecologically" linked to this curriculum development is simple to describe but challenging to practice. This professional development is understood as the cultivation of the abilities to engage in the above curriculum development. Educators must develop their inquiry and instructional capacities so that they can facilitate courses of study as instances of democratic living. They cannot do this without becoming connoisseurs and critics of the democratic good life. This is a tall order, potentially involving years of disciplined study. Ideally, this professional development work begins in preservice teacher education (teacher preparation) and then extends through induction (usually the first two years of a teacher's career) into a wide range of collaborative, supervisory, inservice, and graduate school activities. Just as the 3S perspective on student learning serves as a general referent for curriculum development, the seven modes of inquiry in Chapter 3 function as a general referent for professional development. The adult developmental considerations in Chapter 4 are an important dimension of this work, and one of the three commentators in Chapter 6 provides a more detailed discussion of the necessary professional development.

Organization development (OD) is understood as specific collaborative activities that build a local work culture that nurtures and sustains the necessary curriculum and professional development activities. According to Schmuck and Runkel (1985), there are three phases of OD. In phase I the focus is on examining how members of the school community communicate, cultivate trust and positive regard, and address areas of conflict. Establishing healthy working relationships is a central feature of this initial OD work (Hargreaves, 1995; Lieberman, 1995). Because most educators have been socialized to work independently, learning to work collaboratively typically means giving themselves permission to talk about their work and beliefs far more intimately with a larger circle of colleagues than they have ever been comfortable with.

In phase II attention turns to the critical assessment of organizational life. Educators identify concerns, gather and analyze data about their own beliefs and work, engage in collaborative problem solving and planning, and analyze the overt and covert meanings of their work culture. Phase III translates the communication and critical assessment work into action plans. The focus is on collaboratively addressing concerns and problems that have been identified. The action plans are based on the group's core beliefs and on the data derived from inquiring into the school culture (Sergiovanni, 1992). Problems are agreed on, goals are established, activities are developed, a time line is set, responsible parties are identified, and the assessment of progress and accomplishment is planned.

With reference to the practice of curriculum wisdom, these OD phases are handled in a particular way. The focus of the trust building is on cultivating mutual respect and regard through a shared inquiry-based work life. The critical assessment addresses the institutional structures that inhibit, constrain, and/or prevent the practice of curriculum wisdom, and the general analysis of these structural obstacles in Chapter 4 serves as a referent for this work. Finally, the collaborative action planning focuses on constructive institutional change. The work structures should serve inquiry-based problem solving, not vice versa.

Collectively, the OD activities are guided by such questions as

- How can we learn to trust one another's professional judgments as we work to transform courses of study into instances of democratic living, and how can we base this trust on the fact that each of us is cultivating our capacities to inquire into the democratic good life in our own unique ways?
- How can we collaboratively work together in the facilitation of courses of study as democratic experiences? In the context of our individual inquiries into the democratic good life, can we identify common ground for our work? Can we collectively envision ways to practice curriculum wisdom?
- What institutional structures are obstacles to our curriculum wisdom practices? How can we change these institutional structures? How can we establish a work culture that nurtures our curriculum and professional development work?

The public school superintendent who is one of the practitioner commentators in Chapter 6 provides a more detailed discussion of this OD work.

The necessary community development is a very challenging form of public intellectual leadership (Henderson & Kesson, 2001). The overall goal is to foster the creation of supportive "public spaces" (Greene, 1988; Macpherson, Aspland, Brooker, & Elliott, 1999) for curriculum, professional, and organizational development work. In our current circumstances, public perception of quality education is, generally, closely tied to standardized-test scores. The political logic is basic: quality education correlates with high test scores. The fact that students who test well may not have acquired a deep understanding of subject matter in a context of democratic self and social learning is, generally, not part of public understanding.

The purpose of the community education in this book is to reeducate the general public. This is what Eisner (1994a) describes as "educational criticism." The goal is to elevate the "curriculum literacy" in a society. The local community must be taught that quality education in a society with democratic ideals should be indexed to instances of democratic education, not to standardized test scores.

Henderson and Kesson (2001) discuss three phases of this public intellectual work. Begin by identifying a "public" with which to communicate. From the point of view of this book, this would mean finding curriculum stakeholders who would be open to learning about the value of approaching curriculum work as a wisdom challenge. Next, create ways to inspire this public. For example, organize public forums so that compelling stories of professional curriculum inquiry and student inquiry learning can be shared. Finally, involve this public in collaborative problem solving. Seek their input into the necessary curriculum, professional, and organization development changes.

References

Ackerman, D. B. (2003). Taproots for a new century: Tapping the best of traditional and progressive education. *Phi Delta Kappan, 84*(5), 344–349.

Dewey, J. (1963). *Experience and education.* New York: Macmillan. (Original work published 1938)

Eisner, E. W. (1994a). *The educational imagination: On the design and evaluation of school programs* (3rd ed.). New York: Macmillan.

Eisner, E. W. (1994b). *Cognition and curriculum reconsidered* (2nd ed.). New York: Teachers College Press.

Greene, M. (1988). *The dialectic of freedom.* New York: Teachers College Press.

Hargreaves, A. (1995). *Changing teachers, changing times.* New York: Teachers College Press.

Henderson, J. G., & Kesson, K. R. (2001). Curriculum work as public intellectual leadership. In K. Sloan & J. Sears (Eds.), *Democratic curriculum theory and practice: Retrieving public spaces* (pp. 1–23). Troy, NY: Educator's International Press.

Lieberman, A. (Ed.). (1995). *The work of restructuring schools: Building from the ground up.* New York: Teachers College Press.

Macpherson, I., Aspland, T., Brooker, R., & Elliott, B. (1999). *Places and spaces for teachers in curriculum leadership.* Deakin: Australia Curriculum Studies Association.

Marsh, C. J., & Willis, G. (2003). *Curriculum: Alternative approaches, ongoing issues* (3rd ed.). Upper Saddle River, NJ: Merrill/Prentice Hall.

Schmuck, R., & Runkel, P. (1985). *The handbook of organization development in schools* (3rd ed.). Prospect Heights, IL: Waveland.

Sergiovanni, T. J. (1992). *Moral leadership: Getting to the heart of school reform.* San Francisco: Jossey-Bass.

Snyder, J., Bolin, F., & Zumwalt, K. (1992). Curriculum implementation. In P. W. Jackson (Ed.), *Handbook of research on curriculum* (pp. 402–435). New York: Macmillan.

Walker, D. F. (2003). *Fundamentals of curriculum: Passion and professionalism* (2nd ed.). Mahwah, NJ: Lawrence Erlbaum.

Wiggins, G., & McTighe, J. (2001). *Understanding by design* (Special ed.). Upper Saddle River, NJ: Merrill/Prentice Hall.

Yeh, S. S. (2001). Tests worth teaching to: Constructing state-mandated tests that emphasize critical thinking. *Educational Researcher, 30*(9), 12–17.

Chapter 6

Three Practitioner Commentaries

INTRODUCTION

We invited three educators to comment on the implications of practicing curriculum as a wisdom challenge. These practitioners—a public school teacher, a teacher educator, and a public school superintendent—represent important curriculum stakeholders in democratic societies. The classroom teacher's commentary, which comes first, is the longest because it provides the most in-depth analysis. The other two commentaries are deliberately shorter owing to space limitations and to avoid redundancy. The teacher educator's commentary is interesting in that it is based on two years of research into the challenges of teaching the arts of inquiry to future teachers, and the superintendent's insights result from several years of district-wide reform experience.

A TEACHER'S COMMENTARY

The Way of Living Lens

My wife's maternal grandfather, Bertil Anderson, immigrated, penniless with only a first-grade education, to the United States in 1930.[1] The only thing he brought with him from rural Sweden was his skill as a carpenter and a desire to improve the future fortunes of his family. As I write today, behind me on my wife's side of the office, sits one of the most elegant, sturdy (and heavy I might add) desks you will ever find. It was hand crafted, a high school graduation present for my wife, by Bert when he was in his eighties. As I was formulating this commentary, my wife and I discussed the work of her grandfather; she said, "He left a legacy; he didn't just slap wood together."

Bertil Anderson made a living building things, as many men do, but he was different. He was a master craftsman, a connoisseur. He knew about different woods and finishes. He understood various "joineries" and how to construct furniture for strength, functionality, and beauty. His work fed his family, became loving gifts, created a place

---

[1]Commentary written by Dana Keller

to store books, or added beauty to a room. His work was an expression of himself and his feelings for other people. His work was part of what defined him as a person, and he nurtured and sought perfection and expression in it. Again my wife explains, "His craft echoes the spirit of the man—his ethics, vision, connection to others and the world."

A natural extension of his vast knowledge, dedication, and skill was his critical nature about other people's projects, and he did not always keep his opinions to himself—to do so would be to turn his back on his craft. When my father-in-law had a house built around 1970, Bert, tools in hand, would walk around the worksite hollering, "Doesn't anyone here own a level?"

To some degree this book is reminiscent of Bert's hollering. In an environment of one-size-fits-all educational programs and state- and nationally-driven testing, this book screams, "Does anyone here have a level?" All of us in this book have come together on the worksite to offer a better way to build this house, or maybe a better way to operate the industry altogether. There must be a balance; there must be a way to teach creatively in the face of test-driven policies.

I am a teacher and I am developing my own connoisseurship and critical capacities. I am not alone. I work with other people in a complicated social and organizational structure—in a particular work ecology. I am responsible, to varying degrees, to all parts of the system, but I am the practitioner, and how well I do my job—how well my work directly affects the lives of my students—is of primary importance. My craft is informed by my growing connoisseurship and criticism, and that is what I have been asked to share with you. After describing my curriculum development approach, I will share how this work is linked to the rest of my "ecology." I will talk about professional, organizational and community development.

A Paradigm Shift

Once a teacher enters the authentic space of the arts of inquiry, his or her actions are set in motion through curriculum enactment. Here the teacher's developing judgment affects not only him or her but the lives of the students who perform in the environment. The goal, of course, is to create a more meaningful and developmental experience for the students and the teacher. It is, in a small space and for a relatively short time, the creation of a culture. This book has introduced the tools for developing this classroom culture. Inherent here are hidden or null curriculum issues and what I call "the new expectations." You have been introduced to most of these ideas already, so my goal is to bring attention to them in the context of the sample unit that I will be discussing. This vision may be defined differently a year from now. Remember, the goal is to "transform courses of study into instances of democratic living."

Different people can understand curriculum differently, but I resonate with the wisdom orientation. Wisdom, it seems, is both a way of knowing and a way of acting. It comes with experience, but not in a straightforward way. If two people of equal age can be assumed to have reasonably similar experiences, why then might one be seemingly become wise and the other a grumpy curmudgeon? Why might one of these people seem to have grown from experience and perhaps taken to nurturing the young while the other feels shortchanged, angry, and bitter? Differences in wisdom are mainly due to a person's approach to life's experiences.

There is no precise model or protocol for practicing curriculum wisdom. Perhaps, within the parameters of democratic responsibility, there are as many ways for people to undertake their wisdom journey as there are people. I have always been one to think deeply about learning and culture and society and how they affect and inform teaching. Early in my career, I could tell that compliant students and units that were appropriately formed in the Tyler Rationale just did not feel like good teaching and quality learning. I felt there was more and have been inspired by Dewey's (1930) perspective:

> We have seen that a community or social group sustains itself through continuous self-renewal, and that this renewal takes place by means of the educational growth of the immature members of the group. By various agencies, unintentional and designed, a society transforms uninitiated and seemingly alien beings into robust trustees of its own resources and ideal. Education is thus a fostering, a nurturing, a cultivating, process. All of these words mean that it implies attention to the conditions of growth. (p. 12)

Reading Dewey and similar works started me thinking that there is so much more involved in gaining an education than learning material or passing tests.

I also came to understand that different peoples of the world with different religions or under different governments would need to be educated differently. For instance, a teacher in a totalitarian society, who taught his students the moral value of a government run by the people, would not be preparing students—at least in the eyes of his government—for their future good life. As I came to perceive and understand this political-educational connection, I came to see how complex and rigorous this journey was going to become. I began to envision what a quality democratic citizen is, what he or she does, and how I could start to lead my students in that direction.

I set out to define the democratic good life, particularly as it pertained to what values I should be instilling in and modeling for my students. I began to question more deeply what skills students should be developing and what material they should be studying. I defined, in the context of considerable thought about our culture, what is particularly important for students. I developed six categories of skills or abilities that I considered crucial to the democratic way of life: understanding over knowing, self (student) planning/regulating/evaluating, social wisdom and tolerance, technology, communication, and the definition of self. I was only vaguely aware that I was really using an unsophisticated version of inquiry artistry to work out my goals in terms of the 3S scaffold.

This thinking has metamorphosed into a new document that I am working on in which I outline a foundational belief system from which I will operate. It is a living/breathing document in which I lay out my assumptions about student roles, teacher roles, school roles and assumptions about curriculum, the nature of learning, and—specific to my discipline—the nature of language development and purpose. For example, one of my working assumptions is students, like all people, are meaning makers, creating and reacting to a private, personal reality that resides both apart from and within the context of the greater social reality. As you will see, this belief and the others guide my curriculum decision making. Of course, if I believe this about students' natures, then I need to nurture it in students as part of my curriculum. My students' ability to be creative meaning makers is not going to be well reflected in a "test-driven reform" environment, so I need to be sure that part of my classroom curriculum provides the necessary information to do well on these tests.

This wisdom challenge is hard work. It requires disciplined study! In so many ways, from so many sources, I must balance an infinite amount of information, opinions, beliefs, etc. As I discussed in Chapter 1, the more I search for answers, the more questions I seem to be left with. This is where the arts of inquiry come into play. The scaffolding for this work is the 3S perspective on student learning and the visionary design process. As part of my commentary, I will present a unit design that I will be enacting with my students in the near future. The unit design is presented in Figure 6.1, and my discussion will directly refer to its specifics.

Desired Results: Overarching Understandings	Determining Acceptable Evidence	Plan Learning Experiences and Instruction
Subject Matter To create a meaningful connection through language arts to the Civil War unit in history, mostly through biography, historical documents, and poetry. To study verse and prose, as a retrospective of history, through literature study from the Gettysburg Address through Toni Morrison. **Self** For the students to gain an empathetic perspective of their place in American history. For students to explore their own historical biases and prejudices. For students to explore and develop a sense of responsibility to the greater good of all people. **Social** For students to understand that the human behavior of the past has had influence on the human condition of today, and that human behavior today has a bearing on the human condition tomorrow. For students to develop a perspective and a respect for the struggles of others, particularly African Americans.	• Responses in a reader response journal—many teacher-formulated questions, room for student expansion • Essay • Individual conferencing • Class and small-group discussions • Group project and performance • Narratives and dialogues written by students from the perspectives of historical figures • A response to an article on reparations to slave families • Discussion and analyses of literature	1. Start with individual inventories created from the essential questions. 2. In groups, students share their responses and prepare a presentation of their discussion based on consensus but with note taken of the strong dissenters. 3. Open to a classroom discussion that pulls specifically to the essential questions. 4. Introduce literature packet that I have created. It contains work from the Gettysburg Address to slave narratives to "I Have a Dream" to Maya Angelo, and many in between. 5. Introduce structured response journal that requires and guides in-depth analyses of the literature, authors, and attitudes of the times from Lincoln to the present. 6. Progress though the work will take about three weeks, including watching "I Have a Dream" on video, listening to Maya Angelo on tape and watching an interview, and listening to Langston Hughes poetry on tape.

FIGURE 6.1

Visionary Design with 3S Scaffolding

(continued)

Desired Results: Overarching Understandings	Determining Acceptable Evidence	Plan Learning Experiences and Instruction
Essential Questions 1. Do the cultural, familial, and economic issues created during the time of slavery still affect America today? 2. What changes in the perspective or feelings of African Americans are represented as the literature progresses from slave biographies through Toni Morrison; how does this reflect the social/cultural changes that occurred throughout time? 3. In terms of attitudes, form, theme, author purpose, writing conventions, grammar, and style, how do the works of African Americans differ from the verse and prose you have been exposed to? Explain. 4. Is the concept of equal rights a goal that has been reached? A goal we are seeking? A myth but we should work toward it anyway? A myth and we may as well relax about it? Use your deepening understanding of history and literature to build your case. 5. Knowing what you now know, are you in any way responsible to the plights of others? Why or why not?		7. Reading will be done silently, chorally, as a class, me reading, or reading along with tapes, depending on class interest, resources, and most appropriate dissemination of message. 8. In groups, students will pick from one of many reading/writing projects to facilitate, explore, reflect, and share their growth during these experiences. As groups and with individuals, I will hold planning and writing conferences. 9. Each student will write a perspective essay on his or her unit learning experiences as well as complete the extensive response journal. 10. The unit will conclude with the turning in of the journals and the essays, the sharing of the projects, and a discussion of the essential question, perhaps with debate.

FIGURE 6.1

As you have learned, the 3S perspective is that subject-matter understanding should be facilitated in a context of democratic self and social learning. There are many people who might debate this, believing that schooling is only about subject matter instruction. What I have come to understand is that 3S is not a way of looking at and structuring curriculum; it is a curriculum scaffold that is sensitive to the way life is actually experienced.

As you can see in Figure 6.1, I have detailed the desired results of the unit in terms of democratic subject matter, self, and social learning. These results statements are often further detailed, either formally or informally, in terms of specific performance outcomes that are outlined in my district's curriculum map. This is particularly true for subject matter. The student learning goals develop from and are guided by my developing picture of the democratic good life; thus, those considerations guide my decision making in terms of unit design, environment, and expectations.

For instance, as I stated above, I believe that students are meaning makers. Actually, I believe that adults, as responsible democratic citizens, must be strong meaning makers. They must be critical of masses of information and endless stimuli in order to formulate individual realities and perceptions from which they problem solve—everything from life decisions to voting choices. Further, I believe that if students are to be good meaning makers, any unit that nurtures that truth will need plenty of room for freedom, exploration, choice, interpretation, and expression. Interestingly, if one looks at the difference between the kid and grown-up worlds, such freedom is one of the differences.

I contend that if we want kids to be good meaning makers as adults, practicing these skills should be part of their education. This learning is planned for and is structured by the self and social parts of the 3S curriculum triangle. The balance, and it is a tricky task, is to allow for all this while still focusing on the subject-matter concerns that may require teacher guidance (and show up on tests), such as the need for correct interpretation and, perhaps, matters of grammar, punctuation, form, etc. When 3S instruction (or what I will call transformative teaching) is being enacted in the face of high-stakes standardized tests, it can be tough to balance the needs of both. However, I am inclined to believe that transformative teaching so rises above the requirements of test-driven reform that the needs of the test can, almost invisibly, be absorbed into the greater scheme. However, there are other factors at play here that I will touch on later.

I turn back to the unit in Figure 6.1. If students are to become meaning makers for their futures as democratic citizens, they will need to understand not only the interrelated aspects of language but how language can express perspectives about the culture in which they live. Thus, as I work in a very homogeneously white district, we study many of the other groups who comprise our American culture—for this unit, African Americans.

Slavery, the Civil War, Reconstruction, and so on are topics covered in history class, so I have aligned my African American Perspectives unit with the history schedule. If you look at Figure 6.1, you will see that we not only look at slave and wartime literature but also bring our study right through the Civil Rights Movement and to the current year. One of our essential questions to which we are seeking answers is whether or not (or how) African-American experiences and perspectives today are affected by history and if our conclusions about that play out in the study of the literature. This kind of study is akin to the issue of whether schools should teach that America was discovered or conquered. We have had some issues in our district with people who believe the roles of minorities should not play a significant role in our curriculum. I bring this up because this is a good time to discuss bias, which we will look at in more depth when we discuss hidden and null curriculum.

Educators who believe that we should teach that America was discovered by European explorers or who downplay the roles of minorities in history bring a certain bias to the class. However, my way of teaching, putting the spotlight upon peoples other than those whom my students may be engaged with on a daily basis, shows a bias as well. The avoidance of bias is impossible; what the teacher must be concerned about is whether or not the inherent bias is fairly in line with supporting facts. This is a gray area that is complicated by the fact that my biases about others may be implied rather than directly communicated. Part of the hidden curriculum may be my own unconscious views.

Toward the end of the unit the students and I examine the issue of slave-family reparations with the help of current literature. This topic encompasses areas of personal judgment: attitudes about African American people, beliefs about the roles of government, and political stance. All of these are important parts of self and social learning, requiring individual interpretation. Thus, I must be careful to not overly bias this study. To facilitate democratic self and social learning I must allow my students to explore and debate their growing beliefs. Balancing all of this—nurturing these ideals in each student, allowing for and managing all the different points of view—is tricky. The transformative educator teaches and passes on culture more by managing and nurturing democratic exploration and expression than by using literature to form the students' thinking to some dogmatic view of proper democratic living or believing.

As teachers set aside or at least confront all the biases, we can pave the way for self and social learning that are designed into the visionary unit design. So, the materials I pick, the freedom I give to the students (including the right to pick more materials), the combination of guided teaching and wide-open exploration must come together to create an environment where the subject matter is studied and practiced; the views, beliefs, and attitudes of the authors are understood, debated, and empathized with; and each student's meaning making is nurtured, pushed, and evaluated for future development. This balance, at this point in my wisdom challenge, is how I understand and allow for 3S-scaffolded curriculum.

Any teacher who is sensitive to 3S design is going to be sensitive to hidden and null curricula. These issues are closely tied to the bias I spoke of above. There is no way, as with bias, to eliminate hidden and null curricula. They exist in everything from teacher dress to the food served at lunch to the bell-driven schedule or walk-in-a-quiet-line environments in which kids are asked to function. The question is, are the influences of these curricula going to be left to chance or confronted and crafted?

Null curriculum, which refers to the messages sent to students by what is not studied, has an effect on the portrait of the world that teachers paint for students. Students who are taught history in terms of the successes and conquests of white, Christian immigrants (all others omitted or downplayed) will have a very different view of America and history than students who are taught the roles of various people in the formation of this country. The fact is that historical (and current) reality, within objective occurrences, is a matter of perspective. There is no solution to the problems created by null curriculum, but the goal is to be aware of it, to determine its impact, and to make adjustments or raise awareness as needed. For instance, while I want to give my students a picture of the lives of others in the world, I must be careful not to neglect the history, values, and goals of the cultural subgroups to which my students belong.

The hidden curriculum is, perhaps, more complicated and influential. One example of hidden curriculum would be that schools consistently prompt kids to be unique individuals. Yet, certain modes of dress, beliefs, and levels of creativity are not actually supported. Students also craft hidden curriculum. For instance, while most people respect intelligent and successful students, how well are they nurtured by the social expectations of the collective student body? What is the pressure on a top-performing student as opposed to a top-performing athlete? The effect of the hidden curriculum on girls and minorities has been a topic of considerable study in recent years.

When a teacher really stretches the classroom parameters to individual exploration, there is the potential for more conflict. Thus, a hidden curriculum concern is that biases and opinions are managed rather than any one becoming dominate over the others, leading to narrow mindedness, exclusionary behavior, or downright prejudice.

Teacher beliefs, personality, or even traits can establish a hidden curriculum. For instance, early in my career the rumor came back to me that I did not like the girls. Having been raised by, the brother of, and married to strong women, I didn't perceive myself as sexist, but apparently my female students had a different perspective. When I sought the assistance of an administrator, she helped me see that my dry sense of humor and tendency to playfully tease was perceived differently by girls than by boys. I had an empathetic adjustment to make in the way I dealt with my students. Had this not been brought to my attention and confronted by me, what kind of influence would the hidden curriculum that I was unintentionally creating have on my students, both male and female?

Becoming aware of and dealing with bias and hidden and null curricula is part of the doubled problem solving, referring to enacting means/end and means/visionary end processes, that teachers must undertake in order to produce 3S scaffold curriculum; this is done through the arts of inquiry.

Visionary design is not only a method for unit design that travels a path of establishing goals, conceiving of questions, determining evidence of learning, and then planning the activities, but it is part of an inquiry cycle of connoisseurship, criticism, and planning. There is much overlap, but the connoisseurship informs the planning (in this case the actual unit design), and the criticism includes criticism of student work, the value of the unit, and the teacher's performance. This criticism is guided by the inquiry artistry discussed in Chapter 3. Rubrics are one of the tools for this work, and I will look at those below when I discuss evaluation.

I understand the visionary design process as both an adaptation and an expansion of Wiggins and McTighe's (2001) backward design. While Wiggins and McTighe's self-declared focus is on subject matter, the visionary extension of their design ideas incorporates the 3S scaffold. This is the foundation on which the unit in Figure 6.1 was developed. As I set out to design a unit that explored African American literature and experience, especially as it related the history unit, I first laid out the "overarching ideas" and/or "essential questions" that I wanted my students to explore (see Figure 6.1). These questions become a starting place, a guiding force, and an ending place for the unit, and the students or I can expand them as we discover new things. Generally, these questions cross and combine subject matter-learning with democratic self and social learning. In terms of this unit, I made a pragmatic choice to have the questions focus on the self and especially the social learning. I would then slip in the subject-matter goals. Too many essential questions create too little focus, and I wanted this unit to be, ultimately, more about the examination of, understanding of, and empathy toward the lives and perspectives of the authors.

From these essential questions, I crafted the general "desired results" and then the "acceptable evidence." What a teacher views as acceptable evidence relies heavily on that person's vision of the democratic good life and views about students. If you look at the "evidence" section in Figure 6.1, you may notice that there is no test mentioned. This is not the manifestation of some hatred of tests. I do use tests as a measuring device, but only once or twice a semester and only with material that lends itself to tests, and those tests are carefully crafted. For this unit, it was my pragmatic decision not to use a test. Tests, while valuable, can trivialize material, creating a situation where preparing for the test becomes the focus of the study rather than preparing for an authentic demonstration of knowledge and skills. A final thought on tests. When I use them, they are never a full measure of students' learning, but one of many chances for students to demonstrate their learning.

Many of the acceptable evidence options I require are supported by scholarship, but I designed them by watching great teachers and by studying how adults learn in the real world. Adults tend to learn by receiving incoming information through TV, books, magazines, newspapers, classes, training, discussions with other adults, etc. They connect that learning in some way to previous learning, and a developmental cycle continues.

For instance, after watching part of a Public Broadcasting Service (PBS) special about inquiry-based education, I learned that more information is available on the PBS website. When I go there, what I read will be connected with my previous knowledge of the subject. Certainly, what I learn will become part of the dialogues that I will have about inquiry-based education, and my knowledge of it will be reflected in my authentic use of what I have learned in discussions, my classroom (projects), and my writing. My use of my new knowledge will further develop my understanding of inquiry-based education, which will then prepare me for new, future knowledge.

Although research is available, we do not need it to tell us that this is how learning occurs. We know it because this is how we do it every day. Thus, I contend that this is how teachers should ask students to learn and be evaluated. That is why on my acceptable evidence list there are such things as essays, individual conferences, group projects, public (class) performances, and discussions. These evaluations are congruent with my teaching style, and both the evaluations and my methods are congruent with the beliefs I hold in terms of curriculum and democracy.

As I have discussed, once a unit gets rolling, the students and I often craft its personality as we go, which often leads to new directions in evaluation. However, I always want a place to start. If nothing else, a beginning rubric gives the students some idea of the kinds of things I will be looking for in my evaluations and the kinds of things I want them focusing on. Both the focus and the evaluation criteria are negotiable on an individual basis, as long as the changes are planned before new directions are taken and they are up to the rigor standards and have a specific purpose. Such changes will be drafted and documented in learning journals, but we need a document as a starting point for the curriculum development.

I have created a rubric for this unit. It is informed by an even more general rubric that I have developed to oversee all classroom activity, and the sample rubric will be made more specific as need be for individual elements of this unit as they mature. Rubrics pose a bit of a conflict. They enable us to capture the entirety of what is going on in a classroom or the learning that occurs during a unit, so teachers need to use them as a guide but hardly a rigid yardstick of student expectations. Rubrics offer students a vision of what is expected of them, and they offer both students and the teacher a tool for critique. My criticism is enfolded into my connoisseurship. I need to make continuous informed judgments about a work's worth and then come up with suggestions for improvement. A good rubric provides a basis and a tool for this continuous critical analysis. It is, of course, important that all rubrics are congruent with the word and the spirit of the desired outcomes, the activities of the unit, and the democratic wisdom that informs them all.

It is worth noting that some teachers might not feel comfortable with the flexibility of this unit (which is designed into all my units), but I enjoy creative flexibility, and it offers my students meaning-making opportunities and gives them a sense of personal responsibility. This fits with my "democratic morality" and is part of the self-learning part of the 3S design. It may not fit with another teacher's vision. As I work through this process of "visionary design," having direction for both desired results and acceptable outcomes, I begin to create the unit.

Chances are that by this point, my head is full of ideas and I have been jotting them down wildly on notebook paper. I have a general model I follow—a personally meaningful structure that is built around my developing professional beliefs—that guides my decisions about how to best enact the 3S scaffold. This model is not something you have studied in this book, but it is the basis for why I design units the way I do, which is tied into my search for the wisdom space. Generally, I believe that to nurture my students I must allow them a high degree of freedom, an expectation of creativity, the space to plan and develop projects, time for development, an expectation of self-maintenance, the evaluation of projects as they progress, and high standards for responsibility for workshop, on-task (individual and teamwork) settings.

Basically, I build an environment of freedom and creativity but with the burden of development and responsible behavior weighing squarely on the students. Into this environment I flood quality resources, ideas, coaching, and my own perspective as needed. I try to build an environment where the students are immersed in the topic and where they and I must work together to form and define the work and the spirit of the atmosphere. This is my version of the democratic classroom, but have no doubt of who is in charge. If individuals or the group get too far away from the goal, especially in terms of behavior, fairness, rigor of expectations, or openmindedness, I will redirect them. I consider my classroom democratic, but my interpretation has little to do with making decisions on the basis of a majority vote. I recognize that this curriculum wisdom work is all about professional judgment. After all, my students aren't that mature; furthermore, even though more mature adult democratic citizens have a lot of freedom, when the rules are broken—especially when someone else's rights are affected—the law steps in. So, using the 3S scaffold, visionary design, and my model that is informed by my definition of the democratic good life, I produce a flexible plan to guide us through an exploration of the "essential questions."

Before I comment directly on the systemic reform lens, I want to touch on student expectations and unit evaluation as they pertain to the unit and my classroom. Different teachers require different skills of the students they teach. One of the guiding beliefs I have that helped form my vision of my classroom is that, in general, I do not believe that kids in our culture are asked to work at a level that is anything close to what it is they are capable of and that much of what they are asked to do (even if it's hard) is often not purposeful or substantive. I believe kids need to work hard but on important, growth-enhancing work, and that the responsibility for designing, creating, developing, maintaining, finishing, and evaluating that work lies squarely on the guided shoulders of each student (as it is for adult democratic citizens). This level of authentic responsibility creates an environment in which real skills and knowledge are manifest and from which deep subject-matter understanding, deep self-understanding, and deep social understanding will come—to say nothing of real, deep self-esteem. These beliefs may be more a matter of psychology, but they are part of my search for wisdom.

Finally, I want to touch on the arts of inquiry. All of the work that goes into transformative teaching does not cease with the final evaluation. The unit's effectiveness can be evaluated by reevaluating the outcomes that occurred in terms of the 3S's to see if the unit were as comprehensive and valuable as what was planned. This can be one part of the evaluation of the unit, and changes and improvements can be made for next time.

For example, the unit I share here is improved over last year's unit, with more to come. Last year I designed this unit parallel to an American history unit. It will be stronger if the history teacher and I sit down and actually work together on a comprehensive unit. Also, I have not covered all the voices that I perhaps should. I wish to add more slave narratives and the work of Frederick Douglass, which was absent last year. My own development is an issue. I am working very hard to relearn a good bit of American history and to read a great number of works that I have either never been exposed to or have not read in years. My connoisseurship in this particular area is weak, and it will take some time to develop. Finally, last year I underestimated the amount of time needed to cover the material well, and the unit had a bit of a plowing-through rather than exploring feel to it. This year I either need to narrow the unit's focus or allow more time for it.

Visionary design, like all good unit planning, is not an entity within itself. It is informed by a myriad of information and guided by a complex stream of decisions. Not only does a teacher who enacts visionary design need to have a developed sense of what needs to be brought into unit planning but also a strong critical sense from which to evaluate and guide the work being done in the classroom. Further, this teacher must understand that visionary design occurs within a larger ecology.

Systemic Reform

If all members of the educational ecosystem are engaged with the arts of inquiry, change (understood as the coordinated flow of small improvements) should become the defining element of the school system. I discussed my personal curriculum development above, but I recognize that many other curriculum stakeholders are part of the bigger reform picture. I turn my attention to these individuals and base my comments on how my district has supported my own transformative teaching. I particularly want to speculate on ways a school district could evolve into a "transformative space."

One level of change is professional development. If you are like most teachers I have met, just reading the words "professional development" has turned you off. It's amazing how something so important has become so hated. Why? Most teachers I know, if they take the opportunity to learn about and develop new ideas that will improve learning in their classrooms, are thrilled at the prospect. Somehow, district-operated professional development never seems to reach that goal. There are many issues here. Professional development is often added onto a list of already too-many duties and not connected in a meaningful way to actual teaching, or it is brought in by outside professionals with the implied insult that no one here knows this stuff. If any of these things hold true, the feeling I am always left with is that my time has been wasted or that I am being treated like I'm stupid.

In my district we struggle with professional development issues, like everyone else. A few years ago the district implemented a program that required 12 hours of after-school time for professional development. To their credit, the administration did away with the idea after a wave of serious resistance. Now we have two extra days a year for professional development, during which the students stay home and for which we are compensated. There is, of course, much less resistance, but even on these valuable days the information is somewhat disjointed and there is always more work left undone than done.

All professional fields have a component of professional development: teachers, lawyers, doctors, accountants, professors, etc. In general, these professionals (with the notable exception of teachers) are able to integrate professional development time into their work schedules, be it to schedule a day a week with no patients or a portion of every day to read and discuss new research or attend conferences. Certainly, the easy argument here is that teachers have the summer, and that is a valid point. Many teachers do use the summers to take coursework, seek advanced degrees, or attend workshops, but this is independent professional development. It has nothing to with the comprehensive development of every teacher and the system they create.

A teacher's responsibilities can be categorized into four parts: planning, teaching (including duties), evaluating, and long-term and short-term professional development. At the end of an 8-hour day, only the teaching duties are complete. The evaluation duties are done beyond the 8-hour day (either at school or home), which extends the teacher's day to 10 hours, which closely matches a typical workday in many professional fields. Planning, for many teachers, is done on the weekends or even beyond the 10-hour day. Professional development, the work that sustains all the other work, is done a few hours or a couple of days a year, and often with little purposeful direction or in timeslots that conflict with other teaching responsibilities. Such problems exist in all fields, but the issue of professional development is paramount if we are to create truly quality schools.

There are two issues to be solved here. First, professional development needs to be consistent, connected, and purposeful. Second, it requires workload support on a daily or weekly basis. The inclination for administrators is often to work this time into planning periods, but that time is already not enough, and thus professional development time becomes a half-hour blip that is detracting from other duties. I do not fault building-level administrators here; this is a larger systemic problem, and I do not know who has the power to change these problems.

In my district we have, contractually, a comparatively fairly gracious 200 planning minutes a week, and often there are more (although various duties and meetings tend to lower actual planning time). Imagine a work day like this: teach six classes a day for 4.2 hours; deal with maintenance issues, such as monitoring the start of the day, class breaks, and the end of the day, for 1 hour; fulfill "duty" assignments, such as supervising the lunch periods, for 1 hour; participate in department or team meetings for 1 hour; engage in evaluation and grading activities for 1 hour; conduct copying, room maintenance and clerical duties for 1 hour; work on unit development or revision for 1 hour; undertake professional development for 1 hour; and allow for a reasonable amount of time for trips to the bathroom and a lunch for 1 hour. Any reasonable person who looked at this list could hardly argue with the time commitments assigned to these responsibilities. The problem is that the day would be 12.2 hours long.

The solution is a systematic one, and we will look at it more when we discuss those stakeholders, but the time problems only exacerbate the issue of what teachers are asked to do during professional development time. Much like the process I am going through to develop my connoisseurship, professional development time could be used to develop (using inquiry artistry) collective vision, to evaluate and problem solve, to study new scholarship, or to strengthen teacher know-how through reading and sharing ideas. This time could be used for team or department planning of short- and long-term direction. I would even argue that this time could be used for workshop development, textbook writing, or the writing of discipline, theory, or practice books. What better form of professional development than to have school districts become producers of research and professional scholarship, like a university? Could schools actually become learning communities?

In my district we have many quality reform efforts in the works, but perhaps our single biggest struggle is professional development—the creation of a work environment and schedule that allows the stakeholders of the district to work together to create and maintain a shared purpose, plan and problem solve, or bring a comprehensive feel to the students' educational experiences. Thankfully, our district allows teachers the professional freedom and power to cultivate their growth, but the infrastructure to allow this kind of work at a more global level is not fully developed. This level of reform requires systematic change.

To build a transformative school district, the development and empowerment of teachers to enact quality decision-making must be the primary focus. To accomplish this, the manner in which districts organize and manage the work life will have to be drastically reformed. The agenda for this reform would include power structures and schedules as well as priorities, values, and attitudes. Although curriculum priorities and time are conflicts in my district, we actually use our mission statement and strategic plan as a basis of decision making, and all stakeholders have the opportunity to contribute. Also, while our workday schedules are not really geared toward teacher enactment, the spirit of all levels of the administration is. This is not to say that there is no head butting; there is plenty, but teachers who work hard at their own professional development and who want the power of enactment have a good bit of freedom to develop. There are also optional, paid opportunities for curriculum writing during the summer if teachers are interested.

In my district teachers are respected, trusted, and empowered. This encourages curriculum enactment in a "test-driven" policy environment, and stakeholders at all levels are to be praised for this. However, there is another element here. I work in a wealthy, highly educated, relatively homogenous district, and, while we have had to make adjustments to our state's relatively new proficiency test system, the adjustments have been few compared to other districts. In our state students and schools are measured and ranked according to 27 categories; my district has a perfect score of 27. It should be noted that the list of top-performing schools and a list of the state's wealthiest districts are very similar. This correlation is noted and needs to be addressed from a community education standpoint. Teachers have little control over this hidden curriculum matter.

There is an interesting paradox here. Teachers in my district have a certain amount of enactment power in the test-driven reform environment because we do well on the tests. Generally, I believe that as a district we have very little faith in or respect for the tests or the testing. We hardly believe that it measures the strengths of what we are about. Given a few adjustments, we do not teach to the test because we would not lower our expectations to that level. However, schools that are on "academic watch" or in "academic emergency," who have lofty goals just like us, have begun realigning entire curricula to get kids to pass the tests. I have talked to the teaching professionals from these districts, and there is no doubt in many of their minds that they are developing far inferior curriculum in order to get kids to pass the test.

The solutions to these problems are entangled between system level and community level reform. I cannot comment very well on this solution; I am fortunate to lack first-hand knowledge of the conflicts struggling schools are facing. While I would like to see more enactment power given to our district's teachers, at least we perform well enough to be left alone by the state, which is part of the community element of the ecosystem. This contingent of the community stakeholders is driving policy from the national and state levels, but perhaps the most influential stakeholder in terms of student development is the local community. I may feel unqualified to make a judgment about what changes struggling schools need to make, but I can say without a doubt what makes the good districts effective, and while testing may serve some purposes, it will not create these solutions. This would require community change.

I am going to share with you a synopsis of the elements that come together to make us a top-performing school—a school relatively aloof from test-driven reform. First, my district has its share of reality: conflicts, stronger and weaker players, conflicting agendas, us-and-them head butting. These kinds of things are a given, and as I have discussed, we have a very progressive spirit that pervades our administration and our staff. Good things happen in our school, but let's look beyond that.

As I have come to know many teachers from other districts, many in real trouble, I have been amazed at how similar talking to them is to talking within my district. These teachers have, for the most part, goals, attitudes, training, and ideas similar to ours. They have strong altruistic spirits and are optimistic and dedicated, just like us. This, however, is where realities part. The stories of these teachers tell of professionals who feel strangled by higher authority, be it from the state testing level or from implementation-biased administration. These teachers are often told what to do and how to do it. These issues, of course, are systematic ones, and I only know one side of the story, but the ecological obstacles are more widespread than just micromanaging administrators.

The kindergarten teachers I talk to reflect pictures of students who come to school underfed, dirty, and completely unprepared for school. Many kids who come to kindergarten have not even been taught their colors or their numbers and letters. The highly prepared kids are few, and throughout their entire educational experience they will need to seek stimulation in an environment that must be aimed at their completely unprepared peers. While it is hard to argue with the emotional appeal of the president's "no child left behind" policy, with its goal that all students will be reading by third grade, this goal is the same for disparately prepared sets of children, and it goes against everything we know about learning, especially literacy attainment.

The "team" that educates children is all the curriculum stakeholders: parents, administrators, support staff, teachers, and kids. Everybody has a role. In my district the kids come to kindergarten about as prepared as they could be. This allows the good teachers to teach well, which is reflected on evaluations, which allows for systematic flexibility and creativity, which leads to better teaching and thus better learning. The success of each part of the team improves the value of the whole. My district's parents are highly educated and well off. Thus, our kids not only come prepared for school, they also develop in academically nurturing environments for their entire lives, and this includes the fact that the tangible connection between education and success is in the forefront of their lives every day. As a result, an environment of academic success is easily established.

Whether teaching to the tests will raise test scores will be a matter of history. However, will higher test scores solve any of the problems that create poor education? In other words, will higher test scores (if curriculum changes really provoke them) actually improve education and thus the futures of the kids in struggling districts? This seems unlikely. It is not the point of this writing to condemn testing, nor is it my goal to point fingers. But it does not elude me that, as I untangle the obstacles to quality education, some are school problems, but most are socio-economic-political problems, and those are the responsibility of the citizens of a democracy and the government they elect to represent them—the same people creating the test-driven reform.

Community education may play a driving role in the quality of education, but that is just one part of the equation. Systemic reform is a complex dance with many partners. It will take a lot to transform courses of study into "instances of democratic living."

A Teacher Educator's Commentary

As an early childhood teacher educator involved with a "field-based" teacher education program, I believe the emphasis in developing curriculum wisdom as a foundation for teacher decision making is both visionary and pragmatic: visionary because of the philosophical and moral connections to educating children in a caring, thoughtful, and comprehensive manner; pragmatic because of the guiding tenets inherent in the conceptualization of teacher's curriculum decision making.[2] Liston and Zeichner (1991) advocate that teacher education programs should prepare teachers who understand the purposes of their teaching, who understand developmental aspects of children, who choose resourceful and appropriate teaching strategies, and who can advocate and articulate their teaching decisions. Through field experiences and program coursework integrated with field sites, our students are provided with context-specific learning experiences. As Sarason (1993) argues, teacher education programs often miss the mark in providing future teachers with adequate preparation for work in classrooms and schools. He suggests that a "primary prevention orientation," requiring a long-term perspective view of teaching, is necessary when considering teacher education reform, rather than a quick fix. I have come to believe that the work involving curriculum wisdom, through the cultivation of the arts of inquiry, might be one answer to this call.

Building Inquiry Capacity for Preservice Teachers

One of the courses I teach in our Early Childhood Education Program is "Inquiry into Professional Practice." This is the capstone course our undergraduate students take, concurrently with a 16-week student teaching experience. The required text, *Reflective Teaching: Professional Artistry Through Inquiry* (Henderson, 2001), supports and promotes the idea

---

[2]Commentary written by Richard Ambrose

of developing and practicing curriculum wisdom for our preservice teachers and soon to be first-year teachers. This text is organized around the same seven inquiry modes that are discussed in Chapter 3 of this book.

Throughout our teacher education program, our students are immersed in "inquiry" and "reflection" as a means for developing one's learning to teach. This focus, prior to their last course, primarily emphasizes craft reflection involving the systematic use of observation, interpretation, reflection, and action while focusing on preparing and implementing curricula decisions. What I believe Henderson's "professional artistry" provides for our students is a more in-depth, grounded understanding of the purposes of teaching in a democratic society.

Meaningful teaching requires artistry and tacit understanding coupled with ethical principles and knowledge from research and theory. This type of teaching requires, as Dewey suggested and Henderson promotes, that teachers make decisions on the basis of intellect, not habit or coercion. Jalongo (2002) furthers this notion from the perspective of teachers of young children when she suggests that early childhood teachers need to be caring but also "sufficiently strong-willed to resist constant pressure to fall into habit, routine, and mediocrity" (p. 141). She writes that the myth of becoming an outstanding teacher of young children does not reside only in caring for young children, mastering content-specific knowledge and practices, and meeting the minimum content standards for attaining one's teaching license. Rather, she believes that wisdom about teaching and the needs of young children comes from a lifetime of reflection upon experience, a passion for learning, and accomplishing worthy goals. Accepting Henderson's curriculum wisdom challenge would appear to be a worthy goal.

The ideas involving curriculum wisdom through professional artistry are new for our students and should be integrated within their student teaching experience. The inquiry course is where curriculum wisdom is introduced, to be understood in the context of one's student teaching and in the future and to be critiqued and/or applied in one's student teaching experience through reading *Reflective Teaching: Professional Artistry Through Inquiry*. Preservice teachers respond to peer- and instructor-written prompts, participate in large group and small group discussion of the text and its relationship to their student teaching experiences, and complete a final synthesis piece focusing on their understanding of inquiry and reflection. Much course time is devoted to "collaborative conversations" (Hollingsworth, 1992) to promote the importance of professional dialogue and to emphasize that teaching knowledge is constructed through collegial interactions with others.

More recently, Manouchehri (2002) examined the importance of peer discourse as she studied two preservice teachers in a teamed field-based practicum experience over 11 weeks. Working from social constructivist theory, where teaching understanding is socially derived and individually constructed, Manouchehri suggested that preservice teachers should be provided the opportunity to discuss ideas, articulate their own thinking, and understand other perspectives in the hope that new ideas can be understood in light of one's expanding teaching knowledge. Manouchehri found that the students had difficulty analyzing problems in depth and often relied upon quick-fix solutions derived from intuition and impulse, not on reason. Like Sarason (1993), Manouchehri recommends changing the culture of teaching and suggests specifically the creation of learning environments where teaching is "problematized" and collegial pedagogical problem solving becomes a part of the culture of teaching. Consistent with Manouchehri's recommendations, the use of the curriculum wisdom orientation allows preservice teachers to problematize their student teaching experiences and to analyze them through collaborative conversations. It is the intent of the inquiry course and the student teaching experience to integrate reflection with curriculum wisdom and collaborative conversations in a manner that provides opportunity for professional growth.

Possibilities for Building Inquiry Capacity

The importance of questions in supporting the development of one's professional inquiry capacities is inherent in the work promoting curriculum wisdom. To contextualize and personalize this for our preservice teachers who are placed in districts that vary in size and diversity, we ask them to consider the following questions in the context of their student-teaching placements in specific school settings:

Questions to Ponder: ECED Student Teaching Experience From an Inquiry Perspective

- When discussing teaching and learning with your cooperating teacher, are you able to easily and readily raise questions, share insights, and speak to your understanding of the teaching and learning occurring in your classroom with your cooperating teacher? Are your conversations substantive? What would be an example of a substantive conversation about teaching and learning that is pertinent to your classroom that you have had or would like to have with your cooperating teacher—or is this at all necessary?

- How difficult is it for you to solicit your cooperating teacher's assistance? Over time does it become easier? How risky is it? If you ask for help, what does this suggest to your cooperating teacher regarding your prospects as a future teacher? Are there specific strategies you have used and deliberatively considered when asking for help from your cooperating teacher?

- Continually modifying activities, lessons and ways that you interact with children is the signature of a resourceful, reflective teacher. In what ways do you engage in such modification (self-reflection; discussion with peers, cooperating teacher, university supervisor, other building teacher, parents of the children in your classroom, family members or significant others)? Our program believes that it is important to publicize one's teaching by talking/writing about it. Would you agree that this is important teacher work?

- At the start of your cooperating teacher's career, do you believe that she was more like you or more not like you in her perception of children, teaching, and learning?

- Cooperating teachers do learn from you. Through your modeling and "public discourse" with them, you are able to influence them. Yes, no, maybe?

- What is an at-risk student? What is a not-at-risk student? Is this a pejorative term? Does the label influence how you perceive a child's potential? Can you be an at-risk student for school success and yet be a bright, capable child? What types of labels do children have in your school?

These "inquiry scaffolding" questions (Henderson, 2001) provide preservice teachers the opportunity to both widen and clarify their own and cooperating teacher's thinking about teaching.

Drawing from Dewey's Beliefs about Reflection

I have found it helpful for preservice teachers to examine Dewey's ideas on reflective teaching through collaborative conversations, using his ideas as guidelines/suggestions. According to Dewey, framing a problem, actively considering alternatives, and carefully articulating and thinking about teaching beliefs and practices in a holistic manner involves both rational thinking and emotion. Thinking with one's mind and heart captures this holistic view, and Dewey advocated three necessary dispositions for reflection to occur: openmindedness, responsibility, and wholeheartedness. To be openminded, one must be able to understand one's own view while simultaneously entertaining differing views. This requires one to actively listen to others, even when such views create cognitive dissonance or contradictions to strongly held beliefs. Preservice teachers who display openmindedness are continually asking the "why" of teaching practice.

Responsibility focuses on the consequences of one's actions. In regard to reflective teaching, one must consider the academic, personal, and sociopolitical consequences of teaching actions for children's growth. Being responsible in reflective teaching means thinking about intended consequences and attending to the unintended consequences of teaching practice. Why does it matter, what does it mean, and why should we care become important in teachers' thinking and decision making. Finally, wholeheartedness suggests fully embracing openmindedness and responsibility in ways that allow growth by examining and questioning teaching practices and beliefs. Wholehearted teachers immerse themselves in the problems of teaching, collegially question teaching practices, and strive to sustain high-quality teaching despite the complexity, ambiguity, uncertainty, and demands inherent in a teaching life.

When these dispositions are presented as possible guidelines for collaborative conversations during the inquiry course and student teaching, preservice teachers have the opportunity to critique their own teaching beliefs and practices in a thoughtful, caring way. Because these conversations hold experiential knowledge, unpacking this knowledge in a supportive, meaning-ladened manner enables preservice teachers to understand their own nascent teaching knowledge and that of their peers. Furthermore, it enables preservice teachers to influence and be influenced in developing and refining their understanding of learning to teach, providing both impetus and vision for a good educational journey.

One Possible Format for Collaborative Conversations

Accepting and understanding the challenge of working from a curriculum wisdom viewpoint requires intellect and passion for teaching. Being able to inquire and reflect on beliefs and practices that may be loaded with ambiguity, uncertainty, and hidden unintended consequences may be more difficult for novice teachers than experienced ones. However, learning about curriculum wisdom and applying its tenets to one's emerging practice could change the culture of current practice and influence the socialization of novice teachers. Survival is often a theme encountered when studying the practice of beginning teachers (e.g., Kauffman, Johnson, Kardos, Liu, & Peske, 2002). Can novice teachers understand and apply curriculum wisdom in their student teaching placements? Can they do the same as first-year teachers? The following course teaching strategy offers possible insight into such possibilities.

```
┌─────────────────────────────────────────────────┐
│                  ECED 40125                      │
│       Dialectic Response Cues for Course Text:   │
│   Reflective Teaching: Professional Artistry Through Inquiry │
│                                                  │
│   Chapter_____                          │
│                                                  │
│     1. One question/comment/insight:             │
│                                                  │
│                                                  │
│     2. How does this relate to _____ (your current │
│        student teaching experience, thoughts on children, │
│        teaching, schooling, diversity, equity, curriculum, │
│        assessment, etc.):                        │
│                                                  │
│                                                  │
│     3. After discussing with my small group, my thoughts: │
│                                                  │
│                                                  │
└─────────────────────────────────────────────────┘
```

FIGURE 6.2

Inquiry into Professional Practice

Students are asked to respond to three prompts, as presented in Figure 6.2. After reading a designated chapter from *Reflective Teaching: Professional Artistry Through Inquiry* (Henderson 2001), preservice teachers write their responses to the first two prompts and bring them to class for discussion. After small group discussion of the text and their responses to the first two prompts, they are asked to respond in writing to the third prompt. I collect the written pieces to review for understanding of the text and their thinking about their work.

The following snippets of student writing come from reactions to this teaching strategy, and I hope they provide insight into the building of inquiry capacity. The examples were collected during fall semester, 2001 and spring semester, 2002 and are the basis of a preliminary analysis of preservice teachers' understanding of this work. The selected written responses represent emerging patterns or themes from a pool of 60 preservice teachers in the last semester of their early childhood education undergraduate program.

The Challenge to Understand Curriculum Wisdom

These student comments represent what I consider to be examples of the challenge to understand curriculum wisdom. The complexity of thinking about and practicing teaching appears to be in the forefront of preservice teachers' thinking. Inquiry capacity building may be at odds with the current culture of schools, and confronting the system might be overwhelming for first-year teachers. Furthermore, that this type of work is not an easily taken stance for professional development; rather, it may be beyond the "mechanics of teaching" that may impede embodying an inquiry capacity. "Can first year teachers practice curriculum wisdom?" appears to be inherent in the thinking of preservice teachers.

■ I understand that teachers need to always be willing to try and learn new things. One thing I do not understand, however, is how a teacher should be uncertain. Sure, we will not always have a solution to every problem; but why say that we are uncertain, when we are full of knowledge?

■ I am wondering how you keep up with your teaching, inquiry, and reflection? Especially your first year. Is this something that you learn to do as you teach more and more? How do you fight the system year after year?

■ We had a lot of good discussion about this chapter and related information; however, we seem to only connect to the text when it is something that is visible within our classrooms or education.

■ I most related to the conclusion of the chapter when the author talks about beginning teachers feel that they don't have the time or "energy to cultivate a sophisticated inquiry repertoire." This relates to me in my current student teaching. Right now, I feel I am so busy and so concerned with methods and the mechanics of teaching, that it's difficult to cultivate that inquiry repertoire. Thinking ahead to the time when I have my own classroom, I know I will want the absolute best for my students; so hopefully, I will muster up the energy and make the time for these inquiries.

■ I have some questions about how to foster acceptance of all diversity, thinking about the third "S." I know that I can expose them to different cultures and educate them about different people. But how can I encourage an acceptance of diversity?

■ Henderson states, "to challenge the status quo requires courage and conviction." My question is, as a new teacher, when is it okay to do this? If I lose my job by "challenging the status quo," won't that affect my ability to work in another school district? It is difficult enough to get a job as a new teacher, I don't want to lose one, but I don't want to go against my beliefs either.

The following comments suggest a nascent understanding of curriculum wisdom.

■ I never really thought that children did things just because of habit and coercion. It makes so much sense to me to have children do things because it is appropriate and because they have the knowledge to choose their behavior based on their experiences and knowledge. We have to try to get them to do things, not as much out of habit but because it is the right thing to do.

■ I think disciplined inquiry is a skill that will develop over time. Instead of forging ahead with a new idea or plan, taking the time to consider all sides, taking into account everything involved, being open to others' ideas, and thinking of a variety of outcomes are not only "teacher" skills but life skills. I hope we can teach or introduce our children to this method of solving problems or implementing new ideas.

■ It is hard to think about school as a democracy because I don't think any of us have ever thought about it in this way. Our concerns are with the children and to encourage individual growth for individual children.

■ I believe this relates to my current teaching experience, particularly because I am in a kindergarten classroom, because (although I am not exactly sure how) I think it is extremely important to begin to instill how important public moral inquiry is to being a successful member of the community/world.

■ One group member wondered if ignoring children's interests takes away the "color and passion" of education. In response I thought of the Inquiry Scaffolding again. Asking yourself, as a teacher, what your students are interested in, what their perspectives are, will lead you in planning meaningful learning experiences for those children. Continuing to understand the children's perspectives will also guide/modify your actions throughout the instructional moment. We must constantly ask ourselves these questions in order to preserve the "color and passion" of learning in our classrooms!

■ Page 45 in the *Reflective Teaching* text talks about establishing a public moral inquiry or social philosophy including matters of inclusivity, constitutionality & reciprocity. This section helped me to guide my thinking towards my own social philosophy. When considering my philosophy, I need to consider my audience, our political foundations, and my approach to communication and teaching. I've considered my audience and have considered my approach to teaching; however, I have never considered the political foundations and rights that validate me as a "teacher" and my students as "learners."

■ After today's discussion I also realized the reasons why we teach. We are teaching to help children develop and become citizens of the world, where they can make choices that will lead them on the road to happiness. This idea was something I haven't considered before. It was an eye-opener.

The "Why" of Teaching

Why one teaches typically embraces the purposes and ends of teaching. Values and beliefs about purposes and ends typically do not become important if preservice teachers are passive in constructing their teaching knowledge by readily and uncritically accepting how schools and classrooms function. The why of teaching is captured in different ways through the following reflections:

■ Just the other day, I was placed in a position where I was really asking why. I had been asked to cover a teacher's classroom and for the past two days, the children's behavior had been terrible. I had trouble keeping the class quiet and getting work done. The children totally ignored me when I talked. By the end of the second day I was exhausted and knew that I could not stand another day like the last two, so I sat down and began to consider what I could do differently. First I thought about why I was asking the children to be quiet all the time, and I realized it was because I was concerned about what the other teachers were thinking. I am in a school that values a quiet classroom and feels that a quiet classroom equals a well-disciplined one. Right away I knew that I had to be less concerned with keeping the children quiet and more concerned about just making sure they were working. Then I thought about why the children were talking and realized that there were a couple reasons. One, the routine of the day had been totally thrown off because of practice for a concert and the fact that they had a substitute. Two, they became bored quickly with copying work into their books and with the few worksheets the teacher had left for them to do. And three, I had a very different attitude about discipline in the classroom (than the teacher), and I think the children could sense the difference. The teacher usually keeps the children at their seats, quietly working and uses many different behavioral management techniques to keep them there. I enjoy group work and moving around the room; and I feel that children should learn to do things because they want to, not because they will get a reward or because they are afraid of a consequence. In preparation for the third day, I decided that I needed to judge the noise level by my own standards and always consider why I was telling children to be quiet; that I needed to respect the way the other teacher taught, even if I did not agree, because that is what the children were used to; and finally that I was going to prepare a lesson that involved more than just copying and worksheets. The routine of the day was also back to normal. The day went so much smoother, and I have more experiences to think about and draw from.

■ As I read the chapter I thought about the individuals that have made an impact on my life and also guided me in finding out who I am and what my beliefs are. I find myself often wondering about where I will be in the future … will my teaching styles be accepted by others, will I be challenged against my beliefs, how will I overcome these challenges? As a student teacher, I also tried to look at the values I reflect in my instruction. To me, this has been a challenge to identify these values in my everyday teaching. Sometimes I feel my beliefs are challenged, but I try to listen to others' ideas and then reflect on what I would do in my own classroom.

- As teachers, we should be working to nurture democratic living in our classrooms—I have never thought about teaching before in this way! Wow! When I first began my field experience and student teaching—I viewed teaching in its most basic terms: teaching children to read/write/etc. I never, ever, thought about the *why* of teaching. What is the reason for teaching these concepts? Why not something else? Why was I taught all of these things? After reading this first chapter, it all clicked for me! We learn and teach specific things to aid children, teenagers, and adults how to live in a democratic society in a free and responsible way. Wow! Am I looking at the teaching profession in a whole new way! After discussing the "why" of teaching to nurture democratic living/society, which is a very eye-opening way of looking at the teaching profession, my eyes have also been opened to thinking about "big city vs. suburban" education. Why is there so much inequity in our schools? I don't think about this as much as I should.

- Personal insight will help me establish myself as a teacher. When I reach the confidence to stand up for what I believe in, provide a "foundation" for my objectives and goals as a teacher, and visualize what I want my students to become, I can be the kind of reflective teacher that can readily articulate my professional stories and my "craft reflections."

Teacher Critique

During student teaching, preservice teachers critique their cooperating teachers' thinking and practice of teaching. Critiquing from the perspective of purposes, rationale, and philosophical orientation (i.e., behaviorism, constructivism) helps them better understand their teachers' decision making. The purpose of this understanding is not to evaluate the rightness or wrongness of teacher decisions but to understand them in light of why certain teaching behaviors and ideas support the school or classroom functioning. This perspective gives our students the opportunity to examine possible competing teacher views as their own views are developing. Furthermore, our Early Childhood Education Program emphasizes influencing others, as well as being influenced oneself, through collegial interactions despite the discrepancies between preservice teachers and experienced teachers in professional experiences. The following excerpts from student writing connect this idea of critique and possible influence:

- I believe that my cooperating teacher is "teaching for democratic learning" and believes that through bettering herself and keeping current on research and theory she is better prepared and able to meet the needs of her students. Many of the other teachers I have come in contact with have the opinion that their current style of teaching and the curriculum they are utilizing works just fine the way it is; they feel they can pull the same materials out from last year and just go on with business as usual. I was very sad to see these attitudes come to the forefront, as I know many of the teachers somewhat personally and considered them exceptional teachers, which in a way they are in terms of the materials they are presenting. The question I am now asking myself however is who are they teaching for? Because in my present view, it isn't to meet the needs of the current school population.

- After discussing in my group, I am worried that I will become that stagnant teacher after a few years in the classroom. We talked about the reasons some teachers get stuck in "a rut." We also talked about some ways to stay "fresh." One thing that I like (after a few years) would be to loop with a class for 2-3 years. That way you must stay on your toes and really think of new and innovative ways to teach.

- I am in a first grade classroom. The first grade teachers (5) are a "teaching team." They constantly "reflect" together, plan together, help each other with teaching problems, make teaching goals together, brainstorm ideas together, etc. The atmosphere is so positive for teaching and encourages me to teach at a high level and cooperate when I can.

- Traditional teachers who feel the need to have control in the classroom (over the children) and encourage conformity would never engage in critical inquiry. In fact, these teachers *fear* such inquiry. Conformity is valued too much. Students who are considered "bad" get this label because they challenge such teachers, and students who are considered "good" conform to such teachers. One child in my placement is, I feel, *very* bright. He constantly questions, inquires, challenges. This is why I consider him to be bright (not because he knows his math facts or can read/write well, although he can and does). He takes everything to a higher level and digs deeper than the other students. However, my cooperating teacher has labeled him as "difficult" or "defiant"—in essence, my teacher has already placed him on her "bad list" (in her mind). He cannot get off this list (because he has already been labeled as "bad"); and as a result, I feel as though his gifts will be suppressed, and his behavior will continually be monitored by the teacher. I celebrate his "defiance" because this will allow him to grow and develop to fulfill his potential despite his teacher's negativity.

- "They must continuously stretch their minds, refine their beliefs, and acknowledge the multifaceted nature of their instructional practices." (Henderson, 2001, p. 73) When I asked my cooperating teacher about how she handles the Native American Indian aspect of Thanksgiving, she stated, "Oh, I stay away from that completely." When I asked her if she was familiar with certain aspects of literacy, she replied, "Probably, you know educational researchers keep re-naming the same concepts." When I asked if she'd ever heard of teaching without rewards for the students, she said she tried it once, and it was a disaster. "You'll see," she added knowingly.

- Through my placement I have been able to see that complying with the "norm" or standard is not a "must." There are a variety of teaching styles which can accomplish the same goals or directives, and I am gaining more confidence in my own ideas and beliefs so that I will hopefully have the courage and wisdom to "respectfully decline" those ideas and practices I am uncomfortable with.

- Another member in my group also brought up the point of how hard it is to put into words what you stand for as a teacher. It's very easy to criticize other teachers' beliefs, but without a classroom of our own who's to say what we stand for?

- I feel that the concept of fear and trust in deliberation has a direct correlation to our experiences as student teachers. It is essential to deliberate with the cooperating teacher on planning and student expectations; although fear and trust may inhibit effective communication. As student teachers, we are typically more inexperienced and may feel intimidated to speak openly and freely. I am fortunate to be in a situation where my opinion is welcomed and appreciated. Often, my cooperating teacher will even directly ask for my views. This caring, comfortable atmosphere extends to engulf the children as well. Children feel comfortable offering their views; they trust that their views will be valued.

The Importance of Collaborative Conversation

A central theme of my reactions to curriculum wisdom work resides in the belief that discussing teaching is necessary for developing one's inquiry capacity. I have come to believe that these conversations about teaching are foundational in understanding and promoting one's teaching beliefs and embedded in an inquiry orientation that facilitates teacher growth. The following comments offer insight into preservice teacher thinking that involves the possible impact of collaborative conversations between peers as one examines curriculum wisdom work and its implications for teaching practice:

- After our discussion, I have come to realize, with the help of a particular group member, that the reason I have become more confident in oral deliberation may be because my collaborating group has also grown and become more knowledgeable.
- Teachers who provide collaborative interactions provide students with the ability to think for themselves in specific contexts and to accept the diverse opinions of others. When open-ended and higher level thinking is not encouraged, a child's self-expression is inhibited.
- After discussing my thoughts with my group, I realize how different each community is and how important it is to make that classroom—community connection and also to look outside that community so that children realize there is more to the world than just the one community they live in and the people that live there. Children not only need to know that different people and places exist, but they also need to develop and understand diverse people and places.
- I would like to read over the 3S's again: (1) Subject Learning, (2) Learning to interact socially, and (3) Seeing yourself as a life-long learner. I did not think on these ideas when first reading the chapter. When talking to a classmate, I realized how important these concepts are in terms of teaching-learning interactions.
- Until I began this program, I was one of those people who felt fear during a deliberation. Someone who thought differently than I did caused self-doubt and intimidation. I was so afraid of being "wrong," I didn't take into account how important changing or redefining my thinking was. Changing my thinking is natural and essential to my continuing growth.
- I really enjoy discussing with a group. It makes me think more in-depth about the material and my thoughts about teaching. I applaud collegial support! The support of my colleagues is what is going to get me through my first year of teaching.

Building Inquiry Capacity: Concluding Remarks

Teacher education programs that attempt to facilitate curriculum wisdom capture the complexity of learning to teach in a moral and intellectual sense. They reach beyond the teacher-as-technician perspective associated with current educational policies. A professional journey facilitated by the arts of inquiry embodies a deep call to teach. I can't imagine a better way to work with young children and their families. The facilitation of inquiry capacities in Chapter 3 should be a central goal of all teacher education programs.

As a teacher educator, I believe that teachers who work from a curriculum wisdom stance have positioned themselves to significantly influence the classroom and school cultures. Introducing this perspective to preservice teachers, allowing them to explore and construct their own understanding of this work, and facilitating instructional methods with this view in mind create a rich foundation for career-long growth.

A School Superintendent's Commentary

This commentary reflects my personal reflections on the three lenses on curriculum wisdom.[3] My comments will particularly address the topics of organization and community development. The foundation of my knowledge in this area stems from 25 years as an educator and 15 years as an assistant superintendent then a superintendent of a public school district. For the past several years my school district has been engaged in reform activities using curriculum wisdom as the basis for the "developmental" work. The district is located in an upper-middle-class suburban setting. It is a relatively wealthy district where the majority of the students appreciate the value of education. The parents not only have high expectations for quality educational services, but they also have the means to provide meaningful educational experiences away from the school environment.

In the eyes of the state, the district is a high-performing district, meeting all 27 standards on the state report card. All but three of these standards are test-driven with minimum levels of acceptable performance. Although the percentage of students who do not meet state standards is low compared to districts with less favorable social-economic structures, it is important to recognize that such students do exist in our district.

The reality is that every education institution has students who do not learn in a prescribed manner, especially if the prescription removes creativity, exploration, and engagement from the learning process. An approach of "one size fits all" is superficial and leaves some children behind. We live in a society that thrives on labeling as a form of either positive or negative motivation; but has labeling in any form motivated students, teachers, or districts to perform differently? Why not put that same energy toward creating a democratic school culture that nurtures curriculum wisdom?

What does it mean for a teacher to become a leader for curriculum wisdom? It means that a paradigm shift will have to occur in how teachers carry out their professional calling. In theory, this leadership, which I envision as deeply transformative at both personal and institutional levels, should be an exciting topic for educators. In reality, the topic makes many educators uncomfortable because it is not technically prescriptive in nature. As pointed out repeatedly in this book, curriculum wisdom is a concept and a calling—a professional idea and a disciplined way of working.

This reform activity is complex work requiring the artistry of a well-synchronized surgical team. The image I have in mind is a team that relies on the sophisticated judgments of each member to maintain the health of their patients. These judgments are not bureaucratically prescribed but are based on years of collaboration through disciplined inquiry. The decisions are based on real problems and are not driven by standardized protocols. Communication, data analysis, and collaborative plans of action are key features of this surgical team's work, and the decision making extends well beyond the operating room. All along the path of a patient's recovery, collaborative decisions are being made. Trusting the judgment of each team member creates an environment that will allow the patient's best interest to remain at the center of the professional work. Building such a professional team does

---

[3]Commentary written by Douglas Hiscox.

not happen by chance. An organization must develop a culture that nurtures this work environment. Otherwise, patients will perish.

Developing the necessary work culture requires constant self-reflection, peer evaluation, deliberation, and communication, all of which requires a certain discipline that is often not found in the education community. Moving an organization to the point of supporting curriculum wisdom is difficult work and potentially hazardous in a professional sense; however, it is important and essential work that elevates the professional stature of education.

Understanding and practicing organization development has been, for me, a continuous area of personal reflection, inquiry, and professional growth. Many of the challenges faced by transformative educational leaders are generated by a rigid school culture that has become fossilized over time. The culture can be described as the organizational structures and the beliefs and values that identify how, why, and what the people within the organization do and say. The activities of a school's culture are embedded in a web of established expectations, operational traditions, problem-solving processes, and evaluative criteria. This is the organizational "climate" (the subliminal feel of a work culture), which determines the level of difficulty for any reform effort.

When addressing the school culture, it is important to reflect upon questions such as What is the culture within the school in which you work? Is the organization design supporting or in competition with the school culture? What is the capacity to systematically transform the existing culture? Can the organization-development activities overcome the resistance that will be met when attempting to alter the culture? Later in this commentary, I will share how some of these questions were answered as my school district attempted to alter the organization's structure.

Organization development is defined in this book as specific collaborative activities that build a local work culture that nurtures and sustains a particular curriculum and professional development. This type of organization development requires a commitment to a professional life of inquiry. The focus is on establishing an inquiry ethic during decision making. Consensus building and collaborative problem solving are handled differently. There may not necessarily be agreement on problem definitions and solutions, but there would be a deep consensus that everyone should be working on integrating the seven modes of inquiry into their decision making. Unfortunately, building this type of organizational consensus is very difficult because there is such a limited understanding of curriculum wisdom in the present education community.

Chapter 5 also discusses three phases of healthy organization-development work. These phases, which often occur parallel to each other, can be described as essential, but difficult, work. The practice of curriculum wisdom involves deep change. Dissonance associated with change is often misunderstood as being unhealthy, but it is an important ingredient in any organization development process.

Phase I focuses on building communication. This raises a central question: How do members of the school community express themselves? The education community is often described as independent and isolated. Collaboration is not a comfortable or a natural activity. Issues of trust, conflict resolution, and moving toward an inquiry ethic are a few of the issues that must be understood and worked out. Productive change begins with the creation of a compelling organizational purpose. When the organizational structure and staff are aligned with the mission of the school, change can happen. The shelf life of a district's mission and vision is extremely short. If the mission and vision are not communicated and do not become part of the district's decision-making process and actions, their significance or purpose will soon be forgotten.

The board of education in a traditional public school, or its equivalent in a nontraditional setting, is a critical setting for organization development work. Their purpose is to communicate the organization's mission and establish policies that will guide others in carrying out the mission. Since these governing bodies do not operate in a full-time capacity; they must build human resource capacity by identifying a leader who can further the organization's mission. From here a long list of other internal human resources are added to the list of stakeholders. Some definitions of school community exclude external human resources; but because I feel the internal and external factors influence each other's actions, I include both groups in the definition. The school community includes parents of school-age children, financial supporters in private or nonpublic situations, registered voters, and special interest groups ranging from athletic boosters to local community governing bodies. As you can see, I see organization and community development as integrally linked. Phase I of the organization development process focuses on how all members of the school community communicate through trust building, conflict resolution, and consensus building. If the internal school community is not communicating, there is no chance that the external school community will successfully communicate.

Ideally, organization development would start with the communication of the organization's mission and vision followed by a plan of action. In reality, however, current cultural patterns often twist, pull, and violate the new mission. The longer the organization's history, the more these cultural patterns are deeply embedded. This tension between old and new culture becomes the catalyst for the organization development through all three phases, and success depends on understanding the complexities of the existing culture. Phase I is a vital ingredient in the organization development process. The degree of professional challenges in this area is directly proportional to the school culture's existing alignment with transformative thinking in the area of curriculum wisdom.

Phase II refers to educators' critical assessment of the organization's life and involves data collection, analysis, and collaborative problem solving. The focus in this phase needs to be on overt and covert cultural activities. During this phase it is helpful to estimate the degree of dissonance that may be encountered when moving to collaborative problem solving. Phase III does not run in complete unison with the first two phases, but relies heavily on the integrity of the first two to bring real meaning and purpose to the process. The action plans created in this phase must reflect everything that was learned in phases I and II, and these plans must become integrated into the communication process. Otherwise, the problem-solving processes will be compromised.

All three phases of organization development rely heavily upon collaboration, and many of the curriculum stakeholders have not been socialized to work in this manner. Obstacles to professional trust permeate all three phases. Teachers or school leaders who may find comfort in operating in isolation often succumb to general social and community pressures to maintain the status quo, and this often includes union leadership. The greatest obstacle is typically a general lack of confidence in the value of honest, open reflection on the need for deep-seated changes.

Why do education professionals who are confident in their convictions often resort to the isolation of their classrooms to live out their passions? Is it there where they feel they can make an impact? Issues of efficacy do, in my opinion, play a major role in the reform process. If teachers/administrators perceive that they have no control over their work environments, they will not exhibit the drive, ambition, confidence, or stamina to even initiate a reform movement. Classrooms and offices are full of dedicated, passionate individuals desiring reform but lacking institutional efficacy–the idea that they can indeed control, alter, or influence their organizational structures.

Phase III action planning is the phase that can unite and energize individuals. As many change theorists have indicated, the process of putting one's goals in writing can be the strongest impetus leading to action. In my experience, the very act of planning and perceiving possibilities seems to empower people to look at incremental steps they feel they can control; as they review the steps they have accomplished, they feel a greater sense of efficacy. They feel they are exerting control over the situation. It may also be compared to the satisfaction one gets when crossing a completed item off a "to do" list. It is this sense of accomplishment, of control, of empowerment, and of efficacy that can help teams move from inaction to action.

As teams develop action plans together, they empower each other by demonstrating confidence in each other's abilities. The confidence is contagious as members see that they have the ability to accomplish remarkable things if they unite in their efforts. To me, the greatest difficulty in education today is that we do not encourage and support collaborative efforts. We accept that teachers work in isolation because the school culture creates an atmosphere that does not challenge this practice.

This book focuses on cultivating and trusting educators' curriculum judgments. Faith is placed in professionals who build their inquiry capacities, rather than in the maintenance of a standardized test score system. In my experience, standardized testing encourages isolation and competition, as well as narrow and superficial solutions to student learning problems. Standards of accountability tied to test scores can blind professionals to the importance of wise professional decisions.

Given the obstacles involved with change, why would a school organization attempt to introduce an interpretation of curriculum as a wisdom challenge? Our society is founded on democratic beliefs, yet little evidence of those beliefs can be found in current curriculum decision making. However, if careful organization development can successfully transform a school culture, quality education will no longer be solely determined by standardized tests.

During the past 4 years, organization development in my district has been practiced in a fairly assertive manner. As I mentioned above, the district has many features that inhibit fundamental cultural change. Early on, teachers were asked to move into academic leadership roles as members of a district curriculum council. The goal was to begin addressing isolation issues. For example, the district has two elementary buildings with the same grade and student demographic configuration. Faculty who taught the same grade level but in different buildings never spoke to one another and, in many cases, had never even met one another. To resolve this issue, educators in each grade and/or subject area were provided with regular work time to engage in meaningful curriculum discussions.

As part of our collaborative work, a year-long district/community strategic planning process was conducted and resulted in the identification of 14 focus areas for organization development planning. The process involved extensive data gathering and analysis from responses of a representative cross section of the school and community-at-large. This process was vital to the transformation activity because it began to define the existing culture and identify areas of the culture that would need to change if the organization was going to develop the capacity to support transformative leadership. Strategic planning is a process used to determine what the organization intends to be in the future and how it is going to get there. Our strategic work extended beyond the typical organizational goals to include principles of democratic living.

All three of the organization development phases support each other and should be carried out in a manner that allows that to happen. Understanding how the representative groups in my district communicated, interacted, and built trusting relationships required the greatest amount of attention and time. The process could not move forward until all of the communication issues were brought to the table, discussed, and resolved. There is nothing prescriptive about any of the phases, especially phase I. The process will take as long as the communication issues dictate.

There is nothing magical about the strategic planning process we used. There are dozens of scripted approaches to organization development, but if the motivation is to move the organization development in a more transformative direction, then the process should move beyond prescription and begin to demonstrate the arts of inquiry. In our case the knowledge and skills for practicing a work life of inquiry were not well developed but proved to be adequate at the time. This was a demonstration of cultural capacity and the importance of understanding the organization's capabilities. Building cultural capacity is a constant work in progress that should never reach completion. Successful organizations are constantly redefining and constructing cultural capacity to accomplish their mission. Each of the previous 9 years, the district had worked through organization development issues while building the capacity that would later be the framework for supporting transformative change.

The early phases of the district's transformative change moved at a snail's pace with the constant danger of losing momentum, or even worse, being halted because of the existing culture's needs taking first priority. One may liken the difficulty of this work to the need to change all four tires on a vehicle while it is moving down the road. You first need to gain the trust of the occupants and convince them that it is in their best interest to pull over for a break. During the break the discussion about safety issues around the existing tires is raised and the group decides to change one tire at each stop along the way. Between stops one of the passengers begins to look at the map and suggests a more scenic route eliminating all scheduled stops. If quick, mediated intervention does not occur, the issue of developing the safety capacity of the vehicle is in jeopardy. Since you have developed a trusting relationship, the other passengers feel the original plan should be carried out. It is also agreed, considering the safety upgrade of the vehicle, that a return trip along the scenic route would be a positive experience.

At this point in the organization development framework, teachers are beginning to collaborate, interaction time has been created, and action plans are ready to be enacted. The first real "gut check" occurs at this point. Is the work crew ready to begin the remodeling, knowing full well that some people will become unnerved when their comfort zones are infringed upon? During the time it has taken to get the organization in a ready position, personnel have changed, board members have come and gone, and community stakeholders have moved. Once again I want to emphasize the constant attention that must be given to constructing and reconstructing the "critical mass." The further along an organization is in the transformational process, the greater the attention that must be given to nurturing a critical mass of transformative leaders. If not, one will quickly see the dominant existing culture weaken the framework while retreating to a safer position of status quo.

In my district expansion of the district's leadership support team became critical to move the process forward. The existing leadership design was predominantly a hierarchical model allowing autonomy within the confines of each of the four buildings. Building leaders interacted very little. Like the teachers, they were also working in a comfort zone of isolation. The phases of organization development were the same but much more difficult to implement because the leadership team was going to be asked to support the necessary changes while remaining responsible for the current work structures.

Challenging people to move out of their comfort zones becomes a question of individual and group readiness coupled with cognitive ability. These two areas proved to be the greatest obstacles facing the district's organization development. Trust issues were challenged when a leadership model was built suggesting a collaborative inquiry decision-making process that would move the team out of isolation. At this new level of capacity building, all three phases of organization development were once again carried out while members continued to build the critical mass of curriculum council members and other teacher leaders with the introduction of a district-wide professional development process.

The district's professional development process initially focused on introducing the language that would strengthen the cognitive readiness of the faculty, including the leadership team, as they embarked on a transformation that would cultivate curriculum wisdom. At this point, the notion of quality curriculum judgment became very challenging because of the issues of accountability. The existing culture had been accustomed to the tools mandated by state or local policies while demonstrating little, if any, ownership. A professional development process that supports sophisticated inquiry and professional responsibility was threatening to the dominant existing culture. Readiness and strength of the transformative capacity was seriously challenged by the existing culture.

Reluctantly, those curriculum stakeholders who were married to the existing culture allowed the transformation to continue, but under a watchful eye. Teachers, administrators, and occasionally, a board member experienced challenges. The continued work of building the organization's transformative capacity resulted in development of new hiring criteria that included an understanding or demonstration of inquiry readiness, a redesigned mentoring process for all new teachers and administrators, and an invitation to all faculty to participate in a newly designed professional development process that would support curriculum wisdom through sophisticated inquiry.

Throughout the first year, as participants in the new professional development process began to demonstrate movement toward a new democratic professional life, the existing culture made strong overtures to smother their efforts. The second year attracted greater interest from the faculty, but continued resistance from a divided leadership team challenged all efforts to continue building the necessary critical mass. The third year involved moving the critical mass to a new level by developing a support team of faculty that had begun to effectively practice curriculum wisdom.

As might be expected, a reform process that challenged the "mediocrity" of current curriculum decision making increasingly threatened the faculty. For many, the referent for "professional excellence" was meeting state minimum-standard proficiency scores, and that was now being questioned. It quickly became apparent that a new form of isolation was occurring. Participants in the professional development process were isolating themselves, or being isolated from, the previous culture. This, coupled with the expected operational challenges facing every public school, seriously reduced trust among the stakeholders.

At this point three organization development successes had been achieved. A curriculum council had been created; a supportive strategic planning process had been established; and a transformative leadership team had been organized. All three of these structural achievements became closely woven tools that nurtured the organization's transformative capacity.

Seven years after beginning efforts to build the cultural capacity that would support a democratic professional life, the district has only been successful in creating what some might describe as an isolated reform subculture. Teachers who are demonstrating curriculum wisdom have produced evidence that their students have benefited by being engaged in the discovery of knowledge in a more democratic learning process. Yet, constant resistance from the dominating existing culture continues to undermine any transformative efforts and reestablish the organizational status quo.

This experience exposed several realities. First, the type of professional development needed to support curriculum wisdom will more readily occur on a personal or individual level. This reality highlights the differences in cognitive readiness of individuals and large groups. Is it possible to transform an organization that demonstrates a wide range of readiness? Second, the existing culture is well defined by many years of public education policy, union activity, teacher training programs, and district tradition. In this environment, is it possible to sustain the energy level long enough to create the necessary supporting capacity? Why have all forms of education reform within the existing culture been so difficult to successfully sustain for any length of time? Is it possible to create a critical mass capacity that will transform the existing dominating culture found in traditional public schools?

I now turn my attention to the community development that supports the curriculum development, professional development, and organizational development activities. This area of reform requires the same kind of work and tenacity as the other three areas.

The scope of the community development work naturally moves beyond a school district's, or any educational organization's, geographical boundaries. Community development activities are situated in an educational policy environment that has overlapping local, state, and national political jurisdictions. Acknowledging this complexity raises a whole new set of questions. What is the political energy that is driving the existing culture, and what is the capacity of the education community as defined within the existing political agenda? How does that cultural message become generalized at the local organization level? What is the impact on curriculum development, professional development, and organization development when the prevailing political agenda does not recognize these areas beyond that of accountability through standardized testing?

During my district's mission to build curriculum wisdom capacity around curriculum, professional, and organization development, efforts were also started to address the larger community capacity. In the following example the three phases of community development that were presented in the first section of the chapter are very much present.

Reform centered on curriculum wisdom is difficult because there is no critical mass that presently exists allowing its political voice to be heard. The question becomes, how does this voice get heard and who should be listening? How does this process of communication and trust building occur so that it does not fall victim to resistance from the dominating culture?

The district's efforts began on several fronts. Communication was started with local political leaders including the school board, city and township leaders, local state representatives, an education liaison from the governor's office, and various department contacts within the State Department of Education, including the state superintendent. After 2 years of meetings and various forms of interaction, I came to the conclusion that this part of the reform development would move the slowest because the culture is so engrained in a political arena that relies upon the most popular decision to remain favorable at the polls. The work here is about moving the dominant political voice of accountability through test scores to a voice that speaks about a balanced accountability and responsibility founded on the practice of wise curriculum judgments through a life of professional inquiry.

It is not practical to think that one voice will stop and another will be heard. Within the community, trust was being built, data was gathered and analyzed, and action plans were established; however, it became apparent that little was going to happen within the existing culture without a great deal of sustained attention. This type of cultural reform requires time, patience, and constant attention, which are not typically afforded to the reform efforts since it becomes threatening to the existing culture. The existing culture will typically begin to demand the same time, patience, and attention as the emerging reform culture. This results in reproducing the status quo since the critical mass of understanding has not been altered. Adherents of the existing culture will utilize the available resources to attempt to smother any type of curriculum wisdom reform efforts. The heart of their arguments is that public schools must demonstrate improved student achievement through test results. Everything else is superfluous.

When the discussion turns to the importance of educating for democratic values, few take issue with embracing the idea, and some even suggest that the present culture is already supporting such values. If that were truly the reality of the present education culture, excellent schools would be recognized for supporting students who demonstrate an understanding of subject matter and society through a personal life of inquiry. The 3S learning would be the referent, not the test score. Building the community capacity to understand this shift in focus is a basic connoisseurship challenge that educational leaders must confront.

As I have reflected on the reform journey within my district, I have come to an understanding that there are two fronts of curriculum wisdom reform that are necessary and must occur simultaneously. The first front of reform activity should be experienced in the preservice years of all professional educators. This would include preservice programs for teachers and for administrators. It appears that the arts of inquiry are being introduced to at least some recent teacher candidates in northeast Ohio, which is illustrated in the teacher educator's commentary that precedes mine. This preservice reform is critical, as it provides a less threatening environment to explore and practice a professional life of inquiry. Developing an understanding during preservice activities provides the skills necessary to cope with the cultural resistance that will be encountered in an actual work environment.

Preservice teachers need help in developing strategies and skills to help them better cope with the negativity that may be present when they share new and developing ideas with persons within the existing school culture (Rust, 1999). Rather than revert to the safety of the known, teachers must receive support and strategies that allow them to develop confidence in their own inquiry abilities, thereby creating the impetus to take children further.

The second front is within the practicing culture. As Guskey (1990) states, "Practitioners often need more than one year to grow comfortable with any change. For the majority of teachers, the first year is a time of trial and experimentation" (p. 73). Support during this period of experimentation is essential. Without it, Guskey (1986) reports, many teachers will not be able to see the potential benefits of a new strategy or program and are less likely to stay with the new strategy long enough to refine their use of it. They will often abandon their efforts and return to the old familiar strategies they have used in the past (McBee & Moss, 2002). Without continuing professional development support, it is unlikely that teachers will overcome the anxiety related to attempting new ways of instructing students (Joyce & Showers, 1995).

As an experienced educator, I am encouraged by the increased number of teacher candidates who have been exposed to various notions of reflective practice. As I have attempted to highlight within this commentary, the role of educational leaders within the reform movement must be to foster a sophisticated inquiry that upholds democratic ideals within the practicing culture. To accomplish this noble endeavor, the education community at large must embrace democratic principles by fostering opportunities for students, teachers, administrators, and community members to build their inquiry capacities.

References

Dewey, J. (1930). *Democracy and education.* New York: Macmillan. (Original work published 1916)

Guskey, T. (1986). Staff development and the process of teacher change. *Education Research, 15*(5), 5–12.

Guskey, T. (1990). What to consider when evaluating staff development. *Educational Leadership, 47*(2), 73–75.

Henderson, J. G. (2001). *Reflective teaching: Professional artistry through inquiry.* Upper Saddle River, NJ: Merrill/Prentice Hall.

Hollingsworth, S. (1992). Learning to teach through collaborative conversation: A feminist approach. *American Educational Research Journal, 29*(2), 373–404.

Jalongo, M. R. (2002). Who is fit to teach young children? *Early Childhood Education Journal, 2*(3), 141–142.

Joyce, B., & Showers, B. (1995). *Student achievement through staff development* (2nd ed.). White Plains, NY: Longman.

Kauffman, D., Johnson, S. M., Kardos, S. M., Liu, E. & Peske, H. G. (2002). Lost at sea: New teachers' experiences with curriculum and assessment. *Teachers College Record, 104*(2), 273–300.

Liston, D. P., & Zeichner, K. M. (1991). *Teacher education and the social conditions of schooling.* New York: Routledge.

Manouchehri, A. (2002). Developing teaching knowledge through peer discourse. *Teaching and Teacher Education, 18,* 715–737.

McBee, R. H., & Moss, J. (2002). PDS partnerships come of age. *Educational Leadership, 59*(6), 61–64.

Rust, F. O'C. (1999). Professional conversations: New teachers explore teaching through conversation, story, and narrative. *Teaching and Teacher Education, 15,* 367–380.

Sarason, S. B. (1993). *The case for change: Rethinking the preparation of educators.* San Francisco: Jossey-Bass.

Wiggins, G., & McTighe, J. (2001). *Understanding by design* (special ed.). Upper Saddle River, NJ: Merrill/Prentice Hall.

Chapter 7

Two Teacher Narratives

INTRODUCTION

In this chapter we present the narratives of a teacher and a teacher educator who understand and value the practice of curriculum wisdom. They both tell stories of being called to the professional life of inquiry as described in this book. Their narratives extend the commentaries in Chapter 6. As they share their experiences, they provide personal perspectives on the feasibility of practicing curriculum wisdom. Unlike the practitioner commentaries in Chapter 6, they were not asked to use the book's terminology. Their stories of curriculum enactment are told in their own language.

A TEACHER'S STORY

Sometimes I imagine a new Gap commercial.[1] In mine, there are about 15 people, diverse in age, gender, and race, all dressed in white T-shirts and khaki pants, sitting very straight in identical chairs. On the screen in white letters appears these words: "Reality: it's here to stay." But then above each person's head appears a "think cloud" and inside the cloud is each person's very different reality.

I am very conscious of this reality theme. I hear it all the time. "But, Sheri, the reality is... ." It is a continuing topic in my conversations with colleagues, administrators, and even friends. I hear it so often that it has produced in me a great deal of internal dissonance regarding my own conception of reality and others' perceptions of *me*. What could it be in my own words and actions that provokes others to tell me about what is "real?" How do I reconcile my sense of being out of step with the world with my very human need to be a part of the larger order? Or do I need to?

I have learned only recently that my need to reconcile seemingly mutually exclusive yet coexisting events or concepts is misguided. Day and night occur simultaneously, lips smile while eyes don't, and a classic story can begin with, "It was the best

---

[1]Narrative written by Sheri Leafgren.

of times, it was the worst of times." I have decided, therefore, that I can be out of step and still a part of the parade, and there are plenty of others drifting along the perimeter and weaving in and out of the lines with me. Greene (1988) shares her version of this struggle: "Revisiting the notion of a finished, predetermined, objective reality, I became fascinated not merely with multiple modes of interpretation, but with all that fed into interpretation from lived lives and sedimented meanings" (p. xii). If I were sitting with Maxine Greene right now (I wish!), I don't think she would tell me what reality is.

Billy Bob Thornton, during an interview on Bravo's *Inside the Actors Studio*, told a story that resonated with me in its pleasant ambiguity and its meaningful authenticity. He told of watching a lone diner in a restaurant and feeling happy that the person had found time to be alone and had something to eat, and at the same time, feeling sad that the person was alone and **needs** something to eat.

The authors of this book offer a similar contradiction in Chapter 3 of "playful serious-ness, or serious playfulness," musing that this may seem like too much of a paradox to deal with. But not for me. As a kindergarten teacher, I live my days with 5-year-olds who allow me to share their place in the space between fantasy and reality. I like it there. I find that I truly enjoy not knowing, revel in ambiguity, and love the surprises that each twist of the kaleidoscope offers me (more on the kaleidoscope later).

I wonder sometimes if my attraction to kindergarten is due to my playful nature, or if I can remain playful in my dotage because I live in kindergarten. I think both. Paley (1997) illustrates her version of playful seriousness as she shares this story:

> In college I was taught to study the great thinkers by reading their books.... We were to enter into a dialogue with the author, discussing his ideas with the help of the teacher and bringing up questions of our own. In my case, the questions did not emerge until much later. Apparently, I needed classroom after classroom of young children demanding to be heard before I could identify my own voice and imagine my own questions. (p. 43)

I, too, have grown in my ability to negotiate my way in the world and in beginning to un-derstand myself via seeing and hearing through the eyes and ears of children. Of interest, and perhaps related to this question of causality, is my decision two years ago to join our urban school system's newly converted African-centered primary school. My experience in the classroom has been predominantly with African-American children. To learn more about the children I teach, I have sought out people who could teach me about African and African-American cultures and also read books and articles to supplement my understandings. I was especially struck by Chandler's (1999) examination of "the wisdom of those ancient civiliza-tions that did not disassociate the philosophical, spiritual, and material realms of life" (p. 10). Chandler wrote his book as "an attempt to recreate this holistic experience in hopes that a synthesized view of life will become the perspective of the twenty-first century" (p. 10). I found such articulations of a holistic, organic, African-centered philosophy very appealing, and I began to see important parallels between African-centered pedagogy and "best prac-tices" in early childhood education.

It intrigues me that the authors of this book discuss ancient wisdom traditions and the value of paradox. Consider their description from Chapter 3: "To dwell comfortably with contradictions, to rest content with not knowing, to move ahead, mindfully, in the face of chaos, confusion, and uncertainty is to be spiritually awake, and wise like a fool." Paley (1981) describes a kindergarten discussion on the magic and science involved in cooking stones for stone soup. She notes about the children, "The endless contradictions did not offend them; the children did not demand consistency" (p. 18). To me, there is a parallel spirit among children and ancients. I have often commented that children's eyes seem to be more open than ours; it must be their spiritual awareness that I sense. I feel that the ancient wisdom traditions share much with the joyful sprit of childhood.

It was this connection that led me to seek a position at the school where my story takes place. I had long been seeking a place where childhood would be nurtured and celebrated, a place where it was openly acknowledged that the traditional educational system was failing many children, and a place where everyone wasn't so *sure* of themselves and of their next move and the one after that. When I interviewed at this public school, I asked the panel if they felt a White teacher would be welcomed by the parents and community. Their response validated my presumption of the school at the time. They were seeking to staff the new school with teachers who were open to new ideas, comfortable with ambiguity, and willing to take part in a collegial process of adapting the broad vision of Afrocentrism to an urban public school setting. It seemed just what I was looking for.

I must offer a caution to this happy tale, though. Sometimes there is a space between the envisioning and the enacting. As W. Chandler (personal communication) laments, "The problem I have with some scholars and their interpretation [of Afrocentricity] is that it is something formulated with their intellects and NOT their souls and hearts. The essence of what would be called Afrocentricity is founded within a spiritual base that is rooted in the practice or doingness of specific belief systems."

Truly, I am back in kindergarten in more ways than one, operating on a daily basis in the space between fantasy and reality, between what I thought it would be and what it currently is—for we are still a public school in a large urban district. The district itself is wallowing in rules, mandates, procedures, and hierarchies. Therefore, the school is struggling to find its way, trying to maintain a vision and enact it.

Yet, we are all indoctrinated to a vision already in place and are expected not to question it. I recall the orientation provided by my big city school district to all first year teachers. We were given a book about how to "manage" our classroom (and the children in it) via a huge variety of Machiavellian machinations and manipulations. Seventeen years later, incoming teachers are indoctrinated to urban education in the same way, and it isn't any different in our African-centered school. It does seem perfectly logical that the most practical and efficient means to socialize children (to manage their behavior) is to structure the environment and the procedures so as to preempt or prevent "misbehaviors." But being neither perfect, nor necessarily logical, and disagreeing with the presumption that the goal of schooling is to control children in order to make efficient their acquisition of knowledge, I am challenged to look beyond the craft of management to the art of negotiating an authentic caring exploration into democratic living: to nurture in the children an ability and desire to use their "human intellect for generous… and generative purposes (Henderson, 2001, pp. 6–7)." Ironically, this daunting challenge likely requires my imperfection and illogical notions. The notion of practical wisdom as fallibilistic, contextual, contingent, and holistic (Cherryholmes, 1999) implies a high degree of unpredictability in curriculum work and, therefore, the need to be flexible.

The authors of this book speak of the "process of envisioning and enacting a good educational journey"; as we work hard to translate our educational visions into curricula, we remain pragmatically humble, recognizing that "perhaps our vision of the good journey is mistaken." I try to embrace this notion of fallibility with the best of my courage and humor, for it is this willingness to take a risk—to perhaps look foolish—that allows me to genuinely reflect, deliberate, and act. Part of this joyful venture into the unknown aspect of moral judgment involves practicing the arts of inquiry in Chapter 3.

The authors of this book offer metaphors of a hologram to describe the inquiry map. I liken using this map to a peek through a kaleidoscope: playful, always unpredictable, and influenced in its ever-changing permutations by an interplay of the colors and shapes inside. Unlike looking through a telescope, which might clarify what I am seeing, the kaleidoscopic nature of the inquiry map instead offers a look at the beautiful complexity of its components. Each twist and turn offers a different view; each view evokes a different response.

As a kindergarten/first-grade teacher, my moral judgment is in overdrive on a moment-to-moment basis, and there are many stories to tell about the struggles in envisioning and enacting the democratic path. I could tell stories of abandoned basals, unsolicited missives to superintendents, refusals to administer mandated tests, apologies to children for careless words or acts, mobilizations of parents, morphed curricula, sobbing retreats from staff meetings, balks at state Department of Education mandates, alternative learning environments and materials—all tales of reflective inquiry in various forms. However, the one I have chosen to share with you, a tale of first graders and lines, is a clear illustration of peeking through the many inquiry lenses in order to enact curriculum wisdom.

When I began my kindergarten placement at the African-centered primary school, I was fortunate to be given a class of delightful and very individual children. We bonded so firmly that we lobbied to continue our relationship, and I was permitted to follow my class of 13 to first grade the following year. We did welcome one additional student to our fold, a boy from the next class named Daiyaan, a lively child who I had coveted from the moment I saw him and who I requested as soon as I knew I was being "promoted." I mention this because Daiyaan is a pivotal part of the story and I sometimes wonder if this is because he did come later to us. It is midway through this first-grade year that this story takes place.

It was a typical day. (Or should I say, "It was the best of days, it was the worst of days."?) The children were joining together in one of our ubiquitous lines when Jalen left the line to return a crayon to his desk. When he attempted to move back into his space, Deverette shouldered him away and said, "You have to go to the end!" Jalen tried to shove his way back in, and a scuffle ensued. They both fell, and as the line disintegrated and then reformed, each child had a place, but the grumbling and discontent were palpable. This wasn't the first time the class had experienced a "space-reclaiming" incident, and I realized that while there were school-imposed "line rules," we had negotiated no mechanism in our classroom for returning or not returning to a space in the line. The result was a kind of case-by-case basis of sometimes saving spaces and sometimes not, which had served us well in kindergarten but somehow was not working for us in first grade. So the following morning the class addressed the issue as a topic in our daily meeting: "Should we save a space for someone who leaves the line?" During the discussion, the issue grew to include saving spaces on our gathering carpet as well.

When the meeting began, I wondered what would become of the issue. I could not anticipate what the children would say or how the decisions would be made, and—contrary to the admonishments of classroom managers—I did not have a preplanned conclusion. This was partly because I didn't really have a preference, but more importantly because I fully agree with Dyasi (1995) that "the notion of beginning without conclusion is what creates opportunities for students to exercise their ingenuity" (p. 161).

In fact, much of the joyful playfulness of genuinely sharing the process of problem solving is due to the possibility of surprise: "… consequences of free action… are to a large degree unpredictable" (Greene, 1988, p. 46). While I did begin to develop an opinion as the meeting progressed, I did not share it at the time because of concerns that my feelings would eclipse those of the children.

Over the course of the meeting, the children had the opportunity to share their opinions and feelings on the issue, and as I listened to them, the question that I was ambivalent about to begin with (finding reasons of my own to save and not to save) became much more important to me. The reasons the children gave for saving or not saving were extremely telling about how each interpreted the act. Their voices intensified in me in Greene's (1988) words, "an uneasiness … an anxiety about what is being communicated to the young, about the culture we are perpetuating" (p. 1). In the end, 4 of the 14 children had shared reasons that spaces should not be saved. In listening to their rationales, I heard echoes of grown-ups in their words, themes that I imagined they heard from adults, things they believed:

- "People in the line did what they were supposed to do, so why should they move back for the ones who didn't?" (Perhaps echoing the grown-up question, "Why should my taxes pay for some welfare mother who didn't finish school like I did?")
- "They should have remembered whatever they forgot or listened to the directions." (Perhaps echoing a grown-up position on the letter and not the spirit of the law.)
- "If you are responsible, you won't lose your place; and it isn't someone else's responsibility if you aren't." (Perhaps echoing the grown-up who docks the pay of a man whose car broke down on the way to work.)
- "Move your feet… you lose your seat!" (Daiyaan is perhaps echoing the unspoken thoughts of many grown-ups, "I've got mine, too bad about yours!")

It seemed that the words spoken by these four children indicated a tendency to adopt a harsher, less generous attitude toward perceived weaknesses, perhaps a survival of the fittest mentality. I wondered about this; and as with many things I wonder about, I sought out the advice of an "elder."

Volunteering every day in our school and serving as counsel to both teachers and children is a group of mature (over 55) African American men, organized as the Council of Elders. On one occasion, one of these elders, Jumanne Mweusi, shared a story with me to illustrate his view of the contrasts between Eastern and Western (and what he also refers to as Southern versus Northern and Afro-centric versus Euro-centric) ideologies:

It was said that in Greece, when a young boy was born, he was dipped into the icy stream. And should he survive, then he was thought to be ready, to be prepared for Greek life. Whereby in Africa, it's the opposite. It was thought that the life was so young, so fresh and so tender that the only thing you would want to do was to protect it in any way that you could. Like the Greeks were saying let the child come in prepared to deal with the elements. And it is a shock… a system shock. And we say, no, we don't believe in that form of shock. Africans offered a welcoming into warmth instead of the cold.

The four children who took the "no saving" stance seemed to be taking on the Greek or Western philosophy as summarized in the above story, tacitly agreeing that it's a cold, cruel world and that is what we had better prepare to be a part of. Insight into this point of view is provided by Haggerson's (2000) discussion of European and African epistemologies: "Eurocentric analysis is viewed as linear. Rooted in empiricism, rationalism and scientific method and positivism, its aim is prediction and control. African epistemology... is circular... and seeks interpretation, expression, and understanding without preoccupation with verification" (p. 33). Capra (1984) adds an additional comparative perspective: "In contrast to the mechanistic Western view, the Eastern view of the world is 'organic'. For the Eastern mystic, all things and events perceived by the senses are interrelated, connected and are but different aspects or manifestations of the same ultimate reality." (p. 10)

Even as I write these words, I am reflecting on my own inadequacies in some of the aspects of practical wisdom: I do tend to think in dualistic modes, organizing my thoughts in binary categories—not holistic at all. It's especially interesting that I am using a dualistic notion of Eastern/Western to criticize Western, yet the very practice of employing binaries is a Western/rational construct. Another paradox!

It seems to me that the function of our schools appears to be to toughen our children, to deemphasize playfulness, to foster academic success at all costs: to be prepared (as all "education governors" and "education presidents" seem to exhort us) to "compete and win in a global economy!" What does this say about the world we are preparing them for? Postman (1995) asks, "What kind of public does public school create?" (p. 18). He asks this question because "public education does not serve a public. It creates a public" (p. 18). Consider what "public" must be: the marriage of the individual and the group. No one member can live the democratic good life without a balancing of the good of the one with the good of all. It is a terrible responsibility borne by schools, yet so many educators barely give a second thought to what we might be creating (actually perpetuating) in our short-sighted decision making. I remember reading in a novel about a defense attorney agonizing over how to do her job. She decided she coped the way most criminal defense lawyers did: "Without looking up" (Scottoline, 1999, p. 188).

Perhaps teachers feel they can't afford to look up. If public school does create a public, the inverse is also true. As the public is less willing to value the ethic of care and to engage in authentic discussions and communication, the schools find little time and space for such values. If we looked up, we'd see just how sad that is.

I look up. While I see for myself, much of the context must come from dialogue with others, not only the children with whom I share much but with colleagues and other adults. As I struggle with my moral judgment, I sometimes seek out the feelings and opinions of others to play against my own. Because the "saving spaces" issue seemed so ripe with moral implications, I wondered what other teachers of young children thought and did in similar circumstances. So I asked. At my school, in my university classes, in conversations with teacher friends, and in the context of informal conversations, I shared parts of the story. Many of the reactions were similar to the ones paraphrased here:

- How will they learn responsibility if they aren't penalized?
- It isn't fair to the children who DID remember if the other ones get to come back.
- I always tell my children that they need to remember their things before they come to line. I planned for this and we have the same line order for everyone every day. If

the student isn't ready when it is their turn, then they lose their place and go to the end.

- ▪ That situation would never come up in my class. My students know that they have an assigned place in line and are expected to be there every time—with all the materials taken care of. If they bring a pencil with them, I take it!
- ▪ I will tell them, 'If you snooze, you lose!'

Not one of these teachers quoted above felt that the priority should be on maintaining spaces for others, on reflecting how saving or not affected the children, or on the lessons taught by their policies. Many questioned why such an issue would ever arise since it could be prevented so easily through proper preventive procedures. But consider, "When conformity is fostered, democracy is inhibited. If teachers do not develop their capacity to 'confirm' the unique voices of their students in caring ways, they are simply not in a position to teach for democratic living" (Noddings, 1984 in Henderson, 2001, p. 73). What are we teaching our children when we emphasize efficiency over empathy, accountability over respect, goals over generosity, control over kindness, and dogma over democracy? As Silberman (1970) has posited, "We will not be able to create and maintain a humane society unless we create and maintain classrooms that are humane" (p. 524).

In practice, democracy is taught as a way of government (the three branches, the electoral system, majority rules), as a civics lesson, rather than as a lived event shared among the community of learners housed in the schools. We should inquire if schools are more interested in teaching facts about democracy and studying democratic underpinnings such as Washington's cherry tree and Lincoln's beard than engaging children in democratic processes and inquiry. Lost to habit, custom and rules are opportunities we need to develop human intellect for **generous** and **generative** purposes. These concepts nurture my critical awareness of how the implicit or "hidden" curriculum in my own classroom affects the well being of the children in my care. These ideas don't tell me what to do; they do validate a moral sensibility that influences each decision I make.

At that first class meeting on saving spaces in line we were unable to come to an agreement about whether to make saving spaces consistent but did agree to pay special attention to incidences of children moving in and out of spaces as we made lines and gathered on the carpet over the course of our week. Ostensibly, our goal was to solve the problem of spaces in line, but truly, the practice of attending to feelings and variations and results afforded much richer lessons.

Fortuitously, the very next day as the children were lining up from gym class, two events occurred simultaneously in different parts of the line: In the front part of the line, Ramia left to retrieve her shoes and also Dallas's. As she returned, Dallas wrapped his arm around her shoulder and guided her back into her place in line. At the same time, Tevin had left the line to get his forgotten shoes and tried to return to his place in front of Daiyaan. "NO!" Daiyaan yelled and forced Tevin back out, and a struggle for place ensued. We had another meeting as soon as we returned to class, while the incidents and feelings evoked by them were fresh in our minds. I wanted to be sure the children were making fully conscious decisions based on real events and the real emotions precipitated by the events.

As the children talked, they spoke of the hurt they saw on some children's faces when denied a place, and of the "glow" on Ramia's when she helped Dallas and he welcomed her back. They spoke of feeling like they didn't matter to people when they couldn't get in. The children decided they would like to save a space for a child who forgot something and that once a child had a space next to a friend on the carpet, that friend would keep that space, too. Except Daiyaan. Daiyaan said he still didn't want to save spaces. That's not what they do at his house. In a situation where custom and order is the "end" and democracy itself is a list of rules, no deliberation is necessary: "Majority rules"—hence the introduction of the new classroom rule that would require each space to be "saved." We must reflect, though: Was the most valued end to merely make the decision to save or not to save, or was it to use "human intellect for generative and generous purposes?" So there was no rule made. The process of discussion and looking carefully at one another and at feelings was enough to cause the children to rethink their behavior toward each other and the imposed situation of lines. Most children conscientiously left spaces for children who left their place, and the most generous and generative acts were directed toward Daiyaan.

The children in the class, on their own, when leaving a place in front of Daiyaan generally didn't even try to return there. Most children, most of the time, made their return to the end of the line when they noticed they would need to reclaim a space in front of Daiyaan. The children didn't make a new inflexible rule as I might have. They respected Daiyaan's feelings enough to read his face and adjust to his needs, and on his part, on many occasions, Daiyaan let people in even when they hadn't been in front of him to begin with!

This end was one of the most instructive for me in this story. It showed me that while I may have been practicing what Kohl (1994) refers to as "creative maladjustment" and what Garrison (1997) terms "outlaw logic" by not imposing a common rule for lines, the children adopted those practices much more profoundly in spontaneously adapting to one child's needs. It mattered more to them that each person's feelings were considered than that their new "system" had been put in place. Kohl's inspiration for "creative maladjustment" was a speech given by Dr. Martin Luther King in 1958. King said, "… there are some things within our social order to which I am proud to be maladjusted and to which I call you to be maladjusted" (King, 1992, p. 33). Kohl (1994) expands on King's celebration of maladjustment, resisting unquestioned authority and routine by creatively "learning to survive with minimal moral and personal compromise in a thoroughly compromised world… Creative maladjustment is reflective. It implies adapting your own particular maladjustment to the nature of the social systems you find oppressive. It also implies learning how other people are affected by those systems" (p. 130).

The children's logic was grounded in their intuitive sense of fairness and empathy. Mine was merely a lesser focus on procedure, but each was conceived with a conscious moral justification in mind. Initially, I had assumed that once we had determined the new procedures for spaces, we would make that the rule! The children didn't make that assumption. They looked past that bureaucratic end and demonstrated to me that the visionary end that they valued touched on the feelings of classmates and the spirit of community. As I reflect back on these unexpected, serendipitous, incidental ends, I am reminded of Rivkin's (1991) comment, "I do not like reductionist thinking. It always leaves out something and its conclusions are too constructed—something in me always wants that left-out part, perhaps even more than the included part" (p. 68). Dewey asserts (in Garrison, 1997, p. 81), "Thinking has to operate creatively to form new ends."

There were layers of ends in this story:

- The children wouldn't be likely to push or fight in line anymore.
- The children felt like they have a "space" within the artificial and social constraints of the school: lines, gathering places, etc.
- The children had opportunities to act generously.
- Individual feelings were respected.
- The well-being of the group was nurtured.
- Children had the opportunities to work cooperatively to solve problems.
- Democratic ideals were practiced and lived, not just discussed.
- I learned about the children.
- The children learned about each other.
- The children learned about me.
- Each child learned more about him- or herself.

Except for that first end (children wouldn't fight in line), none of these were the overt, original goals of our discussions. These ends derived from the means, just as the means themselves evolved as new ends emerged. In the words of Quinn (1992), "As we make our journey here, we're going to be reexamining key pieces of (the) mosaic... And when we're finished, you'll have an entirely new perception of the world and all that's happened here. And it won't matter in the least whether you remember how that perception was assembled. The journey itself is going to change you" (p. 40). Just so!

This story is not intended as a how-to story. There are many different ways we could have worked through this problem. I don't experience our solution as THE RIGHT way. If I was trying to solve this problem on a different day, or if I was in a different mood, I might do things differently.

Henderson (2001) describes the willingness to play with perspectives as the "carnival" side of democratic living. He uses Bakhtin's (1984) definition of carnival as a place that lies outside the established social order. I feel that of all places to adopt a "carnival" attitude—places where people "can let down their social guards, relax and perhaps even mock the more sedate and somber sides of their lives" (Henderson, 2001, p. 74)—the spots where children gather should be first in importance. Henderson adds, "Without moments of intellectual play, the forces of habit and custom too easily dominate the power and independence of human intellect" (p. 74). One child, Maalik, demonstrated his ability to play with an idea through his contribution to one of our discussions. When some children struggled with the idea of people who forgot things being able reclaim spaces in front of people who didn't forget, he defused the power of that dichotomy through his carnival-like explanation: "They didn't forget their stuff. They just remembered late!"

Maalik intuits the "double good," seeing past the practical "they should have remembered" to his more generous and playful rationale. As I pursue the double good and doubled problem solving of curriculum wisdom, my relationship with children like Maalik helps to keep my eyes soft and open, a nearly constant influence in my inquiry lens, one that colors my reactions to readings, conversations, observations, and experiences.

I live in paradox. I laugh and I cry every day of my life. Even when I know the science of the water cycle, I still think rain is magic. And while I know that school is to prepare children for life, I don't believe it is a life we know about yet. Taylor (1968, in Silberman,

1970) claims, "Preparing to become a teacher is like preparing to become a poet, the preparation begins in a decision to be something, a commitment made about one's life and the purpose of it" (p. 380).

My purpose, my calling, lies in making a caring space for children: a free, humane and **joyful** place. This is my vision in broad strokes, and I look to the children to influence the enactment.

One of the terms used by the children in my first grade classroom is "big hearted." Aisha once said to Gavin, "I think your heart just grew two sizes bigger," referring to the Grinch whose heart grew upon acting generously to the Whos in Whoville. Perhaps if we consider developing heart as well as mind and body in our schools, we could learn to grow enough space there for EVERYONE in our hearts. And the ones who are a little late in coming, we can save their space. Can't we?

A TEACHER EDUCATOR'S STORY

> There is absolutely no inevitability as long as there is a willingness to contemplate what is happening. (McLuhan & Fiore, 1967, p. 25)

I've been asked to comment on the themes in this book as someone who for 20 plus years has been interested in promoting democratic life through teacher education.[2] As I've read the emerging manuscript, grappling with its sophisticated ideas and multiple frameworks, my struggle to find my own voice and to contribute meaningfully to a conversation about curriculum wisdom has crystallized around several core responses. One is captured in Jack Nicholson's comment to Helen Hunt in the movie, As *Good As It Gets*. Impatient and frustrated by Nicholson's evasive, inexpressive behavior, Hunt says to Nicholson, in effect, "C'mon. Say something nice to me." Twitching and initially silent, the incomparable Nicholson eventually responds, "You make me want to be a better person."

In a heartfelt, nonhyperbolic way, that's precisely how reading this book has made me feel. I want to teach better, read more, write more, research more, and understand more. I want to be a greater force for good in the world, make a bigger impact. Beyond that, I want to be a better father, soul-mate, lover, friend. More than ever, I want to confront and embrace my insecurities, push limits, take risks, connect with others, and live with greater passion and integrity.

During one of his presidential campaigns, Jesse Jackson said, "Purpose gets me up in the morning." This book rises with a spirited sense of purpose, with the kind of conviction and hope reflected in the section-opening quote. What inspires me most is not just the book's elegant arguments and eloquent prose, nor its compelling aspirations and informative frameworks, though each of these are certainly a dynamic part of my enthusiasm. What moves me most is the book's Gibraltar-like integrity. Passionate in its pragmatic pursuit of a "deep" democracy, the book persistently defies dogmatism. Invitational and not ideological at its core, the book, like strong democracy at its best, is fervently and forcefully nonfanatical.

---

[2]Narrative written by Thomas Kelly.

Practicing its essence, this book has led me to examine, refine, and relate my own essential practices. Below I share a number of these. Three purposes guide my commentary. I want to instantiate selected major concepts in this book, demonstrate the book's vital influence on a practicing teacher educator, and underscore the fundamental worth and feasibility of taking the challenging democratic journey the authors so well frame.

Critical Democratic Pedagogy: The 3 C's and the 3 A's

My vision of the purposes of education in a democracy has undergone progressive if halting change over the past 20 years. A significant recent development is linked to research that a colleague, Mark Storz, and I have conducted on secondary student teachers' perceptions of what we call "critical democratic pedagogy" or CDP. How do the students understand its meaning, benefits, applications, and difficulties? The previous semester the students had taken a course from me in which I asked them to read Shor (1992); Kohn (1996); Newmann, Secada, and Wehlage (1995); Wiggins (1998); and Fisher and Ury (1981). They were interviewed at the start and conclusion of their student teaching experience. Our analysis of the data regarding the meaning and benefits of CDP identified six themes. Resonant with this book's seven modes of inquiry and 3S learning frames of reference, the six dimensions are choice, community, critical consciousness, advocacy, authenticity, and accountability.

Student choice involves soliciting and empowering students' voices in the classroom, structuring guided opportunities for responsible decision making, and providing individualized options within the curricular, instructional, and assessment domains.

Conceiving of the **classroom as a learning community** entails deliberately attending to the social relationships within the classroom and seeking to cultivate such psycho-social dynamics as a sense of belonging, trust, care, respect, empathy, and joy. Relationships are seen to have a significant effect on achievement. Given that conflict will arise in any group, in classrooms seen as communities wise curriculum pays deliberate attention to cultivating a distinctive democratic art, constructive conflict negotiation. In addition, as this book demonstrates, a wise curriculum is holographic. It seeks to locate and judiciously honor the unique in the common and the common within the diverse. Put differently, it hopes to forge a disciplined balance between individual interests and the common interest. A wise curriculum will help community members examine the nature of their positive interdependence and the value of an ethical call to be one's brother's/sister's keeper.

Promoting **critical consciousness** involves helping students consider their ideals in terms of the good life and examining the dynamics of power, justice, and equality to determine the fit between the ideal and the real. This critique is not only directed at the macro level. It is also applied to the micro level of the classroom in two senses. One entails reflection on the curriculum's purpose, relevance, and selective biases and/or omissions. The second involves an ongoing examination of classroom practices in light of priority values associated with a good life for all. Do teachers and students walk their own talk in terms of content, instruction, management, assessment processes, and interpersonal relationships?

Insight into problems is a first step. Identifying discrepancies between the ideal and the real provides a platform for taking informed action to diminish the discrepancy in service of a better world. This activist **advocacy** identifies students as courageous citizens-in-the-making and propels them into active participation in the significant issues of the school/broader community.

A wise curriculum, directed toward enhancing the quality of life within an aspiring democracy, will also engage students in **authentic work, pedagogy and assessment**. In general, authentic work is characterized by addressing real-life problems that demand high standards of resourceful, intelligent adjustment. Where feasible, students enact the assessment task in front of an audience selected for their capacity to provide motivational and/or expert commentary.

CDP, like the seven modes of inquiry and the 3S framework, far transcends a basic proficiency orientation. Because it requires robust multidimensional artistry as implied above, it holds teachers **accountable** to challenging standards of student achievement. Consistent with the 3S framework, this accountability to subject matter is complemented by accountability to oneself and to the standards of respectful and caring social interaction. Each of the preceding five CDP dimensions contributes to a continuously renewing classroom culture through a constant teacher self-critique and student critique of the teacher and classroom experience. For those committed to CDP, accountability is not a dirty word. It is a pragmatic moral command to integrate CDP's dimensions in order to optimize the good curricular journey for all students.

I am pleased to report that while prospective teachers and teaching candidates with whom I've recently worked note various conceptual and pedagogical challenges to implementing CDP, the overwhelming majority of them indicate that the basic enterprise of CDP is worthy of their personal identification and ongoing professional development.

Teachers Are Already (Tacit) Democratic Visionaries: Autobiographical Archeology

The six dimensions of CDP have been enormously instructive as I've worked with teachers and administrators to articulate a guiding vision of critical democratic practice and address its concomitant challenges. In this section I want to emphasize my belief that there already exists in the sedimented experiences of educators and their students a motherload of potential understandings, capacities, and dispositions—latent transformative democratic identities, if you will—waiting to be mined and refined, made kinetic and catalytic. This belief is rooted, at least in part, in preliminary but promising curricular efforts at facilitating what I'm terming "autobiographical archeology" or AA. Let me briefly describe one such effort.

This effort has involved conceptualizing a set of **g**enerative **u**nderstandings and **t**ransformative **s**ensibilities (what I call GUTS) that might be considered fundamentally preconditional to optimal engagement in systemic democratic reform efforts in the multiple interdependent spheres (e.g., cultural/educational, political, economic) where it holistically needs to happen. If these psycho-philosophical GUTS are present as part of one's fundamental identity tapestry (FIT), they can propel a can-do orientation toward resolving certain dilemmas, which Newmann (1975) has identified as inherent in political advocacy work. When these GUTS don't fit an individual's make-up, then resistance, discouragement, and disengagement will characterize that individual's response to the democratic wisdom challenge. Implicit in the prompts below, these GUTS reveal significant features about an individual's convictions, conduct, and self-concept and their responsible reconsideration of each.

I have asked students to respond in writing to selected prompts. A current set of prompts includes these:

- *Sense of Efficacy*: Briefly describe an example when you didn't think you could do or learn something that seemed too difficult, but with effort, assistance, and time, you succeeded.
- *Thoughtful Open-mindedness*: Describe a situation where you came to reconsider the truth or wisdom of a particular belief or value in light of new perspectives gained. Considering this in a context of a sense of efficacy, what significant lessons do you draw for helping students overcome internal barriers to constructive change?
- *Public-Minded Beliefs*: Briefly describe two to three specific beliefs/values you passionately hold and wish more people did because if they did, the world, not just your world, would be a better, more just place.
- *Courage to Confront Authority*: Briefly describe a situation where you felt that a superior of yours (parent, teacher, boss, other) created or condoned some injustice and, despite your fears, you confronted that superior and felt proud of yourself, regardless how the situation turned out. What concrete implications would this experience have for you as a teacher seeking to promote deep democratic culture?

In general, I have been impressed by students' memorable experiences, important insights, strong convictions, and genuine concerns in response to these prompts. Overall, my own pedagogical experiences, outlined throughout this commentary, together with the frameworks provided in this book, persuade me that with instructive scaffolding students do possess the GUTS for advancing the curriculum wisdom challenge that democratic societies so compellingly pose.

In summary, I believe the potential payoff of AA for envisioning and enacting the good democratic journey is substantial. I look forward to expanding and researching my efforts in this regard and encourage readers to join in systematic autobiographical excavation inquiry at their own archeological work sites.

The Pragmatic Prescription: Co-constructing a Democratic Culture

Several years ago, I attended a workshop by Grant Wiggins, a connoisseur of educative assessment. He told a story about asking a question of Lee Shulman, then the head of the National Teacher Assessment Board. Grant asked Lee what research was revealing about the differences between effective and ineffective teachers. Paraphrased, Lee said, "We're finding that one variable significantly differentiates between the two: The ability to accurately describe one's own classroom."

I share this story with my students, and in the ensuing discussions, several key points generally emerge. Effectively describing one's classroom entails attending to students' psychological experiences. A focus solely on external behavior or on objective test results is inadequate. In order to describe students' tacit processing of their classroom experience, teachers must recurrently solicit formal and informal feedback from them. Pragmatic principles reign here: Teachers are fallible, internal learning processes are complex, contexts are dense, and indeterminate moments are fleeting and irreducibly contingent. The net result is that drawing unconfirmed inferences is inherently unreliable, fraught with likely distortions and self-projections. Being deliberately provocative, I would say this: Teachers who have an enacted policy of not regularly soliciting feedback from students are being more than merely presumptuous, authoritarian, evasive, and/or lazy; they are being professionally irresponsible.

Of course, there are many understandable reasons why teachers might not routinely seek students' feedback about the class experience. Content coverage demands are so high. Time is so short. Teachers really do know how to read student body language and their informal comments. Many students are inexperienced, immature, and oppressed by multiple forces. All these factors lead to feedback that can be uninformative, silly, and mean-spirited—in short, unnecessary and rightly dismissed.

Despite these considerations, my own experience has me standing squarely in support of soliciting feedback from students on what they're finding helpful and not helpful and what we might do better. I support solicitation of student feedback on both educational and prudential grounds. It is educationally wise for the message it exemplifies, the desirable outcomes it generates, and the requisite preconditions it compels. What it exemplifies and generates is an affirmation of each of the six dimensions defined above. Student voice is directly solicited, as is their input in improving the curricular experience. Collective deliberation about how best to integrate individual, group, and teacher/curricular interests reflects central dynamics within the community. This deliberation, facilitated wisely, will entail critical considerations about the practical and visionary purposes of the curriculum. Concurrently, the teacher, through encouraging collective critique and modeling public self-examination, will illustrate the power of walking the talk and moderate students' learned hypersensitivity to hypocrisy.

Furthermore, the feedback and its related deliberations on improving the classroom experience are themselves a form of authentic student public advocacy. This advocacy seeks to make the whole classroom community more accountable to standards of conduct and achievement that, with wise teacher guidance, will be meaningfully discussed, periodically reviewed, and collectively owned.

Besides these benefits, soliciting productive student feedback requires that a certain set of norms and capacities be consciously nurtured. One way to interpret some of the reasons cited above for dismissing student feedback is that the requisite norms and capacities have not been adequately established. Ongoing research by Ferguson (1999) is pertinent here. According to Ferguson, every classroom needs to satisfactorily address a basic set of interrelated tasks for optimal social and intellectual engagement. These tasks include establishing trust and interest; striking a balance between teacher control and student autonomy; helping students become ambitious learners with minimal ambivalence; sustaining industrious student engagement, even in the face of setbacks; and consolidating one's learning and confirming its utility for future learning. His research is identifying promising interventions to fulfill each of these five core tasks. Applied to our context, Ferguson's research suggests that norms of trust need to be established, the role of student autonomy legitimized by teachers, the worth of the curriculum affirmed by students, and the capacities of students to provide constructive feedback modeled and explicitly taught by teachers.

As these tasks are achieved, the power of student feedback to support a democratic process and the democratic end-in-view of ongoing classroom renewal will be greatly magnified.

Beyond these multiple educational reasons, soliciting regular student feedback is prudent for two reasons. First, I am liberated from the solitary burden of being an omniscient mind reader of students' reactions. Getting students' oral and/or written feedback regularly allows me, in collaboration with students, to make the kind of responsive adjustments that can lead to greater student engagement and achievement within a culture of democratic practices. Given that my continuing aspiring identity as an effective educator in large measure depends upon the realization of these two broad goals, I am doing myself a generous psychological and professional favor. I wish all teachers would come to construe student feedback in a similar vein.

Framing Controversial Discussions

The proper role of student voice in the classroom is just one of countless issues open to disagreement among reasonable educators of good will. How might teachers come to feel comfortable and capable dealing with the multiple controversies circulating within the overt and latent curricula? Given my two decades of teaching discussion facilitation, I know that leading effective issues discussions involves the arts of disciplined inquiry. Unfortunately, if my unscientifically confirmed hunch, based on informal discussions with nationwide colleagues, is correct, it is an artistry that is generally overlooked in professional development at all levels. And democracy suffers because of it.

My own approach might be summarized as follows. After critiquing both absolutist and radically relativist perspectives, I propose to my students that a compelling end-in-view for teachers leading discussions of controversial issues is to foster in discussants the capacity and commitment to express **informed and personally reflective perspectives** on matters affecting personal and public welfare. Being informed speaks to the capacity to render an impartial and accurate representation of all the relevant competing perspectives around a particular issue. Personally reflective perspectives refers to a discussant's current reasoned and intuitive assessment of where she or he stands on the issues addressed.

Without claiming that this dual end-in-view is uncontroversial, I will say this: It is a rare person who proudly states either of the following. "I firmly believe the following, and I know my view is uninformed." "I believe you should listen to me and try to understand what I have to say, but I definitely believe I shouldn't have to do the same for you." It would appear that recognizing and respecting the basic worth of another human being is a core value in a democracy, requiring an active responsibility toward mutual inquiry and informed understanding.

Regarding the development of personally reflective perspectives, a strong democracy cannot thrive if individuals are narrowly informed, however deeply. The democratic polis envisioned in this book demands active, self-examining citizens, individuals who aspire to advocate their own points of view even as they acknowledge the ambivalences of continuing, open-minded inquiry. At its best, their advocacy is essentially inspired by a passionate commitment to realize their personal interests while advancing the public interest.

Having generally addressed this section's heading, let me turn to its pedagogical application. The **best case fair hearing** reflects a high standard of access and material integrity by which teachers can be assessed. Did the teacher ensure that all perspectives relevant to the examined controversies were well represented and thoughtfully considered? This standard would be met if the most articulate spokespeople for the diverse perspectives were present and attested that their viewpoints were accurately and fairly portrayed.

A complementary robust standard, viewed from the lens of student achievement rather than teacher pedagogy, is the Oscar nomination. Do students understand relevant, competing perspectives so well that they could win an Oscar nomination for their empathic, nuanced portrayal of these alternative standpoints? The explicit goal is not to ensure that students agree with these diverse perspectives. That destination is dangerously directed toward indoctrination. Rather, the intent is to inspire and assess students' imaginative exploration of the "other"—an educative journey inevitably leading also to enhanced self-discovery.

As Elbow (1986) explains, this sympathetic exploration of the other is enriched by another deliberate heuristic, "methodological believing." Perhaps less familiar than its opposite twin—methodological doubting or systematic skepticism—methodological believing involves intentionally taking a generous, affirming stance toward the other, seeking to find what is valuable and intriguing about the other's beliefs and behavior. Methodological believing seeks to suspend premature doubt to enhance deep understanding. Without denying the realm of irreconcilable differences, this method intentionally embodies one of democracy's defining goals, respecting the inherent worth of the other. As such, it tends to reflect the kind of strong democratic talk (Barber, 1984) that can nurture win-win dispositions between diverse, even antagonistic, individuals.

I now share three observations about my sustained experience with these perspectives. First, the vast majority of teachers are initially daunted by the complexity and unpredictability of the facilitation challenge. Representative metaphors they've created to describe their experience of leading an in-class issues discussion with peers include juggling eggs and facing the fear of your insecure skill level; prompting a cat to come inside, knowing it may sit still or take off suddenly, in either hoped-for or unexpected directions; acting as ringmaster of the Barnum and Bailey's Circus; directing traffic at rush hour; or trying to get an older senior citizen to drive the speed limit.

Second, students' metaphors convey a gestalt quite well. It takes sophisticated artistry to orchestrate the host of strategic intuitions and judgments instrumental to leading dynamic discussions. For example, it takes structuring an engaging, focused topic; helping discussants analyze key ambiguous terms and prioritize central value conflicts; evoking broad, equitable yet probing participation; promoting respectful and challenging student-student interaction; encouraging alternative viewpoints while identifying common ground; modeling nonevasive self-disclosure without stifling dissent; examining issues in the specific case while testing tacit principles in analogous cases; eliciting genuine student voice while expecting Oscar-nominating role-taking of oppositional perspectives; and insuring best case fair hearings without overly directing.

Third, despite the substantial challenges of striking these elusive balances, it's been my unequivocal experience that professional development directed toward enhancing teachers' artistry in conducting discussions pays off considerably. Teachers clearly get better the more they practice and receive quality coaching.

Can Truth and Youth Speak to Power: Advocacy Projects

In my own childhood, conflict was frightening, making my flight response a psychological imperative. Since physical flight was not an option, I would characteristically suppress and submit rather than confront and negotiate. In the absence of disciplined inquiry and supportive guidance in the arts of conflict negotiation, any moral exhortations to confront conflict and negotiate with authority stood not a whimper of a chance to penetrate my wall of panicked incompetence.

Years of informal "therapeutic" education and marriage with a remarkably sensitive woman, together with my evolving commitment to CDP, among other things, have helped me develop the GUTS and FIT that radically altered my reaction to conflict. These dynamics have also shaped my aspirations for educators in an aspiring democracy. For some time now, I have taught courses on conflict negotiation that feature *Getting to Yes: Negotiating Agreement Without Giving In* (Fisher & Ury, 1981). Through readings, teacher demonstrations, student role-plays, and reflective critiques, students are expected to integrate into their resourceful repertoire the four main "Getting to Yes" (GTY) principles. Adapted for educational settings, these principles and their related skills include:

- *Separating the person from the problem* by using reflective listening, noting the strengths of others, and "reframing" others' offensive behavior to affirm underlying unmet need (e.g., student boredom might be seen as an unfulfilled desire for intellectual engagement; complaints about teacher favoritism become desires for fair treatment, etc.). By refusing to villainize the other, one enhances the likelihood of constructive problem solving;
- *Explicitly confirming common interests* between conflicting parties, further setting the stage for collaborative problem solving;
- *Exploring or proposing (but not imposing) options for mutual gain*; and
- *Using and honoring objective criteria* to maximize the likelihood that agreements achieved are mutually perceived as fair, noncoerced, and worthy of sustained commitment.

It has been my consistent experience that judicious pedagogy on my part can lead to substantial growth in students' GUTS and a FIT more empowered to confront the challenges of building a democratic culture. Filtered through the powerful lens of this book's inquiry artistry map, I now construct that conflict-confronting judicious pedagogy in the following terms:

- *Attending closely to students' experiences with conflict and the associated FIT that has developed.* Allowing students to select for role-play practice the problematic experiences most salient to them enhances their perceptions of purposefulness and their willingness to address personal sources of resistance (poesis);
- *Giving conflict negotiation a curricular emphasis within the larger ends-in-view frame of educating for democratic participation (Edelsky, 1997) within an aspirational democracy.* This establishes the basis for a doubled problem-solving consciousness (i.e., attention to the practical and the visionary, the short and long term) that, ideally, should permeate the enacted curriculum (polis);
- *Balancing a focus on GTY skills acquisition with the artful adaptation of those skills in authentic, if at times simulated, contexts.* Pursuit of this balance involves

discrete exercises devoted to particular skills (e.g., reflective listening, reframing, confirming common interests); relatedly, it involves practice in giving and receiving feedback constructively as well as small group role-play and structured critique. (techné, poesis, praxis);

■ *Emphasizing strategies that convey to diverse others a deep commitment to understand their world view and enhance the deliberative capacities to work collaboratively to achieve realistic common ground* (dialogos and phronesis);

■ *Attending to the multilayered causes of conflicts.* Without doing so, problem construction and problem-solving interventions will likely be flawed and fragmentary (praxis);

■ *Recognizing the importance of displaying impartiality and fair-mindedness as a foundation for reciprocal respect with diverse others.* Achieving the judicious emotional distance that this fair-mindedness often demands is particularly difficult when one is embroiled in a conflict, especially one involving charges of personal culpability. This paradoxical demand for detachment and high-mindedness when passionate and prudential engagement may also be warranted makes realizing this balance distinctively impressive, indeed emblematic of the intimidating yet inspiring nature of the curriculum wisdom challenge this book helps us understand and confront (theoria).

As an extension of praxis work, I have recently designed a political advocacy project that asks pre–student teachers to identify an important problem in their field they want to address constructively. My current scaffolding has them explaining explicitly what changes they are seeking, why the problem has significant implications for democratic education, what multilayered obstacles must be addressed, what conflict negotiation principles and action interventions need to be exercised to what audiences, and how these proposed interventions show both sophisticated and nuanced understanding of oppositional forces and desired changes.

I have been encouraged by the seriousness of student efforts, the quality of their proposals and, once again, the keen role of clear and compelling standards and scaffolding in elevating or depressing student commitment and performance. Projects have advocated the implementation of service learning, the creation of a writing tutoring center, the minimizing of high-stakes standardized testing, and the redesign of content and access requirements across the range of academic ability and subject area.

I envision this advocacy as an important contributor to the GUTS and FIT desirable for advancing the democratic curricular wisdom journey. My initial experience leads me to believe that students are quite capable of realizing this importance as well.

Looking Backward Is Super-Visionary: Constructing Critical Authentic Curriculum Projects

For many years I have taught courses in which a major goal has been to help participants develop critical authentic curricular projects of the kind presented in the above teacher commentary. My evolving efforts have come to focus on synthesizing Wiggins (1998), Wiggins and McTighe, (2001) and Newmann's (1995) work on designing authentic curriculum, with Shor (1992) and Freire's (1970) emphasis on critical democratic pedagogy. These two strands—the authentic and the critical—are integral components of my six-dimensional framework (CDP), which fundamentally animates my own curricular vision, which is further enhanced by the arts of inquiry. What I want to emphasize in this section is a message I've sought to convey throughout my commentary. That message is analogous to the one repeatedly and prophetically whispered to Kevin Costner by a super-visionary voice in the movie, *Field of Dreams*: "Build it and they will come." To a great extent, this is a core hopeful message of this book. Create a vivid, aesthetically appealing structure that captures your dreams of the ideal, and others from all over, as if attracted by a magnetic force, will make the great journey to participate in a deeply satisfying, even spiritual experience.

From my experience, I believe students can and do rise to the elevated level aspired to by a curriculum when they experience that curriculum in three interrelated ways: **meaningfully multidimensional** so as to activate a desire to exert holistic, synergistic effort (e.g., in the intellectual, emotional, aesthetic, and ethical realms); **well-structured** so that effort can be channeled productively toward clear-enough standards of performance; and **challenging** so as to inspire sustained superior efforts, often involving risk-taking and resilience in the face of frustrations and setbacks.

The scaffolded format of my current version of a critical authentic project (CAP) involves students creating a culminating unit project that answers to the following questions:

- What are the central goals and essential questions of the unit that the CAP is designed to assess?
- How does the CAP engage students in organizing and analyzing information/knowledge?
- How does the CAP explicitly engage students in thoughtful consideration of alternatives?
- What forms of real-world, critical problem posing will be involved?
- What forms of concrete action directed to addressing an inequality/injustice meaningful to students will be involved?
- Who is the genuine audience toward which performance on this CAP will be directed?
- What informative rubric provides students with guidelines about what constitutes poor through superior performance?
- What specific student beliefs, values, and dispositions might need to be desocialized or resocialized?

Let me outline a CAP that answers these questions. Greg Weimer, an undergraduate history major, created a high school economics unit titled *Consumer Economics, Written Across the Lines*. I excerpt Greg's unit extensively because I believe his sophisticated understanding of a CAP and the critical democratic pedagogy within which it is embedded is a stellar exemplar of the critical, fair-minded, advocacy-oriented curricular work this book fosters.[3] Selective concepts to be understood include

- What it means to think and read in the critical paradigm, especially with regard to the textbook.

---

[3]We also wish to posthumously honor Greg Weimer as a dedicated student and exemplary teacher.

- The difference between learning the information in the book and thinking about what is in the book.
- The basic concepts of the American economic system (e.g., resources, supply, demand, markets, etc.) that are found in the book.
- Other concepts of the American economic system that are not found in the book (i.e., disposal of used products, labor practices).
- The four pillars of capitalism, circular flow, and what is missing from the "four pillar" model and the "circular flow" model.

Selective skills/capacities and attitudes to be fostered include

- Thinking and reading in a critical paradigm.
- Thinking critically is a good thing to do.
- Applying conclusions of critical thought in a constructive manner is a good thing to do.
- The American economic system is not without fault, and is one of many possible systems.
- The American economic system is successful in many ways, but also harmful in many ways.

The overarching or essential questions the unit addresses include

- What is economics?
- How should this textbook be approached by a reader?
- Is the picture of the American economic system painted in this book accurate?
- What is the value of thinking critically?

Greg handed out the following written description of his culminating assessment project.

> The Capstone Critical Authentic Performance Task (CAP) for this unit will be a simulated meeting of the Junior Achievement Textbook Review Board. Students will participate as members of the board, authors of the book, representatives of special interest groups, concerned parents, students, teachers, and economists. Each student will be given an identity as well as a political viewpoint several days in advance. It will be each student's responsibility to decide where such a person would stand with regards to the textbook and everything we learned about it in the previous two weeks. Proposed changes to the text, prepared by the students and myself, and also passed out in advance, will be debated by all present. Each student will have prepared a brief detailing his or her position on each proposed change, using argument and evidence for support. I, the teacher, will moderate the debate. Votes will be taken on the proposed changes.

Greg indicated that potential audiences for this simulated meeting might include the school principal, other economic teachers, a Junior Achievement representative, and interested parents.

Greg identified two specific beliefs students might currently hold that would need to be desocialized (Shor, 1992) because they could depress student engagement or distort understanding of important unit concepts.

- What the textbook says is correct and complete.
- Even if we disagree, there is no way we can ever change what a textbook says.

Greg's rubric establishes four criteria ranging on a scale from 0 (absence of the given behavior) to 5 (outstanding performance). These criteria are worded as follows:

- Student demonstrates a clear understanding of the material as presented in the textbook.
- Student demonstrates an ability and willingness to think critically about that understanding.
- Student accurately portrays his or her role and viewpoint. Student behaves in a manner appropriate to the activity.

In his written self-assessment of the unit in light of peer and instructor feedback, Greg highlighted a number of areas of which he was proud and several reservations he had. Here are a few selections from that self-critique:

> I think my unit does a very good job at integrating many components of Ira Shor's *Critical Democratic Pedagogy*.... When it was necessary for me to lecture or simply provide information to the students, I always attempted to front load student input and back load my input.... I know I will have to lecture quite a bit in (a particular) lesson, but letting the students get their ideas on the board first gives them the sense that what is coming out of my mouth is supplementing something that they themselves started. And this is indeed the case.

> I am a strong supporter of the idea that political action should be the end of education, and so I attempted to design my CAP so that students were required to think and act politically. Furthermore, I think my CAP is an activity that can easily be adapted so that the students can use what they learned in the classroom to actually address JA representatives or the real authors of the textbook. According to its literature, JA is very interested in receiving and applying feedback from students and teachers. Perhaps we will get to see if they are telling the truth.

> I am most insecure about the idea of balancing the actual content of the book with my ideas about learning to be a critical thinker. They are both of the highest importance, I think, and it will be hard to give them both the attention they deserve.

Though Greg's understandings and capacities regarding CDP and CAPs were exceptional, my experiences with other students confirms all of the points I make in this section of my narrative. Done well, CAPs reflect the kind of meaningful, well structured, challenging curricular experience to which most students respond quite well.

Doubled Problem Solving: Particularizing the Real While Advancing the Ideal

In this section I discuss several extensions I hope to incorporate, stimulated by my reading of this book. The first involves the practice of doubled problem solving. Opportunities are ubiquitous within professional development for situating immediate practical problem solving within an explicit end-in-view vision. My work in a seminar with student teachers affords particularly robust opportunities. I'll illustrate with two sets of opportunities. One is at the heart of the emergent curriculum—pressing concerns regarding their field experiences about which student teachers seek catharsis, support, and advice. At the semester's beginning, issues of motivation, management, and cooperating teacher–student teacher relationships typically take center stage. In the past I've sought to facilitate various interventions (e.g., timed advice-giving, spontaneous role-plays) that, while reflecting the need for judgment and re-sourcefulness, tended to emphasize specific "how to" strategies. How to apply GTY negoti-ation principles to the issue at hand was often a perspective I'd probe. Done well, I'd also encourage broader causal considerations of the problem, which transcended a message that mere technique could solve the complex issues often embedded in the situation.

Fundamentally, though, I have overlooked incorporating the visionary frame when facilitating discussions within this emergent curriculum. Influenced by this book, I will fa-cilitate inquiry of the following nature: In addition to promising short-term impact, how does this intervention advance your long-term, sustaining goals for this student, for other peers, for the class as a whole, and for your view of the good society? Have you articulat-ed these goals to yourself and to your students? If so, how do you assess the efficacy of your message? What implications are there in the presenting problems for any modifica-tions of your message? If you haven't articulated your goals well to yourself or your stu-dents, why not? How can possible obstacles to desirable articulation be effectively addressed? What are possible consequences of the proposed intervention(s) that might obscure the im-portance or undermine the realization of your visionary goals?

A second book-inspired extension I'd like to mention is conducting a program of ac-tion research projects that examine the relationships between critical authentic assessment (CAA) and high-stakes standardized testing. Questions that would focus inquiry include ones like these: How authentic are standardized proficiency tests in the different subject areas? Can a combination of proficiency-test preparation and authentic assessment pro-jects enhance proficiency performance while also enhancing democratically desired out-comes not adequately measured by high-stakes standardized testing protocols? How do different groups (e.g., students, teachers, parents, and policy makers) envision CAA and high-stakes standardized testing fitting into their ideal assessment program? What actions by whom would they recommend to better achieve their ideal? What are the similarities and differences between the perspectives of these different actors/audiences? What kinds of evidence, arguments, and actions directed toward what audiences would best advance the status of CAA?

Performing and reporting on action research projects has been a regular part of our student teaching seminar. There is consistently a powerful concern among student teachers about the significant and problematic influence of proficiency testing on what goes on in classrooms. These concerns can be intensified by seemingly countervailing seminar im-peratives to enact CDP and CAA. To help frame this set of problems as a curriculum wis-dom challenge and to enhance a sense of collaborative inquiry, I hope to include student teachers in this very significant action research program.

Concluding Comments

In closing, I would like the reader to consider these two perspectives:

> The day will come
> when nations will be judged
> not by their military or economic strength
> nor by the splendour of their capital cities and
> public buildings

but by the well-being of their peoples:
by their levels of health, nutrition and education;
by their opportunities to earn a fair reward for their
labours; by their ability to participate in
the decisions that affect their lives; by the respect
that is shown for their civil and political liberties;
by the provision that is made for those who are
vulnerable and disadvantaged;
and by the protection that is afforded to the
growing minds and bodies of their children.

(Anonymous)

It is hard. It's supposed to be hard. If it wasn't hard, everyone would be doing it. That's what makes it great. (Tom Hanks as Jimmy Dugan in "A League of Their Own")

It is my unequivocal conviction that the ideas and spirit conveyed in this book will hasten the advance of that glorious day in the journey of humankind. It is one of the greatest aspirational undertakings imaginable, a defining democratic vision, one wholly worth our most animated, disciplined, and sustained efforts.

References

Bakhtin, M. (1984). *Problems of Dostoevsky's poetics.* (C. Emerson, Ed. and Trans.). Minneapolis: University of Minnesota Press.

Barber, B. R. (1984). *Strong democracy: Participatory politics for a new age.* Berkeley, CA: University of California Press.

Capra, F. (1984). *The tao of physics: An exploration of the parallels between modern physics and Eastern mysticism.* new York: Bantam Books.

Chandler, W. (1999). *Ancient future: The teachings and prophetic wisdom of the seven hermetic laws of ancient Egypt.* Atlanta: Black Classic Press.

Cherryholmes, C. H. (1999). *Reading pragmatism.* New York: Teachers College Press.

Dyasi, H. (1995). Is there room for children's inventive capacity in the curriculum? In W. Ayres (Ed.), *To become a teacher: Making a difference in children's lives* (pp. 153–161). New York: Teachers College Press.

Edelsky, C. (1997). Education for democracy. *Democracy & Education* (pp. 48–51). Athens, OH: Institute for Democracy in Education.

Elbow, P. (1986). *Embracing contraries: Explorations in learning and teaching.* New York: Oxford University.

Ferguson, R. (1999). Social science research, urban problems and community development alliances. In R. Ferguson & W. Dickens (Eds.), *Urban problems and community development.* Washington DC: Brookings Institution Press.

Fisher, R. & Ury, W. (1981). *Getting to yes: Negotiating agreement without giving in.* Boston: Houghton Mifflin.

Freire, P. (1970). *Pedagogy of the oppressed* (M. B. Ramos, Trans.). New York: Seabury.

Garrison, J. (1997). *Dewey and eros: Wisdom and desire in the art of teaching.* New York: Teacher's College Press.

Greene, M. (1988). *The dialectic of freedom.* New York: Teacher's College Press.

Haggerson, N. (2000). *Expanding curriculum research and understanding: A mythopoetic perspective.* New York: Peter Lang.

Henderson, J. G. (2001). *Reflective teaching: Professional artistry through inquiry.* Upper Saddle River, NJ: Merrill/Prentice Hall.

King, M. L., Jr. (1992). *I have a dream: Writing and speeches that changed the world,* (J. M. Washington, Ed.). New York: Harper Collins.

Kohl, H. (1994). *I won't learn from you and other thoughts on creative maladjustment*. New York: New Press.

Kohn, A. (1996). *Beyond discipline: From compliance to community*. Alexandria, VA: Association for Supervision and Curriculum Development.

McLuhan, M., & Fiore, Q. (1967). *The medium is the message*. New York: Bantam Books.

Newmann, F. (1975). *Education for citizen action*. San Francisco: Jossey-Bass.

Newmann, F., Secada, W., & Wehlage, G. (1995). *A guide to authentic instruction and assessment: Vision, standards and scoring* (prepublication draft). Madison, WI: Center on Organization and Restructuring of Schools.

Noddings, N. (1984). *Caring: A feminine approach to ethics and moral education*. Berkeley: University of California Press.

Paley, V. (1981). *Wally's stories: Conversations in the kindergarten*. Cambridge, MA: Harvard University Press.

Paley, V. (1997). *The girl with the brown crayon*. Cambridge, MA: Harvard University Press.

Postman, N. (1995). *The end of education*. New York: Alfred A. Knopf.

Quinn, D. (1992). *Ishmael*. New York: Bantam Books.

Rivkin, M. (1991). What are we interpreting: The data problem. In L. Bergman, F. Hultgren, D. Lee, M. Rivkin, J. Roderick, & T. Aoki (Eds.), *Toward curriculum for being: Voices for educators* (pp. 65–86). New York: State University of New York Press.

Scottoline, L. (1999). *Mistaken identity*. New York: Harper Paperbacks.

Shor, I. (1992). *Empowering education: Critical teaching for social change*. Chicago: University of Chicago Press.

Silberman, C. (1970). *Crises in the classroom: The remaking of American education*. New York: Random House.

Taylor, H. (1968). *The world of the American teacher*. Washington, DC: American Association of Colleges for Teacher Education.

Wiggins, G. (1998). *Educative assessment*. San Francisco: Jossey-Bass.

Wiggins, G., & McTighe, J. (2001). *Understanding by design* (special ed.). Upper Saddle River, NJ: Merrill/Prentice Hall.

Chapter 8

Two Administrative Narratives

INTRODUCTION

In this chapter we present the narratives written by a director of professional development and an elementary school principal. These two administrators, like the teacher and the teacher educator in Chapter 7, understand and value the practice of curriculum wisdom. They also tell stories of being called to the arts of inquiry discussed in Chapter 3.

A CENTRAL OFFICE ADMINISTRATOR'S STORY

As a transformative curriculum leader in a small, public school district in the Midwest, I am challenging myself and inviting others to reconceptualize curriculum and professional development.[1] I am called to a curriculum wisdom challenge to guide teachers and leaders toward a sophisticated life of inquiry that encourages collaboration and breaks the cycle of teachers and leaders working in isolation.[2] Henderson (2001) notes, "professional collaboration should not be confused with congenial social relations" (p. 178). Rather, professional collaboration invites substantive reciprocal interactions that include exchanging, modeling, coaching, supervising, and mentoring. According to Barth (1990), "collegiality requires that everyone be willing to give up something without knowing in advance just what that may be" (p. 32). Therefore, such work proposes distancing ourselves from workshops, and other similar formats, which provide

---

[1]Narrative written by Michelle Thomas.

[2]Henderson and Hawthorne (2000) describe transformative curriculum leadership as a collaborative effort to base curriculum decisions on morally wise judgments as well as a complex set of carefully orchestrated, multileveled reform activities focusing on "deepening" curriculum problem solving in societies with democratic ideals. *Transformation* connotes changes in the power relations between curriculum stakeholders. Curriculum is understood as empowered enactment. Constructing educational purposes, acting on these purposes, and evaluating the results of one's actions are treated as closely integrated and continuously cyclical dimensions of curriculum work. Leadership is understood as a collaborative and inspirational activity.

the answers to our educational problems, and instead experiencing a more sophisticated inquiry journey that invites us to be open to unimagined possibilities and guides our personal and professional growth and development. Professional collaboration occurs when teachers and leaders recognize they cannot improve their craft in isolation from others. Glickman (2002) contends,

> If, as a teacher [or leader],
>
> - I present the same lessons [or information] in the same manner that I have used in the past;
> - I seek no feedback from my students [or faculty];
> - I do not analyze and evaluate their work in a manner that changes my own emphasis, repertoire, and timing;
> - I do not visit or observe other adults as they teach [or lead];
> - I do not share the work of my students [or of my leaders] with colleagues for feedback, suggestions, and critiques;
> - I do not visit other schools or attend particular workshops or seminars or read professional literature on aspects of my teaching [or of my leadership];
> - I do not welcome visitors with experience and expertise to observe and provide feedback to me on my classroom [or leadership] practices;
> - I have no yearly individualized professional development plan focused on classroom [or building or district] changes to improve student [or faculty] learning; and finally,
> - I have no systemic evaluation of my teaching [or leadership] tied to individual, grade/department, and schoolwide goals,
>
> Then I have absolutely no way to become better as a teacher [or leader]. (p. 5)

Moving out of isolation naturally invites professional collaboration, which is the impetus behind the transformative curriculum leadership (Henderson & Hawthorne, 2000) work in my district. To begin, during the 2000–2001 school year, 24 self-selected teachers and leaders in my school district began a collaborative journey to engage in a process of sophisticated inquiry as they carefully examined the impact of such work on their teaching and leadership practices and in turn on their work with students. Using an action research framework (Arhar, Holly, & Kasten, 2001), the group began the journey to develop a culture for professional growth. They learned and practiced cognitive coaching to foster professional collegiality and a responsible autonomy (Costa & Garmston, 1994), while guided by inquiry artistry mapping (Henderson, 2001). Encouraging cultures of collaboration (Fullan, 1993) became a central goal of the reform effort. Our experiences, as supported by the research, revealed that educators who experience such a culture work collaboratively rather than in isolation and take more risks (Little, 1987); commit to continuous rather than episodic improvement (Rosenholtz, 1989); tend to be more caring with students, teachers, and colleagues (Nias, Southworth, & Yeomans, 1989); have stronger senses of efficacy (Ashton & Webb, 1986); are more assertive in relation to external pressures and demands (Hargreaves, 1994), experience more opportunities to learn and improve from one another (Woods, 1990); and have access to more feedback (Lortie, 1975) and opportunities for reflection (Grimmett & Crehan, 1991).

I have spent the past 3 years working on transformative professional development initiatives. As the leader of this process, I embraced the following challenges: the ongoing development of my inquiry capacities; inviting teachers and leaders in the district to engage in the inquiry development process and guiding them along their journey; and providing a safe, caring, nonthreatening milieu for such important work. In recognizing that inquiry-capacity development is lifelong work, we must begin with an introspective or autobiographical component. We must know how we think and act before we can be welcoming to others. Therefore, questions such as: What does it mean to be an educator? What are my professional values and beliefs? How do my actions align with my values and beliefs? How do I meet the needs of students, teachers, and leaders? How do I invite professional dialogue with colleagues? What are the best catalysts for our inquiry artistry journey?

In small group discussions and individual interviews, I have focused on these questions and have discovered four dimensions of commitment to this transformative work: predisposition, cognitive readiness, developmental readiness, and willingness. My working definitions of these dimensions are as follows:

- *Predisposition* provides the foundation to the process and supports the notion that inquiry and reflection require a professional calling.
- *Cognitive readiness* is the foundation for using one's intellectual ability to conceptualize and articulate what it means to be inquiry minded. These understandings and responses are personal and individual and are developed through reading, making personal connections, and engaging in dialogue with colleagues.
- *Developmental readiness* builds upon cognitive readiness through role-playing, journal writing, ongoing dialogue, and action planning that support one's conceptualizations and articulations, which change over time as one develops deeper understandings.
- *Willingness* comes from within; it involves risk taking, being flexible and open minded, and opening one's heart and soul.

Predisposition, cognitive readiness, developmental readiness, and willingness collectively implore educators to trust their professional judgment and engage in an internal change process that, in turn, invites passionate and intellectual discourse, lifelong thinking and behaviors, and connects to teaching, learning, and leadership.

Trusting one's judgment requires internal motivation. What is the role of self-directed learning (Grow, 1991) in a transformative curriculum leadership process? Kegan (1994) suggests,

> Educators seeking "self-direction" from the adult students are not merely asking them to take on new skills, [recognize and] modify their learning style, or increase their self-confidence. They are asking many of them to change the whole way they understand themselves, their world, and the relation between the two. They are asking many of them to put at risk the loyalties and devotions that have made up the very foundation of their lives. (p. 275)

Furthermore, Grow purports self-directed learners are able to

> …examine themselves, their culture, and their milieu in order to understand how to separate what they feel from what they should feel, what they value from what they should value, and what they want from what they should want. They develop critical thinking, individual initiative, and a sense of themselves as co-creators of the culture that shapes them…. Self-directed learners set their own goals and standards, with or without help from experts.

> They use experts, institutions, and other resources to pursue these goals…. [They] are both able and willing to take responsibility for their learning, direction, and productivity. They exercise skills in time management, project management, goal setting, self-evaluation, peer critique, information gathering, and use of educational resources. (pp. 133–134)

As a self-directed, transformative leader who engages in a sophisticated inquiry process and invites others to do the same, I recognize the paradigm shift that challenges one's work-life. These challenges include moving from a primary focus on standardized tests to facilitating student inquiry (Magestro & Stanford-Blair, 2000); to providing educators the time to consider new approaches, systematically examine their practices, and explore applications of what they are learning (Schon, 1983); and to providing professional growth opportunities that engage educators in complex, critical questioning and thinking, inviting them to explore and engage in discourse concerning current educational issues and involving them in systematic school improvement processes such as peer coaching, mentoring, professional portfolios, action research, and specific curricular initiatives as indicated by the district's Continuous Improvement Plan. Such work requires a safe and secure milieu as the foundation for providing intellectually challenging professional growth experiences.

As a result of this collaborative work during the 2001-2002 school year, systemic change continues in the district. We have established a professional norm that provides ongoing opportunities for the district's educators to participate in transformative in-house professional development (Thomas, 2001; Thomas, 2002). This newly designed work culture promotes in-depth studies of selected topics that encourage small group discussions of professional literature, and require projects, activities, classroom implementation, and connections to the growth and development of students, teachers, and leaders. The teachers' evaluations clearly indicated that small group work is critical to the process, specifically, the dialogue, sharing of practices and frustrations, where they plan to go next with the information gained, and how they plan to share with colleagues. This rich feedback supports the need to provide continued opportunities. As Lambert, Collay, Dietz, Kent, and Richert (1996) write,

> Learning communities…require complex, authentic relationships that involve the whole person (all that we are—emotional, social, cognitive, and experiential). They require trust, infusion of new ideas, facilitation, time to honor reflection and learning, and respect for individual differences. On the one hand, we invite and value diversity; it contributes to the disequilibrium that generates energy for learning and for change. On the other hand, it presents a challenge in learning how to collaborate, to listen, to learn, and to respect the multiplicity of thinking in the school community. If members of a school community have not experienced themselves as learners individually, they will not be able to help create learning for others. Learners must be willing to suspend assumptions, respect the ideas of others, and engage in dialogue, continually constructing their understandings. (p. 68)

This systematic and systemic transformative work is in the early stages of leaving its mark on perspectives, policy, and practice in my district.

What is the impact of our transformative curriculum work on the students, on the faculty and the district, and on the public? In a paper I presented at the 2001 American Educational Research Association Conference, I shared a collection of stories regarding the growth and development of teachers and leaders who were engaged in this sophisticated inquiry process during the 2000–2001 school year. One year later teachers who are engaging in inquiry artistry and reflection, along with teachers who have been influenced by these teachers, began to respond to the question, How is the inquiry process affecting students? Teachers told that students welcome the opportunity to express themselves and have their voices heard. Questions are posed, dialogue begins, and thoughts and ideas are embraced. Teachers expressed that they are cognizant of holding back and allowing students to initiate and facilitate discussions. One teacher told how she has provided the opportunity for students to decide how they would be tested, when they would be tested, and to what extent they would be tested. Teachers are developing assignments and projects that encourage students to take a personal stake in their work. Teachers are helping students be more insightful. Teachers are sharing their own inquiry experiences with their students; students are learning the value of inquiry and reflection, and this reciprocal exchange breaks down barriers between teachers and students and, in turn, provides learning opportunities that "enculturate a sense of coming to understand what one needs to know to be competent in the roles one may expect to fulfill in society, rather than in the narrow sense of learning-done-at-school" (Wolcott, 1983, p. 24). Inquiry and reflection are processes that can be experienced throughout a lifetime.

How is this inquiry work reaching out to the faculty? Teachers and administrators who have been engaged in the process are slowly reaching out to colleagues through grade-level, team, or departmental interactions. Teachers are using an inquiry process to help them make practical decisions regarding curriculum alignment, policy and procedures, and professional development needs. In an attempt to encourage a more transformative culture, new teachers in the district are reading about inquiry, participating in discussions, and experiencing the inquiry process through their interactions with other teachers and leaders. Additionally, the in-house professional development program and the Local Professional Development Committee's collaborative project guidelines are developed through an inquiry-based, action research process that aligns with this work.

How will we know when transformative curriculum leadership practices are permeating the district? Practitioners who practice the arts of inquiry will demonstrate their intellect (thoughtful subject learning), generativity (self as a lifelong learner), and generosity (social interaction with diverse others) in the following ways:

- Planning lessons/meetings that promote student/faculty inquiry, allowing students/faculty to find their own meaning that encourages them to make sense of content/topics/issues in their own way.
- Facilitating an atmosphere in which students/faculty generate solutions rather than only listening to answers.
- Confirming the value of alternative approaches and outcomes.
- Presenting meaningful, problem-posing incidents that spark student/faculty inquiry.
- Encouraging students/faculty to explore multiple solutions.
- Expressing sensitivity to students'/faculty's needs as they engage in inquiry.
- Carefully observing students'/faculty's meaning-making responses and noting successes or problems.
- Asking questions such as why is that so? What explains such events? What accounts for such actions? To what is this connected?

- Recognizing and embracing the existence of many plausible and illuminating interpretations of the same stories and human events.
- Determining how interpretations relate to the school community and the community at large.
- Actively supporting imaginative problem solving.
- Asking questions such as what does it matter? What does it mean? What does it illustrate in human experience?
- Questioning attempts to apply universally "valid" principles.
- Deciding if one is willing to agree to disagree.
- Allowing for personal passion and expression.
- Asking questions such as how and where can we use this knowledge?
- Knowing students/faculty well enough to incorporate their cultural framework into the lesson/topic/experience.
- Questioning all dogma and encouraging a healthy skepticism.
- Asking questions such as from whose point of view? From which vantage point? What is assumed or tacit that needs to be made explicit and considered? Is it plausible? What are the limits? So what?
- Creating evaluations that allow for diverse perspectives.
- Taking time each day to reflect, to contemplate, and to regenerate.
- Asking questions such as how does it seem to you? What do they see that I don't? What do I need to experience if I am to understand? What was the person feeling, seeing, and trying to make me see and feel?
- Engaging in recurring cycles of instructional study, application, observation, and reflection.
- Stating the best way to educate for moral competency, personal ethics, character development, and citizenship.
- Asking questions such as how does who I am shape my views? What are the limits of my understanding? What are my blind spots? What do I misunderstand because of prejudice, habit, or style?

Although we are in the early stages of working with an arts of inquiry process, the teachers, students, and leaders who are committed to the process continue to challenge themselves as they work collaboratively to respond to the questions above. As expectations continue to increase, a broader question now exists: How do we go public with this democratic inquiry artistry work? Going public (Palmer, 1998) with beliefs and values about organizational change requires a security founded in knowledge, conviction, and the support of others. Without the support to develop dialogic relationships with other school districts, conversations may never be initiated or may be abandoned. Furthermore, precipitating change in a high-achieving organization has not been without its challenges. Most significantly these challenges have been associated with political constraints (teachers' union, state mandates) and the dissonance associated with the fear of the unknown. What is known about change theory can be applied to experiences throughout this inquiry initiative: lack of change is comforting; establishing change is painful, and as a result, little incentive for change exists; significant change takes time; and change is a process, not an event (Fawcett, Brobeck, Andrews, & Walker, 2001). At this early stage in the process of transformative curriculum leadership work, going public continues to involve uncertainty, controversy, some resistance.

Although this work seems to be somewhat enigmatic, as a self-directed, transformative curriculum leader, I continue to forge ahead. Since my journey is one that is embedded in inquiry, I am prompted to look at the business of schooling in a nontraditional way. My vision for this work is one where the school is a community of learners. School is a place where everyone (students, teachers, and administrators) is teaching and learning; the administrators are learners, facilitators, coaches, and mentors displaying behaviors they want students and teachers to adopt. The major responsibility of the adults in the community is to be actively engaged in their own learning, to make their learning visible to others, to enjoy and celebrate their learning, and to sustain their enthusiasm. School is a place where teachers, principals, and district leaders talk with one another about practice, observe one another engaged in daily activities, share their knowledge of their craft with one another, and actively help one another develop inquiry capacities. School is a collegial milieu that provides adults and students the opportunity to engage in daily staff development, since everyone is a staff developer for everyone else. This school builds a community of learners who take responsibility for developing a repertoire of strategies that invite them to engage in continuous professional growth and to avoid stagnation. School is a place where diversity is welcomed and applauded; differences are looked for, attended to, and celebrated. We ask ourselves the question, How can we make conscious, deliberate use of differences in social class, gender, age, ability, race, and interests as resources for learning? School is a place where people ask why things are the way they are. Nothing is more important to building a culture of inquiry. Finally, since teachers, students, and administrators have the opportunity to be leaders, they also have the opportunity to make what they believe in happen.

My work affords me the opportunity to begin to open the doors to this transformative school by promoting life-long learning, professional and student inquiry, active and engaged learning for students and educators, and ongoing growth and development. Collectively these essential elements provide positive, substantive, sophisticated educational experiences for students, teachers, and leaders. I chose to become an administrator to introduce these elements and develop a working knowledge of them with teachers and leaders. My belief about the importance of this transformative approach is validated every time I observe traditional approaches prevailing in classrooms (i.e., sage on the stage; students working independently on a daily basis with little interaction with their peers and without ownership in the learning process; teacher-directed and initiated topics and projects) and management practices dominating leadership. In order to facilitate transformational change, I choose to be a central office administrator who works with teachers and leaders as they learn to become facilitators, coaches, and mentors for and with their students rather than maintaining the "disseminator of knowledge" status that in past practice was never best practice.

In conclusion, as a transformative leader, my lifelong work advocates the examination of professional experiences and invites a moral wisdom challenge. Such work "encourages practitioners to continue learning how to teach [and to lead]. Inquiry pushes teachers [and leaders] to see themselves as career-long students of their profession" (Henderson & Hawthorne, 2000, p. 41). As I continue to embark upon my life's work, the following questions (adapted from Henderson & Hawthorne, 2000, pp. 63–64) guide my democratic work life with educators:

- What can teachers/leaders problem solve together?
- What concerns are important to each of us? What are the issues that unite or divide us as caring, creative, critical, and contemplative professionals?
- Can I work with beginning teachers in ways that are appropriate and supportive? How can I work with experienced teachers in ways that respect their experiences yet encourage them to engage in continuing reflective inquiries?
- How can all of us work together to encourage and challenge each other's reflective inquiries?
- How can we show tolerance and forgiveness in conversations with diverse others?
- Am I willing to raise questions of what can I do and to acknowledge what I can't do?
- Am I willing to accept varying degrees of developmental readiness in my colleagues? Can I accept my own developmental challenges?
- How can teachers become politically active in publicly responsible ways?
- What can we do to empower ourselves as ethical professionals?
- How can we affect the structural basis of the problems and concerns we identify?

These questions provide a catalyst for cultivating our inquiry capacities. Is it not morally wise to use our intellect for generous and generative purposes? After all, in doing so our voices are trusted and respected. We create a safe and secure milieu for inquiry, and for those with a predisposition to the process, we provide time for cognitive and developmental readiness and encourage continued willingness. A dialogic exchange occurs that invites intellectual challenge and stimulation, and future opportunities nurture the leadership capacity of teachers and leaders.

Living a life of inquiry and reflection is a transformative process for teachers, leaders, and students. This cyclical process requires a strong intellect, a developmental readiness, and a willingness to move beyond one's comfort zone, be a risk taker, share ideas, listen to others, model collegiality, and learn and grow: "Unless teachers [and leaders] can hold up a model of lifelong learning and adaptation, [they] are likely to find themselves trapped into obsolescence as the world changes around them" (Bateson, 1990, p. 14).

A PRINCIPAL'S STORY

At the time of the Cuban missile crisis in the fall of 1962, I was just beginning the second grade at our neighborhood public school in Columbus, Ohio.[3] I remember being troubled by this turn of events, having heard the details through conversations at the dinner table. Conversation about world events was common in my home. Although many childhood memories fade over time, I distinctly remember sitting in a living room chair thinking through what I might be able to accomplish if I could just speak to the leaders of the United States and Cuba, hoping to avert the possibility of military conflict. While we might be amused at the naïve thoughts of a child of seven, this vignette offers a view of the early traces of a calling to be about the work of making a difference in the lives of others.

_____

[3]Narrative written by Rebecca McElfresh.

I am the daughter of a musician and an artist who earned their living as a pastor and a teacher. As busy professionals, my parents modeled a passion for learning, for creative expression, for the inner spiritual journey, and for outward expression of their dedication to justice.

For most of my life, one parent or the other pursued formal education through university study. Near my twenty-first birthday, my father completed his doctoral program. Not only do I have many memories of my parents engaged in study at home, but I also remember many lively discussions among members of their fellow scholars as they studied together in our home. Most significant, however, was the modeling of a deep thirst for understanding that moved beyond the acquisition of knowledge to a quest for meaning.

This intellectual atmosphere was blended with an intense commitment to the arts. Our home was often filled with my mother's creative endeavors as she learned new ways to express her creativity through visual art. As a preschooler, I often accompanied her to studio classes and played on the floor with clay while she created and practiced techniques. Our home reflected the importance she placed on the aesthetic dimension. I attended many of my father's performances as conductor of the Columbus Orchestral Society. His piano students were in our home frequently as he sought to provide them with the skills necessary for musical expression. He has supported and encouraged my own interest in vocal music. I have come to understand that this dedication to the pursuit of the arts allowed my imagination to grow in ways that have supported my ability to envision the good life.

My father's role as a clergyman filled my life with the experience of formal religious practice. Throughout my childhood and youth, I remember continually questioning the difference between religious practice, as defined by my family and my community, and my inner hunger for spiritual experience. For much of my life, they have been very different entities. My conversations with my father over this difficult difference between us caused us both to continue to grow in our appreciation for difference. Our deep longing for the pursuit of an inner life was the place we found our common ground.

My siblings and I were also fortunate to have been a part of regular dinner conversations about national and global social justice issues. Embedded in these conversations was our family's rich tradition of spiritual practice. This practice provided a moral intensity for the pursuance of difficult issues. I remember clearly the day my father assisted students as they journeyed across town on yellow busses because of court-ordered desegregation in Cleveland. At the time of his death at the age of 78, his current political project involved issues of human rights for gay and lesbian persons. As a minister with the regular advantage of a pulpit, he directed some of his energy toward this reform within the context of his mainline protestant denomination. Just before his death he joined a local advocacy group with no religious affiliation, consistent with his pattern of having a voice in public spheres as well. I have consistently seen his intellectual inquiry and his sense of a calling to this work have direct results in political action.

My sense of what it means to have a calling is a blend of all of these aspects of my experience and, in many ways, a direct result of my heritage. I was taught, through the modeling and direct instruction of my parents, that the good life entailed a journey of discovery leading to an ever-emerging understanding of one's calling, and that attention to one's calling bore direct relationship to the quality of the good life for others. For this reason, it is my belief that the discovery and pursuit of one's calling is not just a journey for a few, but is the responsibility of all who embrace democratic ideals.

My journey to understand (envision) and live (enact) my calling begins with a commitment to my inner life. It is within this space that I have moved toward what Greene (1995) calls a state of "wide-awakeness." While it is certainly only one component on my journey of wisdom seeking, it is vital that it is the beginning point. What is clear is that my orientation to live out this calling is a way of being and not a role and not only attached to my professional life. Without this inward journey, a life oriented toward wide-awakeness, any attempt to enact the kind of life described in this book would merely be a thin layer and would not be transformative in my own life or the lives of others.

For these reasons, my commitment to this inner work remains primary, and the ways of being that provide this growth are a part of my daily routines. At times when these ways of being slip behind other priorities, I can see my ability to live within this space diminish. Welwood (1996) describes this way of being as being present, being open to the current moment and able to fully process all the emotions and thoughts that various situations bring. He describes our more natural response as being a defensive posture in which we externalize our feelings by giving responsibility to others for our well-being. In doing so, we abandon ourselves at times when we most need to provide support for our own growth as well as the growth of others. He states, "Although 'awakening to the sacred' might sound esoteric, it is, in fact, quite ordinary—for it only involves learning to respond more deeply to what we already experience, and to appreciate what we already essentially are" (p. xiii). Meditative practices help me to create the energy necessary for this very difficult personal work. Attention to my body and the need for rest and a healthy diet is important as well. Alternative stress reduction therapies and Eastern forms of energy balancing, as well as the spiritual practices of a variety of cultures enhance this space for me. Finally, a trusted other who serves as a sounding board and a mirror for my personal growth path has been essential.

Intellectual work supports my calling to a life of wisdom practice. Studying the ideas of others and having the opportunity to reflectively process them in the presence of others who share this passion for the journey of wisdom brings another dimension to this space of wide-awakeness. Great ideas become a place of feasting where another kind of presence can be experienced. In this space our assumptions can be challenged, and we can move beyond current understandings to spaces of greater awareness and possibility. Exploring the edges and boundaries of current thought expands our capacity to stretch toward a space of wisdom. T. S. Eliot (1971) wrote, "Let us not cease from all our exploring, and the end of our exploring will be to arrive where we started and to know the place for the very first time."

According to the heritage given me by my parents, my life is filled with music, visual art, drama, poetry, and literature. The arts have a unique way of developing our imaginations (Greene, 1995), so necessary for the wisdom journey. In addition to singing, I pursue visual art through work with paint and clay. I am often able to understand something elusive as I work with these materials in a creative process. My deepest inquiry has to do with the question of how the arts help us envision the good life and how our collective pursuit of this good life within the framework of democracy can be realized through our aesthetic experiences. With a group of educators, artists, and musicians, I have been engaging in regular dialogue about these ideas through a listserv. Our conversations often take their form in lyric, poem, or visual art.

These pursuits of inner growth, intellectual development, and aesthetic awareness are not put on hold when I walk through the front door of the public elementary school where I am employed as a principal. They are very much a part of my being in every situation in which I interact with myself or with others. In one very important sense, my ability to influence others to pursue their own notion of the good life in a deep and powerful way is dependent on my ability to lead a transparent life, one that is lived before others in a way that exposes my growth as well as my personal challenges. For this reason, I very consciously choose not to separate my life into personal and professional categories. Certainly, I do not contact my stockbroker from my desk at school. I mean that the essence of who I am becomes a part of my life in all situations.

What might this look like inside the walls of a school? How does this personal experience move seamlessly into an organizational culture? In what ways have we practiced inquiry artistry? How does personal and political resistance to this curriculum wisdom work impact us?

My experience with inner growth work is often shared with others at opportune moments, when my intuitive sensibilities determine that my experiences might provide encouragement for another along her own journey. Collectively, meditative practices can be experienced in staff meetings. Responding to the need for stress reduction following much serious illness and several deaths among our staff members, as well as numerous deaths of the parents of staff members, we began to end our staff meetings with meditation exercises designed to renew and empower. It is not uncommon for staff members to join one another for community opportunities that would provide support for this inner growth. This spring a group of staff members attended a workshop sponsored by a local cancer support group. The speaker, Dr. Joan Borysenko, author of *A Woman's Journey to Go: Finding the Feminine Path* (1999), helped us focus on our inner capacity to create positive outcomes from very difficult life experiences. These opportunities to develop, and then share, our emerging intuitive and spiritual sensibilities are important building blocks as we move toward an understanding of the artistry of theoria through which we can continue to envision our work together in the years ahead.

The love of intellectual growth is a part of our culture. The love of learning is demonstrated, at times, through the enthusiastic sharing of course readings, independent readings, and new discoveries coming from the experience of the classroom. More and more, we are finding ways to be together to share what we are learning. Our struggle is significant, at times, as we seek to find meaning from this learning and to find ways to create changes in the learning journey of the students we serve. This is not an easy process. At times we disagree, and we are learning to move within the artistry of dialogos and then to allow our dialogue to move us into phronesis, where our decision making can be informed by our multiple understandings. At times we are frightened by the rate of change. At times we are fearful that to change at all means we were not good enough to begin with.

The arts are a primary way we experience goodness together in community. Each year we have an artist-in-residence, so the students experience a variety of art forms and a variety of artists. Our experiences have been rich for both students and staff. We have come to understand more fully that the arts allow a different way of knowing, opening us to an understanding of ourselves, of one another, and of our communities. During the time of our deepest grief a number of staff members gathered to use visual images to help us understand

our grief. Collages were created and shared, allowing us to understand one another's journey. On a Saturday in February we gathered as a staff at the Cleveland Museum of Art. Our
facilitator led us through the museum, experiencing as we went the manner in which artists
allow their art to express grief as well as hope within our sadness. Experiencing together
the artistry of poesis, we are able to deepen our understanding of the aesthetic element from
which we can derive wisdom for the journey.

At times, the artistry of praxis helps us examine what might, on the surface, seem to be
the simplest of problem-solving situations. Underneath, however, we might discover power
relationships within the community that represent greater societal issues. For example,
during the previous school year a group of volunteer parents assisting children in the cafe-
teria were distressed to learn that it is our practice to ask the students to take turns cleaning
the tables following lunch. Even after health concerns related to cleaning tables were addressed, and we were assured by our nursing staff and by our own research that the children were not using harmful chemicals or risking harmful exposure to germs, the issue
continued to surface. It became apparent that some parents held a belief that their children
should not be asked to do this kind of work at school because they were not asked to do it
at home. Within the context of our very privileged homogeneous community, it seemed
that issues of power relationships were at the core of the disagreement, and it became necessary to contrast these beliefs with our own beliefs about community and our collective
responsibilities to it. Also, that year, after September 11, 2001, we needed to bring the
same critical awareness to our decision making about how we would provide for our students in the days that followed. It was necessary to examine our own motives as we planned
activities. This was a most difficult task for me, as my critical sensibilities caused me to
consider the international power relationships so inherent in this crisis.

Within the school district several central staff members are actively pursuing the
artistry of polis through their advocacy efforts toward envisioning a different way of addressing the issue of accountability. Given the privileged nature of the community and
given the high quality of reflection related to curriculum development, our students score
so well on state-mandated assessments that we have been able to spend some time envisioning other means of measuring the quality of our work for students and the quality of
their learning. Because these staff members are giving this time and attention to state and
federal legislation, they have been able to testify before the state legislature. Often, all district employees have been asked to contact legislators as these issues come to the floor at
the state house. This practice is motivated by a deep sense of responsibility for those beyond our city limits and state borders who are not able to engage in this work.

It is important to understand that while the various inquiry artistries are practiced by a
variety of individuals within our school and within our district, many are still focused on
techné, the consideration of the craft of our profession, as the primary purpose for our
work. Others are able to envision a number of the other artistries within the framework of
their calling. Fewer still have been able to envision and respond to the calling of the holistic notion of the curriculum wisdom challenge described in this book.

My challenge has become a struggle with ways to invite others to inquire with me
about the deeper work of this wisdom challenge. Because I have a formal leadership role
within the organization, I have a variety of venues from which to share my own journey
and to seek out others who have been exploring this path within the context of their

own role within our organization. I have also found it important to find others outside our school district who are seeking to explore this work. It is the very nature of this work that it must be carried out within the context of community, however we might define its boundaries.

Resistance to this work sometimes comes from political realities and sometimes from individuals who are a part of our learning community. Given the nature of the high achievement levels of our students as measured by state-mandated testing and given the desire of district leadership to envision alternatives to this accountability system, as well as a school board supportive of this wisdom work, political realities have not been as significant as personal factors of resistance.

Some are able to dismiss the idea of curriculum wisdom because techné, craft reflection, is the sole means by which they understand their work. For some, the vision of their work stems from a belief that schooling is about helping young people develop skills necessary for economic competitiveness within a capitalist system. The notion of the good life is primarily about material gain. For others, these ideas simply have no relevance to daily living. They envision a good life apart from a journey of inquiry artistry.

Others who resist this work are caught in what seems to be a crisis of identity in which they cannot envision playing a role in envisioning and enacting a different way of being together in community. I have understood this dynamic to be about individual identity in which there seems to be lacking a sense of self-agency and empowerment. In order for an individual to take on this challenge, she/he must have a sense of being able to make a difference, to initiate change that will result in a higher quality of life. These individuals have a tendency to externalize the source of solutions to any problem.

Finally, personal resistance sometimes comes from those who see the importance of this work and have an internal sense of being able to envision and enact but are acutely aware of its challenge. After realizing the commitment required by this work, they choose not to accept the challenge.

I have described the legacy of my parents and its impact upon my choice to be about this work. I have considered the nature of this work, and have chosen to make it my responsibility to engage the world in this way and to invite others to consider it as well. Some have responded to this challenge. My great challenge has become that of addressing those who do not make that choice. Although my critical sensibilities will not allow me to consider that some may never be able to respond to the call to this wisdom journey, I am faced with the practical need to know where to expend the greatest amount of energy for the greatest possible impact.

I have focused the greatest energy on those who see this work as personally relevant and who have the sense of self-agency necessary for this work but have counted the cost as much too high for the time. My hope is that I will continue to be able to help them understand that the cost of not responding to this responsibility is far higher. I sometimes ask them to join me at conferences where others who have taken on this challenge might support them. I ask them to read with me and discuss the implications of our reading. I share my own journey, including its struggles, openly with them.

For those who are facing internal resistance, I have allowed my own understanding of the psychological factors influencing self-agency to guide my conversation. Posing reflective questions seems to be a good way to move others to engage in the self-reflection that is necessary to understand these dynamics. This remains the most challenging aspect of this work. Sometimes I am deeply frustrated by this kind of resistance. At other times I rejoice as understanding develops.

At times this is a very lonely journey. It requires a great deal of intellectual, physical, and psychological energy. It requires a high level of intrapersonal and interpersonal honesty. I am very aware that engaging in this work causes others to sometimes be very uncomfortable.

Clearly, then, there have been other factors causing me to continue to choose this path, given the costs I have considered. Primarily, my courage continues to come from the daily and practical application of these ideas as I watch their transformative power impact one individual at a time. I continue to be amazed by the mystery of this work, by the way it evolves in each individual in a different manner, while at the same time contributing to the whole of the community. I am also compelled to continue to envision a better way for us to be human together as I observe the tragic as well as the transformative ways we have responded to one another throughout history. I sense we have arrived at a moment when our choice to respond will matter greatly.

References

Arhar, J., Holly, M. L., & Kasten, W. C. (2001). *Action research for teachers: Traveling the yellow brick road.* Upper Saddle River, NJ: Merrill/Prentice Hall.

Ashton, P., & Webb, R. (1986). *Making a difference: Teachers' sense of efficacy and student achievement.* New York: Longman.

Barth, R. S. (1990). *Improving schools from within: Teachers, parents, and principals can make the difference.* San Francisco: Jossey-Bass.

Bateson, M. C. (1990). *Composing a life.* New York: Plume.

Borysenko, J. (1999). *A woman's journey to God: Finding the feminine path.* New York: Riverhead Books.

Costa, A. L., & Garmston, R. J. (1994). *Cognitive coaching: A foundation for renaissance schools.* Norwood, MA: Christopher-Gordon.

Eliot, T. S. (1971). *The collected poems and plays of T.S. Eliot: 1909–1950.* New York: Harcourt, Brace, and World.

Fawcett, G., Brobeck, D., Andrews, S., & Walker, L. (2001). Principals and beliefs-driven change. *Phi Delta Kappan, 82*(5), 405–410.

Fullan, M. (1993). *Change forces: Probing the depths of educational reform.* New York: Falmer.

Glickman, C. (2002). *Leadership for learning: How to help teachers succeed.* Alexandria, VA: Association for Supervision and Curriculum Development.

Greene, M. (1995). *Releasing the imagination: Essays on education, the arts, and social change.* San Francisco: Jossey-Bass.

Grimmett, P., & Crehan, P. (1991). The nature of collegiality in teacher development: The case of clinical supervision. In M. Fullan & A. Hargreaves (Eds.), *Teacher development and educational change* (pp. 56–85). New York: Falmer.

Grow, G. (1991). Teaching learners to be self-directed. *Adult Education Quarterly 41*(3), 125–149.

Hargreaves, A. (1994). *Changing teachers, changing times: Teachers' work and culture in the postmodern age.* New York: Teachers College Press.

Henderson, J. G. (2001). *Reflective teaching: Professional artistry through inquiry.* Upper Saddle River, NJ: Merrill/Prentice Hall.

Henderson, J. G., & Hawthorne, R. D. (2000). *Transformative curriculum leadership* (2nd ed.). Upper Saddle River, NJ: Merrill/Prentice Hall.

Kegan, R. (1994). *In over our heads: The mental demands of modern life.* Cambridge, MA: Harvard University Press.

Lambert, L., Collay, M., Dietz, M. E., Kent, K., & Richert A. E. (1996). *Who will save our schools? Teachers as constructivist leaders*. Thousand Oaks, CA: Corwin Press.

Little, J. W. (1987). Teachers as colleagues. In V. Richardson-Koehler (Ed.), *Educators' handbook* (pp. 491–510). White Plains, NY: Longman.

Lortie, D. (1975). *Schoolteacher*. Chicago: University of Chicago Press.

Magestro, P. V., & Stanford-Blair, N. (2000). A tool for meaningful staff development. *Educational Leadership, 57*(8), 34–35.

Nias, J., Southworth, G., & Yeomans, A. (1989). *Staff relationships in the primary school*. London: Cassell.

Palmer, P. J. (1998). *The courage to teach*. San Francisco: Jossey-Bass.

Rosenholtz, S. (1989). *Teachers' workplace: The social organization of schools*. New York: Longman.

Schon, D. A. (1983). *The reflective practitioner*. New York: Basic Books.

Thomas, M. D. (2001). *Contemporary curriculum mindfulness for professional in-service*. Paper presented at the annual American Educational Research Association Conference, Seattle, WA, April, 2001.

Thomas, M. D. (2002). *Reflections from a transformational leader: Inviting democratic inquiry artistry into public education*. Paper presented at the annual American Educational Research Association Conference, New Orleans, LA, April, 2002.

Welwood, J. (1996). *Love and awakening: Discovering the sacred path of intimate relationship*. New York: HarperCollins.

Wolcott, H. F. (1983). Adequate schools and inadequate education: The life history of a sneaky kid, *Anthropology and Educational Quarterly, 14*(1), 24.

Woods, P. (Ed.) (1990). *Teacher skills and strategies*. New York: Falmer.

Chapter 9

Three International Commentaries

INTRODUCTION

The possibility that curriculum wisdom, as both a professional ideal and a vocational calling, could have global relevance is captured in the subtitle of our book: *Educational Decisions in Democratic Societies.*[1] This chapter presents commentaries by three international educators who were asked to consider the feasibility of enacting this interpretation of curriculum wisdom in their cultural contexts. Though their comments are based on a wide range of professional experiences, they are personal opinions only. Their views should not be interpreted as representing the perspectives of other educators in their particular settings. Furthermore, their commentaries are initial responses. Though, as mentioned in Chapter 1, the practice of wisdom has an ancient heritage in societies around the world, this is not true for the practice of curriculum wisdom as presented in this book. It is a new professional idea, and the international commentaries reflect this.

The educators in this chapter share this book's professional vision. All three hope that curriculum wisdom will, someday, become a viable professional norm in all societies that possess democratic ideals. The personal commentaries emerge out of three distinctive cultural locations: a Western "developed" nation (Australia), "developing" African nations (sub-Saharan Africa), and an ancient civilization that is now the largest democracy on the planet (India). Though the commentaries possess a limited geographical scope with respect to the entire planet, they have been included as a way of initiating an international conversation on the professional relevance of curriculum wisdom.

AN AUSTRALIAN COMMENTARY ON CURRICULUM WISDOM

Cultural Context

Australia is a developed independent nation and a member of the British Commonwealth.[2] Its ties are increasingly situated within the recognition of its long indigenous

---

[1]For an important, groundbreaking statement on the importance of approaching curriculum topics from a global perspective, see Pinar (2000).

[2]Commentary written by Ian Macpherson in close collaboration with Tania Aspland, Bob Elliott, and Ross Brooker.

heritage and a desire to be an integral part of the Asia-Pacific region. It is governed by a federal parliament overall, and by state and territory parliaments more locally. For its relatively small population, it is a vast country with pockets of population separated by great distances. Over half its area is desert-like.

Australia's population is multicultural, and a constant challenge is associated with the recognition of diversity on the one hand and the struggle of a national identity on the other. The mix of heritages, the separation of federal and state responsibility, the tyranny of distance, and the ongoing uncertainties about a common national identity combine to shape a cultural context that impinges on all aspects of life in Australia, not the least of which is education.

Introduction

I write this commentary as a member of a four-person curriculum leadership team at the Queensland University of Technology (QUT). We have been working closely together for the past decade. The group consists of Ian Macpherson, Tania Aspland, and Bob Elliott, who are all still at QUT, and Ross Brooker, who is now at the University of Tasmania. All four should be acknowledged as authors of this piece. This commentary is arranged in three parts. First, a broad-brush picture is painted to set the scene; second, we turn to a more specific summary of our recent curriculum work; third, some overall observations are presented.

A Broad-Brush Picture to Set the Scene

Cutting-edge curriculum work in Australia may be viewed as contextual and conceptual; it is deliberatively envisioned as well as collaborative and critically constructed (and reconstructed) and thoughtfully enacted. From this perspective, then, it is a wisdom challenge that contains elements of both democratic envisioning and enacting. It may also be seen as the arts of inquiry in that it is a praxis—understood broadly as a dynamic interplay of theoretical concepts and professional practices.

A conception of curriculum work by the Australian Curriculum Studies Association begins to expand on a democratic wisdom challenge with the following statement (see ACSA website: www.acsa.edu.au):

> Curriculum is the product of social, historical, political and economic forces. It involves the selection, interpretation, representation and assessment of culturally-based knowledge, skills and values. Curriculum work should:
>
> ■ be informed by political, social, economic and historical analysis
> ■ involve explicit identification and evaluation of the values on which it is based
> ■ be a collaborative experience for all participants
> ■ involve collective critical reflection
> ■ be resourced to ensure active participation by teachers, students and parents
> ■ be based on action at personal, school, community and system levels
> ■ acknowledge that individuals will experience the same learning activities in very different ways
> ■ acknowledge that curriculum should be flexible and responsive to the experience of learners.

It is difficult to be certain about how such a view of curriculum came to be in the Australian context. Bill Green, for example, laments the fact that there has not been a systematic documentation of curriculum history in Australia (Green, 2001). One could cast the net more widely perhaps and ask, what is democratic about the Australian way of life? Much could be said about both indigenous and European roots, but in the end, if there is such a thing as an Australian good life, it is underpinned by notions of egalitarianism, "mateship," and a "fair go" for all. These are the roots from which curriculum principles, priorities, policies, and practices emerge. However, it may be better, at this point, to focus more on recent curriculum history, where the focus has been upon learners and learning, and where the concern has been for the inclusion of all learners in terms of meaningful learning experiences and worthwhile learning outcomes—in other words, a "fair learning go" for all.

A recent work edited by Green (1999), containing a set of essays by Garth Boomer, clearly paints a context for the envisioning of curriculum work in Australia. Grundy's (1987) work on curriculum praxis provides a bridge between this sort of envisioning and a way for enacting curriculum work. In this regard, the work of Stephen Kemmis, Robin McTaggart and several others in the area of action research (see McTaggart, 1991) has been significant in shaping curriculum work in critical and transformative terms.

A Summary of Our Recent Curriculum Work

Chapter 1 mentioned our work in curriculum leadership (Macpherson, Aspland, Brooker, & Elliott, 1999), in which we highlight the significance of places and spaces for teachers in curriculum decision making (conceived as curriculum leadership). The notion of places conveys a commitment to the inclusive participation of teachers in curriculum decision making. Teachers lead learning and this is their primary focus in curriculum work! Our focus is on learners and learning, but the centrality of teachers is always celebrated. Curriculum leadership, then, emanates from a "fair learning go for all" perspective as well as from a more ecological than managerial view of leadership. Teachers orchestrate the many factors impinging upon learners and learning, and as they do so, they make informed curriculum decisions. This is their curriculum wisdom in both thinking and practice. It is definitely a challenge for them as they strive to make the rhetoric of democracy a lived reality for both themselves and their learners.

We have sought to reflect on this challenge as we have witnessed and been part of curriculum work. We have done so by traversing a decade of curriculum leadership here in Australia (Macpherson, Aspland, & Brooker, 2001). As a result, we have noted what we have learned about curriculum leadership, what the implications are for teaching curriculum studies in teacher education programs, and what some implications are for supporting teachers as curriculum workers. These are as follows:

What we have come to know about curriculum leadership:

- Curriculum leadership is about leading learning and it can involve a range of stakeholders working in partnership.
- Curriculum leadership is a process involving dialectical relationships among wider contextual forces, ideas about curriculum, organizational structures, and social dynamics within schools and the people who are involved in curriculum. These relationships give

a unique shape to curriculum leadership at each school. Very often, this shape may be viewed as a mystery worthy of unraveling.

- Teachers are central to curriculum leadership because of their professional preparation and ongoing development, but this does not deny the focus on learners and learning in making decisions about curriculum.
- Curriculum leadership is a contested field, which is fraught with complexities and dilemmas. The process of curriculum theorizing is particularly important.
- Curriculum leadership is very much a conversation, if not a spirited debate, about the unfinished business of optimizing learning opportunities and outcomes for all learners. Unfinished business conveys the ongoing nature of the conversations and debates. It does not mean walking away from a task incomplete.

What we have learned about teaching curriculum studies in teacher education programs:

- Constructivist approaches are useful in helping teachers develop understandings and capacities relative to curriculum leadership, as they take account of the dialectical relationships; the contestations, dilemmas and uncertainties; and the processes of critiquing and reconstructing.
- "Teachers as researchers/curriculum makers" is a mindset that is appropriate for the use of constructivist approaches in developing teachers' levels of competence and confidence to engage in curriculum leadership as curriculum decision making within their classrooms and beyond.
- The mindset may develop broadly with a focus on the self at the preservice level; a focus on the self and others at the inservice level; and a focus on the self, others and the cultural context at the postgraduate level.
- Understandings and capacities relating to curriculum leadership are always contextually based and need to be theoretically and critically informed. However, they may focus on the immediacy of classrooms at the preservice level; the need for collaboration beyond classrooms at the inservice level; and the need for wider advocacy in forums at the school, community, and policy levels at both the inservice and postgraduate levels.

What we have learned about professional development that focuses on curriculum decision-making as curriculum leadership:

- There are multiple ways of thinking, and doing, in the field of curriculum. Curriculum leadership is one way to think about and act out curriculum practice that focuses on learners and learning and that values teachers for the central role they play in making a range of curriculum decisions.
- The "what" of curriculum leadership presented above provides the genesis of a navigational tool or diagnostic instrument for teachers to clarify and empower their contributions to curriculum decision making in their classrooms, their schools, and their wider community and professional settings.
- Finding more effective ways of capturing and communicating instances of curriculum leadership continues to be a significant challenge in continuing the conversations and addressing the unfinished business.
- Professional development that focuses on what we have come to know about curriculum leadership is not likely to produce a universal and generalizable set of strategies (or recipes) for engaging in curriculum leadership. However, the "what" does present a compelling stockpile of descriptive case-study data and interpretive insights that are generative for teachers, school and systemic leadership personnel, educational/curriculum policy makers, and other stakeholders.

■ We have developed a draft policy statement for the Australian Curriculum Studies Association for teaching curriculum studies in teacher education programs. In this statement (see Macpherson, 2002b) we (that is, Macpherson, Aspland, and Brooker) characterize teachers as curriculum workers who are contextually aware, ethically sensitive, culturally inclusive, and socially just; critically informed, praxis oriented, and research/inquiry based; learner and learning centered; critically reflective and pedagogically competent; educationally defensible and deliberatively passionate about their beliefs and values; professionally responsible, politically astute, and collaboratively participatory; and transformatively reconstructive.

Addressing this book's wisdom challenge in the Australian context has much to do with the inclusive participation by a range of stakeholders in curriculum decision-making processes. There is wisdom from a contextual, conceptual, and critical perspective (envisioning) and there is challenge from a collaborative and constructed (and reconstructed) perspective (enacting). Envisioning and enacting are inextricably linked in the arts of inquiry, interpreted and defined broadly as praxis, which facilitates a dynamic interplay of theoretical concepts and professional practice. This praxis is the basis for cutting-edge curriculum work in Australia.

The seven forms of interdependent inquiry underpinning the arts of inquiry are significant for spelling out praxis in the Australian context. The ecological view that we take of leadership aligns nicely with the notion of a hologram. In our view, curriculum leadership as a form of curriculum wisdom takes on many shapes. Our curriculum leadership factors, for example, may be observed in many different mixes, and the uniqueness of the shape of curriculum leadership at a particular site has always been important for us to describe and analyze. The forms of inquiry outlined in Chapter 3 provide an excellent platform for examining and transforming curriculum thinking and practice in Australia, both generally and at particular teaching/learning sites. As they work together in a synergy, there is the potential for an ever-deepening understanding of the contextual complexities within which we engage in curriculum work. Of course, it would be dangerous to see the arts of inquiry as a panacea that leads to some sort of utopia. Nevertheless, they provide a worthwhile frame for continuing to narrate what might be called a "never-ending story of never-finished curriculum business."

All of this, however, does not satisfactorily address from a broader philosophical and political perspective the notion of the wisdom challenge being democratic. It begs questions about what is democratic and how education can contribute to ongoing constructions of democracy in the Australian context.

Late in 2001, the Australian Council of Deans of Education published a document titled, *New Learning: A Charter for Australian Education*. The document contends that its eight propositions will shape the future environment of learning. The eight propositions are as follows:

Proposition 1: Education Has a Much Larger Role to Play in Creating Socially Productive Persons. This contention anticipates trends and demands of the new knowledge economy, many of them already visible. A sharp increase in knowledge-intensive industries is occurring, but new learning recognizes that traditional areas such as manufacturing will also be transformed by the rise of information and communication technologies, greater collaboration, and the need for interpersonal and problem-solving skills. Put simply, nations in the new economy are judged not by the value of their fixed capital, but by the skills and knowledge of their workforce. Given this, Australia's current neglect of our education sector is alarming, and a radical rethink of the role of education is required.

Proposition 2: Learning Will Be Lifelong and Lifewide. This acknowledges the greying of the population and the short shelf-life of technological skills. In an era signified by rapid change, the need to promote autonomous learning is paramount. Citizens must learn to learn, throughout and across their lives. "Lifewide" learning recognizes the need for much greater flexibility and diversity of educational experiences: Learning should occur in parks, in pool halls, and outside of traditional institutions. Lifelong learning means that education for most does not end at school or university, and that adult and community education, in particular, is of growing importance. Learning opportunities must be available to those from all backgrounds, of all ages, and at all stages of life. To this end, a national framework for lifelong learning is imperative.

Proposition 3: Opportunity and Diversity: Education is One of the Main Ways to Deliver on the Promise of Democracy. Education promises individuals greater social mobility: more access to material resources through better paid employment, a greater capacity to participate actively in the processes of government, and the personal dexterity that comes with knowing the world. It promises improved employment prospects, increased self-determination, and extended access to the wider world. The key challenge, however, is to ensure that education fulfills its democratic mission, and the charter argues that this challenge can only be met by dedicated programs that address inequality. Targeting disadvantaged and "at risk" groups must be done, not on the basis of moral arguments alone, but also on the basis of the economic and social dangers of allowing individuals and groups to be excluded.

Proposition 4: A New Basics is Emerging. The old basics of the three R's must be reconceptualized in order to reflect contemporary changes to learning. New learning will be general in its focus, rather than specialized on the particular needs-of-the-day. It will be about creating a kind of person, with kinds of dispositions and orientations to the world, rather than simply commanding a body of knowledge. These persons will be able to navigate change and diversity, learn as they go, solve problems, collaborate, and be flexible and creative. Finally, new learning will be increasingly interdisciplinary, requiring deeper engagement with knowledge in all its complexity and ambiguity. The new basics are about promoting capability sets, reflexive and autonomous learning, collaboration, communication, and broadly knowledgeable persons.

Proposition 5: Technology Will Become Central to All Learning. This is arguably more complex than it first appears. Technologies of digitization have the potential to transform learning relationships for the better, but this potential needs to be harnessed. This proposition contends that we need to learn through, but also about technology. Technology is not just a tool for learning, in other words. It should be one of the main things that learning is about—a message as well as a medium.

Proposition 6: The Work of Educators Will Be Transformed. The role of educators will broaden considerably. Individualized programs and customized learning will be common in classrooms of the future, and this will require educators to be highly skilled, attenuated to individual needs, and more broadly knowledgeable than ever before. Already, of course, educators perform one of the most important roles in the economy, and salary and wage packages need to reflect this role better. Moreover, educators require more time for professional development and reskilling, for national and international exchanges, and for collaboration with other local community organizations.

Proposition 7: The Place of the "Public" and the "Private" in Education Will Be Redefined. This proposition tackles the problematic relationship between federal and state governments that undermines schools, vocational education institutions and higher education in particular. It argues that education must be viewed as a public obligation, and that, notwithstanding a moral imperative, the new economy demands that all members of the community have access to quality learning. Demarcating clearer federal/state responsibilities is important, as is a clear commitment from all governments to provide quality education for all, not simply for those born into privilege or wealth.

Proposition 8: The Focus of Education Policy Must Change from Public Cost to Public Investment. This requires attitudinal change, which must come from greater awareness of the importance of education. The charter cites several studies and numerous data that demonstrate the long-term benefits to the nation of investment in education. At an individual level, the data are also clear: Educated individuals have higher employment rates, higher average weekly earnings, lower imprisonment rates, and greater opportunities for continued reskilling. That education is a public investment is a proposition we must accept if Australia is to embrace and thrive in the new economy.

These propositions provide a clue to what is thought to be democratic. The first two frame the envisioning, while the third and fourth elaborate the vision in educational terms. The third begins to elaborate on what the Australian Curriculum Studies Association calls "political, social economic and historical analysis," while the fourth identifies a basis for constructing a view of knowledge. Democracy, then, is conceived more in socially inclusive terms than in purely political terms. The remaining propositions provide ideas for enacting.

Overall the democratic wisdom challenge for cutting-edge curriculum workers in Australia is the ongoing theorizing and transformation of their work. This cerebral activity is the arts of inquiry or, as we refer to it, the praxis. Further, there is a challenge for those who employ, support, and sustain those who engage in curriculum work. Their challenge is to recognize the place(s) of teachers in curriculum work, and to create/facilitate the space(s) for them to exercise their understandings and capacities to engage in curriculum work as curriculum leadership.

Some Observations to Finish for Now

In our paper at the recent Annual American Education Research Association (AERA) Meeting in New Orleans, we (Macpherson, Aspland, Elliott, & Brooker, 2002) reported some observations from our work with people at four school sites in 2001. Teachers engaged in curriculum leadership reflected upon their experiences and recounted them to us. In an ongoing way we worked together to analyze and interpret their narratives. Here is the essence of what emerged:

Any process of change (or curriculum reculturing) is characterised by a multitudinous mix of paradoxes. It is not so much an "either/or" response that is called for, rather a "both/and" response. We identified a number of these that were evident at each of the sites. We then noted that in addressing these paradoxes, we saw personnel at the sites invoking principles associated with a COMMITMENT to a shared vision about the learning journey; COMPETENCE and CONFIDENCE in working with, talking about, and reflecting upon productive pedagogies in the journey towards worthwhile learning outcomes; COLLABORATION in a "learning journey" culture of distributed curriculum leadership; CONSOLIDATION and CELEBRATION of the learning journey through appropriate support mechanisms; COMMUNICATION from the inside out of professional learnings and implications for ongoing support and action; and (RE)CONSTRUCTION(S) of the ongoing journeys.

Based on this understanding, we elicited a number of propositions about an inclusive and transformative discourse about curriculum leadership. These propositions are as follows:

- It is contextualized in a strong sense of community.
- It values the multiplicity of voices from within a school community.
- It relies on the development of a shared curriculum vision in a school community.
- It is best promoted through a common curricular language.
- It juxtaposes broader curriculum initiatives with local aspirations.
- It is nurtured in flexible school and curriculum structures.
- It promotes the reconstruction of curriculum practices.
- It is underpinned by a process of authentic engagement of voices within a school community.
- It positions teachers as lifelong learners.

If all of this is a journey, then the journey has just begun! The discourse for taking us further is multidimensional, as our AERA proposal for 2003 demonstrates (Macpherson, 2002a). The ongoingness of the journey is certainly true in Australia, and the use of the phrase "cutting-edge curriculum work" conveys a sense of curriculum workers in any setting being at many points along the route.

If there is a curriculum wisdom challenge for teachers as curriculum workers in Australia, then there is also a challenge for all who have a responsibility to support and sustain the ongoing efforts of teachers who seek to envision and enact their curriculum work in these terms. It is a recognition of, and response to, this responsibility that will take all curriculum workers further towards the cutting edge.

In terms of curriculum leadership as a democratic wisdom challenge, we take up this responsibility by inviting curriculum workers not to accept the "what is" but to critique it and to envision "what might be." Such critique (which must be ongoing) provides the basis for reconstructing their thinking and practice. A frame for this sort of critique is well explained in the Atweh, Kemmis and Weeks (1998) edited work on action research.

Our concern with curriculum leadership has always been to draw away from a managerial and organizational view of leadership to one that is more ecological as a basis for bringing together the personal, cultural, and moral dimensions of curriculum work. Our curriculum leadership factors are similar, and we always try to stress that there is an inescapable dynamic occurring among them.

The work we have been doing in the reconceptualization of our preservice B.Ed course at QUT has been informed by this thinking. We maintain that reform will not take place through a restructuring (which is more managerial and organizational); there is hope for reform if the process is conceived of as a reculturing where the personal, cultural, and moral dimensions have to be addressed in a more cohesive and holistic manner (see Macpherson & Aspland, 2002). The Australian Curriculum Studies Association in its principles of curriculum reform captures this more ecological, comprehensive view. Systems and schools are beginning to take it on, but it is huge task!

The picture of curriculum work presented here is our perspective of what we observe at the cutting edge. It is a picture painted within the context of current policy documents around the country (and reflected in the Deans' Charter), so there is hope for a brave new world of curriculum work as a democratic wisdom challenge in Australia. It is an unfinished picture, though, and certainly one that we offer as a basis for ongoing challenge, contestation, and critique by both our colleagues here in Australia and overseas.

AN AFRICAN COMMENTARY ON CURRICULUM WISDOM

Cultural Context

The Republic of Benin, known as the Republic of Dahomey prior to 1975, is located in West Africa.[3] With an area of 112,622 square kilometers, the Republic of Benin is bordered on the north by the Republic of Burkina Faso and the Republic of Niger, on the east by the Federal Republic of Nigeria, on the west by the Republic of Togo, and on the south by the Atlantic Ocean. Benin is a multicultural society with 42 different ethnic groups, 55 national languages, and a population estimated at 5,700,000 (52% females and 48% males) in 1996.

Benin was declared independent on August 1, 1960. Following independence, it went through many political upheavals, military coups, and frequent government and ideology changes between 1960 and 1972. The military coup of 1972 was the starting point of a 17-year Marxist-Leninist regime. The regime's centralized system, combined with economic difficulties, led to major social demonstrations between 1975 and 1989. The government held a national conference in 1990 where fundamental decisions were made, namely the abolition of the Marxist-Leninist ideology, the dissolution of all one-party structures, the institution of a multiparty system, and a new constitution outlining democratic government and elections. Along with Benin's radical transition to a society with democratic ideals, was a significant rethinking of the role of education in the development of the country. The period after 1990 opened the door to a democratization of education. The priorities of the government educational policy included intellectual and moral education, the development of critical and creative thinking, the acquisition of skills for lifelong learning, and an emphasis on a curriculum that stresses self-employment.

---

[3]Commentary written by Issaou Gado.

Introduction

This is a critical commentary by an African curriculum scholar on the possibilities of envisioning and enacting democratic curricula in African democratic societies through the arts of inquiry. *Curriculum Wisdom* is a text that "has been created to support the improvement of educational decisions in societies with democratic ideals," and my commentary focuses on educational practices in emerging democratic countries in sub-Saharan Africa. I write from a postcolonial critical perspective, integrating the voices of other African scholars, and I invite other African scholars to reach their own conclusions about the "wisdom" of this book.

Wisdom in the African continent is an old concept that is applied to various educational, political, economic, agricultural, technological, social, and cultural contexts. The *Oxford English Dictionary* definition of wisdom, cited in Chapter 1, applies to African wisdom traditions, and I appreciate the acknowledgement of its ancient heritage in Africa as well as other locations around the world.

The basic structure of African societies is grounded in wisdom. Traditional wisdom in Africa is still cultivated in nonformal educational contexts, which parallel and overlap formal educational settings. Wisdom in education is practiced in administrative and classroom management, school culture, and curriculum development settings because current educational leaders in Africa come from families with strong African traditions. Unfortunately, wisdom in Africa has sustained a long period of colonization and foreign hegemonic domination. In formal education wisdom is failing because countries are espousing and experiencing Western educational values. The basic structure of the education system, largely inherited from the colonial era, is the main reason for this failure (Fafunwa & Aisiku, 1982; Hinchliffe, 1987; Moumouni, 1968; Urch, 1992). The weakness of educational efforts in Africa is often the result of direct transfer of features of northern nations that are unsuitable in the African setting (Pinar, Reynolds, Slattery, & Taubman, 1995).

The central question guiding my commentary is **What are the possibilities for wise decision making in countries with democratic ideals in sub-Saharan Africa**? The way in which African curriculum scholars and educational practitioners answer this question and, thus, enact the professional vision of this book will depend on their attitude and vision for curriculum development. There will, inevitably, be multiple interpretations of this text. Those who like novelty and newness would see curriculum wisdom as the cream of the crop in curriculum development and the solution to educational problems and teacher empowerment in democratic countries. Those who view curriculum as a set of national artifacts may feel that this book's curriculum wisdom challenge is not transferable to their cultural context. Those who see themselves as pragmatist democratic leaders may pick, choose, and apply within the archetypal inquiry domains of Chapter 3. Those who favor globalization and internationalization of curriculum discourse may welcome that chapter's sophisticated arts of inquiry and may deductively derive their own subtheories. A different answer would be provided by aid and funding agencies that decide unilaterally or bilaterally what kinds of curriculum or educational projects are appropriate in sub-Saharan Africa.

For my part, as an ex–doctoral advisee of one of the authors of this book, I have been challenged to think critically for myself; therefore, I will respond to the book with my face turned away from the master. Even though I could have written a commentary in the spirit of "praise the Lord," I have chosen to respond to the questions I have raised from a post-colonial perspective. I will probably dissatisfy those who expect black and white answers and the do's and don'ts of curriculum wisdom and decision making in sub-Saharan African countries with democratic ideals. Though I do not want to portray myself as an expert, I hope my reaction to the book will be of interest to national educational leaders, international experts, and researchers responsible for studying, designing, and implementing educational programs in elementary, secondary, and higher education in democratic societies in Africa.

To meet the curriculum wisdom challenge of envisioning and enacting the democratic good life, the authors have identified seven inquiry domains: techné, poesis, praxis, dialogos, phronesis, polis and theoria. In the context of African societies that have, for so long, been intellectually, economically, politically, socially, and educationally dominated, the domains of dialogos and praxis should be the nucleus of a democratic revival and renaissance. I see the domains of techné and phronesis as closely revolving around this nucleus, while the domains of poesis, theoria, and polis occupy the outer circle in my conceptual framework. My understanding of the relationship of these inquiry domains is depicted in Figure 9.1, and the arrow indicates the entrance of the process.

The relationship between dialogos and praxis needs to be center stage because a post-colonial point of view is embedded in multiperspective and critical inquiries, while techné and phronesis represent the next stage of development in the process of application and understanding of democratic educational decision making. Educational leaders then complete their well-balanced inquiry with the outer-circle domains.

I will open my commentary by presenting the democratization process in sub-Saharan Africa. Without an understanding of the creation and maintenance of African democratic

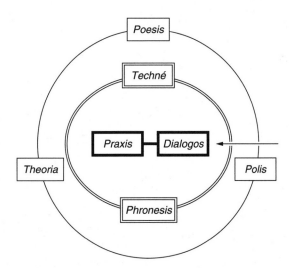

FIGURE 9.1

**Sub-Saharan African curriculum inquiry
from a postcolonial perspective**

societies, my commentary would be lacking important historical context. I will recast sub-Saharan Africa as a continent of multiple educational ideologies. I will follow this by addressing the issues of national educational priorities, the change process or inquiry into a new form of dialogos and praxis as route to good curriculum artistry, and moral and ethical inquiry needs. I will end my discussion of the change process with some recommendations and conclude with final comments.

Democratization and Education

When describing curriculum decision making in African societies, it is important to clarify the birth and maintenance of African democracies and to address the use of democratic language in education. When Dewey (1966) wrote *Democracy and Education,* he was generally referring to countries that already possessed democratic ideals. However, *Democracy and Education* has been studied and applied in sub-Saharan African countries that did not have democratic ideals. For example, under a Marxist-Leninist ideology, Dewey's book was taught to prospective teachers at the National University of Benin; in fact, a professor of that institution was nicknamed "John Dewey" by his students.

Educational goals in Benin were developed with an understanding of democracy under a socialist political regime. In the *National Program of Edification of the New School,* the policy guidelines for educational reform in a Marxist-Leninist regime were titled "Des Principes de Gestion Démocratique de l'Enseignement" and "Gestion Démocratique de l'Ecole Nouvelle" ("Principles of Democratic Management of Teaching" and "Democratic Management of the New School") (Ministère de l'Education Nationale, 1983). The democratic ideals in this literature invited the community, the parents, the students, and the teachers to join in the national educational effort. In addition there was a desire to encourage and foster creativity, initiative spirit, accountability, and an effort to firmly maintain the education system free of foreign domination and interference. Further, it was indicated that the teacher was a facilitator. Statements borrowed from Deweyan pragmatism were used to characterize the "New School" under the socialist system.

The New School was an integral part of society and was conceived to ensure a physical, intellectual, and moral balance for Benin citizens. It was also necessary to decolonize educational services, teaching and learning methods, and the bourgeois mentalities. Similar "democratic and liberatory" educational reforms were undertaken in most sub-Saharan African countries after independence, and Dewey's engaging ideas were used.

The collapse of the communist bloc and severe economic and social problems changed the political and educational landscape in sub-Saharan African countries, and Boafo-Arthur (1999) provides an insightful account of the birth of African democracies. Following the collapse of the Communist bloc, developing countries have embarked on the simultaneous pursuit of structural adjustment and democratization. Some countries, such as Ghana, started with adjustment for almost a decade before democratization. However, the joint pursuit of adjustment and democratization has engendered intense debate among academics and policy makers.

In some countries such as Benin educational reforms have followed political reforms. National conferences are usually a forum where all political sensitivities convene to think about how to provide students, teachers, and parents with experiences that reflect the new democratic orientation. These conferences usually start with a heated debate in which "new" educational leaders express their anger against the failure of the past education system under the former "rotten and corrupted" political regime. In the case of most democratizing countries in sub-Saharan Africa, the same educational leaders who developed the past educational goals, returned their jackets, changed their hats, swore to serve the country and nothing but the country, and learned to use new disenfranchised language to create "new" goals of education.

The case of Benin provides a good example. In the *Actes des États Généraux de L'éducation* (Ministère de l'Education Nationale et de la Recherche Scientifique, 1990), a document created by educational and political leaders after the successful national conference that turned the country into a multipartite democracy, it was indicated that

> Il ne s'agit pas d'inventer nécessairement un système éducatif tout nouveau, mais de s'inspirer des expériences passées en vue d'améliorer les programmes qui existent déjà et de favoriser leur mise en œuvre par un appui financier adéquat. Ce qui a toujours fait défaut, ce sont les moyens pour la mise en œuvre de la politique définie. (p. 32)
> [There is no need to necessarily invent a very new education system, but to take the past experiences as starting points in order to improve the curricula, which already exist, and to foster their implementation by an adequate financial support. What has always been missing are the means for the implementation of the defined policy.]

This emphasizes that there is no need to invent a new education system, but to use the past experiences to improve educational programs that existed and to foster their application through adequate financial support. It also indicates that what has always been missing is the means to implement the educational policy.

Some educational goals that appeared in the new democratic reform were similar to those advocated in the New School reform under the Marxist-Leninist regime. The concern was to make sure that the educational language matches the new democratic political language, and this mind-set about change applies to other newly democratized countries in sub-Saharan Africa.

Some of these national forums were organized with the financial and ideological support of international educational institutions. Educational leaders established the goals of education in accordance with their new patrons—donor institutions, the World Bank, and the International Monetary Fund. After close inspection of the nature of these new partnerships, one may infer that it is all about an African version of "old wine new bottle." Since multiple international institutions support the democratization process, it was not surprising to experience multiple educational ideologies, which can be described as an educational "bricolage"—a multilayered overlapping of reform discourses.

With the rise of new democratic countries in Africa, Dewey might write an African version of *Democracy and Education* and title it *Democratization and Education in Africa*. Democratization is the process of bringing about democracy. African democratic countries are still in the process of democratizing their institutions. The democratic ideals advocated in this book may be welcome and used, even by countries that are autocratic. However, there could easily be a misuse of these ideas not only in emerging democratic sub-Saharan countries but also in established democratic societies. There are also many constraints in the democratization process because the former French colonies have to renegotiate the old international patron-client relationships (Clark, 2002), and any democratic success will be closely linked to these negotiations.

What emerges from this historical overview is that democratizations in Africa have been triggered by economic failure, mass deprivation, popular upheaval, foreign imposition, and democratic incentives (Bates, 1994). According to Aké (1990), the underdevelopment of African countries was related to the lack of democracy. Therefore, democratization was perceived to be the ideal solution. Usually there is a transition to democracy without rupture (Kandeh, 1998). However, some countries in the democratization process quickly move from the conference table to the battlefield.

A Continent of Multiple Educational Ideologies

Educational ideology refers to a body of doctrines, myths, beliefs, or theories of a social movement, institution, class, or large group with reference to some underlying political, cultural, or economic plan, along with the devices for putting the plan into operation. There are many educational ideologies that structure curriculum development processes in the sub-Saharan African democratic societies. The complexity and multiplicity of educational ideologies in sub-Saharan Africa are the direct effect of funding agencies, the global movement of African scholars, and international partnerships.

African educational leaders take short trips to the West and the North to acquaint themselves with current advances in curriculum discourse. International partners and funding agencies provide monies and human resources to strengthen and actualize education systems in Africa. It is also common for developing nations to transfer curricular practices into the sub-Saharan African countries whether they are democratic or not. Because Africans want to bring the best to their countries, the continent has been besieged by multiple curriculum ideologies and various applications of educational theories.

Those who understand this text's curriculum wisdom know that envisioning and enacting democratic curricula is a complicated and reflective conversation with diverse others. In this spirit of an open and "extraordinarily complicated conversation" (Pinar et al., 1995), it is essential that educational decisions be informed by dialogos and praxis. In the sub-Saharan African context, this multiperspective and critical emphasis resonates with Freire's (1985) notions of "dialogical encounter" and "conscientization." However, the term *dialogos* perhaps carries a different meaning in the African context. An African scholar once said,

> I feel that until we recognize that our sense of self depends upon another and that there is no sense of self without there being another, until we recognize that there is a reciprocal relationship, we will be very confined in our thinking and in our sense of place. So the notion of a dialogue is to me very important. But to pick an even better word, the notion of a conversation runs more freely and flexibly than does a dialogue. And so while I would not put out of consideration the notion of dialogue anymore than I would put out the notion of nation, I am bothered by both of those a bit and I would like to see cross-cultural conversations. So the notion of a discourse or a dialogue that moves across cultural and country boundaries is important. I don't think we should lose in any way our cultural identity. But I think we need to honor each other's otherness. (Interview 1, African scholar, 2000)

In this context the dialogical encounter might be an international postcolonial conversation that would lead to an adaptation of curriculum wisdom. Praxis, the integration of critical inquiry into teachers' reflective practices, will develop teachers' awareness of the decision-making process. Praxis would foster the conscientization of stakeholders that would enable them to see the big picture.

National Priorities and the Arts of Inquiry

African educational leaders may be hesitant about any endorsement of democratic wisdom because they believe curriculum work is inextricably linked with national priorities and embedded in national histories and politics (Gado & Verma, 2000). Reid (2000) writes,

> Curriculum is not comparable across nations, and theorists are not dealing with the components of a universal scientific enterprise. National curriculums are cultural artifacts, in the same way that national songs, stories, and festivals are cultural artifacts. Even if they use the same basic materials, what result from those materials has unique meaning for individual nations. (p. 114)

In the spirit of dialogos, curriculum decision making in democratic societies with strong national identities should not echo any standardization, uniformity, or intellectual hegemony. There is some evidence that within national systems of education, a substantial part of the curriculum decision making reflects and promotes the nation's interest. This is probably a major concern because countries with democratic ideals in politics, economics, and social affairs may not necessarily espouse democratic ideals in education.

In most African democratic societies, the control of curriculum development is mainly at the state level. National curriculum leaders appointed by the government carry out the major decisions. As a result, there is a tendency of the people in power to impose their "democratic vision" of good educational practices, and this would be contrary to the spirit of this book. National educational forums establish the priorities for the country. In the future, if these forums would be guided by dialogos and phronesis, they would not accept any curriculum orientation without prior public debate.

Curriculum decision making in the African context is inevitably collaborative and international because scholars and politicians recognize that more and more national borders are very fluid. Pinar et al. (1995) write, "Of course, curriculum discourses must not be sealed airtight within national boundaries. Just as economic, political, and ecological phenomena increasingly ignore national boundaries" (p. 792). This globalization trend can work against the formation of national identities (Gado & Verma, 2000) but could support the broad international focus of this book.

The nature of existing partnerships between developed and developing countries could be a major impediment in educationally envisioning and enacting the democratic good life in the sub-Saharan African context. It is important to critically address the nature of these partnerships, or "patronships." Otherwise, the international encounters will be experienced as monologues by the donor countries. However, the enactment of the arts of inquiry could empower and sensitize some African democratic countries to reject such cultural/curriculum dominance. Reid (2000) articulates the appropriate critical spirit:

> In spite of claims that the patterns and structures of schooling can be conceived of, and determined through an exercise of universally applicable theory, history tells us that the arrangements that nations make for the content and patterns of their school curriculums,

are inextricably linked with themes of national identity and national aspiration.... If then curriculum theory is to make claims of universality, it must operate at a meta-level from which it can treat broad issues of how the forms of learning are related to the uniqueness of the societies that maintain them and their cultural evolution. (pp. 121–122, 113)

The Change Process: Inquiry into a New Form of Dialogos in the African Context

Effective educational reforms in a postcolonial democratic context and the meaning making of curriculum wisdom might require agendas and initiatives with strong local roots and broad participation of those with a stake in educational outcomes, including educational officials, students, parents, teachers, and communities. The democratic change process must be enacted as a transformative curriculum leadership. In sub-Saharan Africa educational decisions may foster voices from diverse communities. African sages understand that within any group or culture there are multiple competing voices and that there is not a single political, religious, cultural, or economic theory that solves all problems (Gado & Verma, 2000). Reform-minded curriculum developers must work with the interconnectedness of ecological, technological, economic, political, religious, cultural, and educational systems.

In sub-Saharan Africa curriculum development and continuing professional development have been rooted in craft teaching. What is required to raise educational consciousness in the newly democratic countries is a move beyond techné and toward praxis. Educational leaders may perceive that praxis might be a chaotic process. I agree with Doll (1993) that

> In order for students and teachers to transform and be transformed, a curriculum needs to have the "right amount" of indeterminacy, anomaly, inefficiency, chaos, disequilibrium, dissipation, lived experience.... The issue is one to be continually negotiated among students, teachers, and texts.... But the issue of the curriculum needing disturbing qualities is not to be negotiated; these qualities form the problematic of life itself and are the essence of a rich and transforming curriculum. (p. 167)

The enactment of the arts of inquiry would include the voices of various indigenous, or politically repressed groups. Envisioning and enacting a democratic good life would empower and enlighten minorities and different cultural groups that may not have official recognition in the curriculum development process. This is also a form of public moral inquiry that requires a transformative curriculum leadership (Henderson & Hawthorne, 2000). Banks (1991) writes,

> A transformative curriculum designed to empower students, especially those from victimized and marginalized groups, must help students to develop the knowledge and skills needed to critically examine the current political and economic structure and the myths and ideologies used to justify it.... The transformative curriculum must help students to view the human experience from the perspectives of a range of cultural, ethnic, and social-class groups, and to construct their own versions of the past, present and future. (pp. 130–131)

This endeavor calls for personal, interpersonal, and institutional challenges. This transformative curriculum work cannot be easily accomplished. Individual and institutional adjustments will be necessary in envisioning and enacting a democratic educational life in sub-Saharan countries. International experts and local curriculum leaders should start curriculum conversations that would constantly challenge stakeholders from diverse socio-cultural and religious backgrounds. Once informed, organized, and cultivated, curriculum leaders should unmask the hegemonic ideology that preserves power in an age of change, unequal partnership, and global colonization (Kincheloe, Slattery, & Steinberg, 2000).

This book advocates this critical transformative stance by using the term *praxis* to "signify action that is grounded in a serious examination of the root causes of injustice, and that is oriented toward human liberation." This critical combat against domination and exploitation has, overtly and subtly, been practiced for a long time in African countries, and it has informed efforts to raise children in a postcolonial cultural context of national independence.

African democratic educational leaders need to be aware that technical assistance in their educational effort can impede rather than promote critical inquiry. Even though the supports of aid agencies are directed toward building Africa's capacity to help itself, the ways that advice or support is transmitted may undermine and preclude educational leaders from envisioning and enacting democratic educational leadership. Democratic countries in sub-Saharan African countries need to be aware of this professional challenge. The following suggestions emphasize democratic and reflective partnerships:

- Coordination of reform efforts at both international and state levels related to national interests.
- Ongoing professional development based on a long-term partnerships between governments and international institutions.
- Coordination among agencies and international organizations driven by state policy and informed by research findings.
- Financial support for developing new curriculum and curriculum materials aligned with the fundamental needs of teachers and students.
- Funds for workshops and educational programs based on research and informed by formative and summative evaluation.
- Government officials critically informed of democratic educational practices. Frameworks, materials, and textbooks relevant to national realities or adaptable to the context.
- Curriculum practices aligned with national standards when they exist and based on common interest, mutual respect and credibility for national "brains."

On Moral and Ethical Inquiry Needs

This section addresses public moral inquiry (theoria) and ethical inquiry (polis). This book is founded on a democratic theoria. This theorizing needs refinement and application in the African context. African scholars believe that educational practices are generated from theoria. However, they do not make theories the core of educational change. An African scholar offers her interpretation of theorizing in the African context:

> Usually in Africa there is not much, though there is a lot of theorizing in the United States and Europe. Their theories may not necessarily be acceptable to us, but nothing stops us from even examining their own theories closely. And that will also be part of scholarship. So using and getting ideas from here and there and then situating our ideas and our own socio-cultural realities will enable us to focus on the things that we need to focus on. And then we can relate with the rest of the world. We cannot afford to isolate ourselves. (Interview 1, African scholar, 2000)

It is important that African scholars think about situating the ideas in this book in their own socio-cultural realities. In the traditional African context theorizing is a daily occurrence for sages who emphasize their theoretical thinking in morality, spirituality, and ethics. Teachers and students who have been raised in the traditional context may consider theorizing about morality and ethics as the "port of entry" of their educational journey.

Morality and ethics are African principles. The essence of curriculum wisdom in the African context should include multiple voices from global communities and promote discourses that address the ecological, moral, spiritual, and theological needs. Pinar et al. (1995) write,

> Moral and ethical issues had been abdicated to the extreme right wing; they are now being reclaimed as essential to the reconceptualized effort to understand curriculum, a project that is hermeneutical in its acknowledgment of its political, theological, practical, and spiritual dimensions. (p. 637)

In various African societies, civic education, now mostly forgotten, has been prominent. We must be aware that the theological, moral, and ethical perspectives of communities are very diverse. As we continue experiencing ethnic cleansing, ethnic slaughter, and religious bigotry and hatred in African countries that are aspiring to democratic ways of living, educational decisions in established democratic societies need to include and reinforce moral and civic education. Public moral inquiry needs to be emphasized. That would deepen our understanding and awareness of African tradition by dialogue and interaction with other traditions without the need to assimilate, annihilate, alienate, or change the other traditions (Gado & Verma, 2000).

Educational decisions in democratic societies need to take into account these elements. This book certainly does not address any solution to these problems. However, it provides a vision and a platform that can support the improvement of educational decisions and the empowerment of stakeholders.

Concluding Comments

The authors state in Chapter 1 that one response to the problem of educational reform is to work on the quality of curriculum decisions. Who would want to challenge such a reform agenda? Who would be opposed to the importance of making quality curriculum judgments? I hope African educational leaders will embrace this book's "inquiry dance" and wisely choose their "dance partners."

The reader also needs to keep in mind that even though African educational leaders, in formal settings, may envision a good educational journey for all children, they do not always have the resources for its enactment. For example, because curriculum wisdom is a personal challenge, the necessary professional development work must be individualized, and this is expensive.

There are already educators in sub-Saharan Africa who, at least tacitly, are working from a democratic wisdom perspective. If they wish to work with the seven archetypal inquiry domains delineated in Chapter 3, they will face enormous psychological, interpersonal, and institutional obstacles. In a standards-based and state-controlled educational system, entertaining a personal challenge of envisioning and enacting a good educational journey may be an act of bravery. If there is a group of challengers who wish to envision and enact curriculum wisdom, they will need to overcome the administrative inertia, gain some national recognition, and have access to funding. This situation is not different even in the United States, where funding for educational programs is generally based on technical and efficiency criteria and not on a critical awareness of democratic morality.

For African scholars who believe that it takes a village to raise the child, they might wonder how this text might accomplish that: raise the child. The text does not provide recipes for teaching and learning. It is mostly designed as a professional development tool. As a tool, the book might serve the purpose of the user and not necessarily that of the authors. In most countries, including the United States, professional development is geared toward craft knowledge. In that context, this book could easily be perceived as too theoretical to be taken seriously—particularly by practicing teachers who are fed up and burned out by years of "lifelong learning" that did not serve their immediate needs.

I have noted how economic, political, social, demographic, and technological forces shape curriculum decision making in the African context. Sub-Saharan African countries with democratic ideals have formal and nonformal programs of education designed to "raise the child" and transmit the society's culture and way of life. If educational leaders in these countries are concerned about educating for a democratic good life, they will need to find a way to adapt this book to a broad range of curriculum, professional, and cultural development needs.

AN INDIAN COMMENTARY ON CURRICULUM WISDOM

Cultural Context

India is one of the oldest civilizations, with a rich cultural heritage.[4] The ancient history of India consists of a span of about 3500 years. India is located in Southeast Asia and is surrounded by Pakistan, China, Nepal, Myanmar, and SriLanka. Bounded by the majestic Himalayan ranges in the north, it stretches southward and at the Tropic of Cancer, tapers off into the Indian Ocean between the Bay of Bengal on the east and the Arabian Sea on the west. India was colonized by Britain for over 200 years and got its independence in 1947. It has achieved multifaceted socio-economic progress during the past 55 years of its independence. India is a vivid kaleidoscope of landscapes, historical sites and royal cities, beaches, mountain retreats, rich cultures, and festivities. Indian civilization has been a complex weave of many traditions and cultures. Given the complexity introduced by differences of race, religion, language, customs and tradition, it is not easy to identify the elements of Indian culture. The effects of past colonialism and the ongoing forces of globalization have further complicated the issue. This interesting interplay sometimes brings the elements of ancient traditions and value-systems and the demands of living in a modern society in direct conflict with each other. The effects of these conflicts can be seen everywhere in the society. Thus, education is not an exception and happens to be one of the places where these conflicting and competing needs, desires, and interests play out in an

---

[4]Commentary written by Geeta Verma.

interesting manner. The conflicting ideas present a different kind of challenge to all the stakeholders in education, who would benefit from revisiting their ideologies in order to accommodate existing demands as well as rekindle India's rich wisdom heritage in a vital and democratic way.

Introduction

My comments address the possibility of practicing curriculum wisdom in the context of Indian culture and society. I begin with a short historical background of the formal and informal education system in India in precolonial, colonial, and postcolonial times. This is done in order to acknowledge the deeply rooted wisdom themes that permeate everyday life in Indian society. These themes are complex, multilayered, and multifaceted and have many cultural roots. India has a cultural heritage that emphasizes the harmonious development of intellect, will, and feelings. Colorful rituals have given scope to the play of imagination, and stories of the epics have provided moral education. Oral discourses on philosophy and religion have helped train the intellect. Customs and folklore, proverbs and fables, mythology and scripture have been passed from generation to generation through folk songs, folk drama, and folk art.

My hope is that this commentary will raise more questions than it provide answers. I hope to open channels of communication and provide some fertile ground for Indian scholars, curriculum leaders, policy makers, and other stakeholders to be able to have vibrant discussions about curriculum wisdom as discussed in this book. My commentary revolves around three questions:

- In the land of sages, philosophers, and social thinkers, how should the educational wisdom traditions that have been practiced for thousands of years be revived (with the assumption that there are at least some educational stakeholders who see a value in reviving the wisdom traditions of precolonial India)?
- How should we re-articulate these wisdom traditions so that they are relevant and meaningful in the contemporary context of the largest democratic nation in the world?
- How do we integrate the democratic ideals of Indian society into curriculum decision making?

My commentary will include a brief section on the educational philosophy of Gandhi and Tagore since their thoughts and experiments provide a deep moral undercurrent for current Indian educational thought. I will be using the seven archetypal inquiry domains used by the authors in Chapter 3 (techné, poesis, praxis, dialogos, phronesis, polis, and theoria) to trace the history of educational trends and to articulate a curriculum inquiry map that would be appropriate for the contemporary Indian context.

Education Traditions and Curriculum Artistry

In precolonial times the children of privileged citizens studied under an individual teacher, a guru, who taught only a few students. Education was considered to be a lifelong process and based on deep-seated and continuing principles. It was evolutionary, integrative, and unitive. The individual was primarily guided by a perennial philosophy that viewed man as a student of life or a seeker of wisdom. As Gandhi (1977) notes, "along with the academic subjects, the emphasis was on the expansion of human consciousness or awareness, in order to sensitize one's perception and enhance the capability for expressing one's creative self in action" (p. 156). The ancient Indian culture placed equal stress on the development of the intellect, intuition, metaphysical doctrines, and humanistic values. It accepted beauty among a multiplicity of races, languages, customs, and manners and provided vitality, resilience, and beauty to its socio-economic existence (Gandhi, 1977). Deriving its strength from its integrity of thought and action, this cultural heritage strongly influenced the individual's socialization, providing a compelling socio-psychological context for educational work. Overall, educational practices focused on developing attitudes rather than stimulating the acquisition of knowledge (Perisaswamy, 1969).

In the scheme of ancient Indian education moral training played a scarcely less important part than mental training: "The development of the inner nature of character of the student occupied a larger place in the ancient pedagogic scheme than the part that deals with the mere intellect" (Patel, 1953, p. 37). This perspective reflects the discussion of good curriculum judgment in Chapter 1 and requires "multidimensional, long-term problem solving" focusing on envisioning and enacting a "good life." Since educators were deliberating over the lifelong consequences of their educational activities, they worked on cultivating the "wide-ranging intellect" also discussed in Chapter 1.

I can describe the enactment of wisdom in precolonial times using the seven inquiry domains. I believe that inquiry modes of phronesis and dialogos were at the heart of educational work. This was accomplished through the customs and folklore, proverbs and fables (thus poesis) and discourses that could be either of a religious or political nature (thus praxis). In other words, phronesis and dialogos were embedded in, and circumscribed by, certain poetic and political traditions. The polis and theoria were outside poesis and praxis, yet they were inside the periphery, as they were the glue that kept traditional society in place. In addition, it was not the prerogative of everyone to engage in all of these inquiry domains. This was particularly true for theoria, which was reserved for the traditionally wise people (religious leaders, community leaders, and others of a comparable status). Techné occupied a peripheral place. This was not due to a lack of emphasis on skilled craftsmanship but simply because it was more matter of fact. Most people acquired a trade by virtue of being born in a particular caste.

Keep in mind that none of these inquiry modes were interpreted in the democratic spirit of this book. They were being practiced in a traditional way. The "masses" had no formal education, except maybe religious teaching passed on from generation to generation—the best in the form of stories, myths, legends, songs, and plays (Gandhi, 1977). There was an everyday emphasis on phronesis (practical, deliberative wisdom) through poesis (soulful attunement to the creative process); dialogos and theoria were off-limits to the common person. In effect, the understanding of life as a wisdom challenge was centered in religious scriptures, as described in Chapter 1.

The advent of British rule in India in the early eighteenth century led to the introduction of Western ways. The British system of education was completely divorced from the Indian traditional milieu. It was different both in its orientation and organizational structure. As a powerful tool in the process of the so-called modernization of the Indian view of life, it caused a "major breakdown in the principles of hierarchy and holism, the two pivotal value systems of the traditional culture" (Gandhi, 1977, p. 158).

This "modern" education system had a deep impact on the education that was provided to students. Completely detached from traditional, dynamic educational practices, the new curriculum focused on preparing Indian students to become important tools in the propagation of British hegemony. This was reflected explicitly in the content and process skills included in the curriculum (Naik, 1975):

> The educational system assumed that knowledge was something which was outside the individual, that it was good for the individual to acquire as much of it as possible and to store it in his brain, irrespective of the fact whether or not it was related to his life and environment, that the individual must be able to recall this stored knowledge whenever needed, and that the mere possession of knowledge was a power or privilege which put the individual concerned above those who did not have it and also entitled him to social and economic reward.... Consequently, this emphasis on information gathering and comparative neglect of social and productive skills became an essential and deep-rooted feature of the new educational system. (p. 46)

Using the seven inquiry domains, I can also describe the loss of wisdom practices during the colonial era. Techné occupied the center of the colonial education system, and this techné focused on the problem of mastering the information that would help consolidate the British Empire. The other inquiry domains were more or less neglected in the formal education of the child. Thus, it can be concluded that the education system introduced by the British government was lopsided, as it emphasized only a narrow training of the mind.

However, this does not mean that educational thinkers and philosophers during colonial times did not advance more balanced educational philosophies, and two prominent social leaders stand out in this respect. The philosophies of Gandhi and Tagore drew from ancient Hindu educational traditions and were applied successfully in the colonial context. I now turn to their ideas.

Gandhi's Educational Philosophy

Gandhi's educational philosophy has its roots in Indian life and culture. In Gandhi's view education is an integrated and indivisible process beginning with conception and ending with death (Patel, 1953). Gandhi believed that education is a pivotal activity for social, moral, political, and economic progress (Patel, 1953). Besides character building, Gandhi made *sa vidya ya vimuktaye* (education is that which liberates) one of the most important aims of education; his emancipatory understanding was quite broad: "Knowledge includes all training that is useful for service of mankind and liberation means freedom from all manner of servitude even in the present life" (Patel, 1953, p. 39–40). This quote parallels the point made in Chapter 1 about practicing a "doubled" problem solving and balancing the spirit and the letter of curriculum practice.

Gandhi (1937) presents a broad, holistic definition of education: "By education I mean an all-round drawing out of the best in child and man—body, mind and spirit. Literacy is not the end of education nor even the beginning" (p. 37). He states that his interactions with students and intellectuals during his travels led him to believe that their education was leading to intellectual dissipation rather than development. He felt that the fault lies with a modern system of education that misdirects the mind and hinders its development (Gandhi, 1951).

Gandhi conceptualizes two sets of educational aims: immediate and ultimate. The immediate aims of education are manifold because they touch life at different points. The ultimate, and by far the most important aim of education, is according to Gandhi the knowledge of God, leading to self-realization, the merger of the finite being into the infinite.

This ultimate aim includes and embraces all his immediate and subordinate aims such as preparation for complete living, adjustment to environment, perfection of one's nature, character-building, harmonious development of one's personality, etc. (Patel, 1953).

Based on his educational ideas, Gandhi proposes a scheme of "basic education" centered on manual labor, to which he imparts a special dignity by making it the pivot of all activities—social, political, educational, economic, and even religious (Patel, 1953). He felt that productive and remunerative educational activities can be the prime means for intellectual training (Perisaswamy, 1969). More specifically, the learning of handicrafts is the pivot around which the teaching of other subjects such as mathematics, history, geography, and biology should revolve. He wanted an effective and natural correlation between craft activities and other subjects, and he felt that the child does not learn exclusively with his mind or with his body, but with his body-mind. This educational method enables the child to grow better, to gain confidence, and to manifest unique abilities. The child learns more quickly by actually doing the thing and by understanding the relationship of branches of knowledge (Perisaswamy, 1969).

Tagore's Educational Philosophy

Rabindranath Tagore was an artist, poet, philosopher, humanist, and educator who exercised tremendous influence on the development of twentieth century educational thought and practice. His reputation as a writer and artist was one that transcended the Indian subcontinent. He felt that education should aim to develop all sides of man's nature, focusing on his physical, intellectual, and moral powers. Tagore (1917) writes,

> The object of education is to give man the unity of truth. Formerly when life was simple all the different elements of man were in complete harmony. But when there came the separation of the intellect from the spiritual and the physical, the school of education put entire emphasis on the intellect and the physical side of man. We devote our attention to giving children information, not knowing that by this emphasis we are accentuating a break between the intellect, physical and the spiritual life. (p. 126)

Scholars who have studied Tagore's educational philosophy comment on his holistic understanding of his education. For example, Mukherjee (1962) writes,

> Tagore's fundamental aim of education as the harmonious development of all human faculties in order to attain complete manhood must have the reflection of his fundamental philosophy of life. The highest education is that, Tagore said, which makes life in harmony with all existences. Harmony with all existence can be achieved only when all the faculties of an individual have been developed to the highest pitch of perfection, which represents Tagore's conception of complete manhood. (p. 266)

Slattery's (1995) conception of a postmodern education that "challenges educators to explore a worldview that envisions schooling through a different lens of indeterminacy, aesthetics, autobiography, intuition, eclecticism, and mystery" (p. 23) strikes a chord with the educational philosophy of Tagore.

Perisaswamy (1976) notes that Tagore's educational philosophy contains three main features: freedom, creative self-expression, and active communion with nature and man. Tagore stresses the attainment of an inner freedom, an inner power and enlightenment. This ideal of inner freedom may be expressed as the liberation of the individual from all kinds of slavery. Therefore, the main characteristic of good education, according to Tagore, is that it does not overpower man's nature but it emancipates him (Perisaswamy, 1976). Tagore's ideas have many parallels with John Dewey's educational philosophy. For example, Dewey's (1966) comment about human freedom is very "Tagorian" in spirit:

> Freedom means essentially the part played by thinking-which is personal-in learning; it means ... independence in observation, judicious invention, foresight of consequences and ingenuity of adaptation to them. But because these are the mental phases of behavior, the needed play of individuality—or freedom—cannot be separated from opportunity for free [physical] play .... (p. 302)

Tagore's educational theory emphasizes the arts and crafts so as to cultivate children's natural creative instincts (Perisaswamy, 1976). Saiyidain (1967) explains,

> Tagore stressed the need to bring education into close relationship with productive work, both as important in itself as a medium for the education of the mind and personality. What he wished to introduce in his school would today strike a responsive chord amongst educationalists of many lands. The various activities, Tagore believed, could bring teachers and students into a vital partnership of effort and also establish fruitful relations between the school and the community. (p. 49)

Gandhi experimented with his educational philosophy in Sabarmati Ashram, whereas Tagore enacted his educational ideas in Shantinikentan. Thus, they were not only educational philosophers but, as described by Henderson and Hawthorne (2000), undertook the moral challenge of democratic curriculum reform by working as educational visionaries, communicating the big picture, practicing systemic reform, engaging in eclectic problem solving, fostering active meaning making, collaborating with colleagues, and serving as public moral advocates.

To summarize their educational philosophies, it can be concluded that both Tagore and the Gandhi accorded the highest place to the "freedom of mind" (Bhattacharya, 1987, p. 53) through the use of different curriculum inquiry domains. As depicted in one of the poems by Tagore (1997), the focus on liberation and emancipation of both mind and soul is a common theme among the prominent educational philosophers of India:

> Where the mind is without fear and the head is held high;
> Where knowledge is free;
> Where the world has not been broken up into fragments by narrow domestic walls;
> Where words come out from the depth of truth;
> Where tireless striving reaches its arms toward perfection;
> Where the clear stream of reason has not lost its way into the dreary desert sand of dead habit;
> Where the mind is led forward by Thee into ever-widening thought and action—
> Into that heaven of freedom, my Father, let my country awake. (p. 51)

Reality versus Illusion: Colonized in Body and Mind

Despite the domineering presence of prominent educational philosophers in Indian educational history, the period of British colonialism has left a deep mark on the contemporary educational system. The contemporary Indian academic community does not treat education as a lifelong process (Gandhi, 1977). Before and during the struggle for India's independence, political and social philosophers commented on the state of education and its impact on the minds of young children:

> There was a general discontent with the then existing system of primary education. The teachers were badly paid and badly equipped for teaching. Education was all bookish; it had no bearing on the daily life of the children, with the result that it never sustained the interest of the children who forgot what they learned in schools as soon as they left them. This amounted to tremendous wastage in time, money and energy. (Patel, 1953, p. xii)

A report by the Ministry of Education (1963) clearly indicates the narrow educational focus that is a legacy of the colonial period:

> Curriculum construction, the methodology of teaching the different subjects at the elementary stage, and particularly the teaching of reading and arithmetic to the beginners, the psychology of child development, the organization of primary schools, the different problems of primary education—these are very, significant areas of research if the teaching in the elementary schools is to be vitalized. (p. 25)

One possible cause for this limited curricular orientation is the evolving political subculture of India, which lacks a certain vitality. Democracy, understood as a moral basis for living and not just as the practice of a particular political system, has many features: a multiparty system, a free press, an independent judicial and legal system, and an existential embracing of freedom (Greene, 1988). India has not yet achieved this cultural maturity, and consequently, Indian education is only in the early stages of democratization. The reality of the situation is that interested groups within and outside the political parties now dominate Indian politics. This has resulted in the emergence of ethnic dynasties, primordial loyalties, divisive regional interest groups, and ideological identity politics (Gandhi, 1977).

The general picture of Indian education is a system that does not cultivate a moral worldview based on enduring democratic values and attitudes. It does not educate for sensitivity, emotional awareness, personal insight, or broad understanding. It focuses only on creating "experts" in the manipulation of material things. In general, education in India has become utterly irrelevant and rootless except for the purposes of awarding degrees and diplomas to swell the ranks of the educated unemployed (Gandhi, 1977). This critical analysis is reminiscent of a point made by Henderson and Hawthorne (2000):

> Most mainstream schools [in the United States] design curriculum according to state-provided textbooks, goals, and objectives. . .each teacher plans specific activities using textbooks and related materials intended to implement the prepackaged design. These individual plans are often referred to as instructional plans, not curriculum plans, implying that teachers themselves do not make curriculum decisions. (p. 83)

Old Wine, New Bottle: Dialogos, Praxis, and Phronesis?

Some Indian educators and policy makers are realizing the shortcomings of the current education system. However, as in the United States, the politics of a narrowly focused technical education, geared toward employment or economic upward mobility, is now deeply rooted in the Indian soil. India may be the largest democratic nation in the world, yet some of the precolonial aristocratic traditions as well as postcolonial manifestations make the picture more complicated. Corruption, bribery, and low-functioning bureaucracy are living realities that one has to consider before proposing any sweeping changes.

In this historical context, I want to propose a curriculum inquiry approach for India based on the Chapter 3 map. Dialogos would occupy center stage. I have in mind conversations between educators and other educational stakeholders on the enduring values of postcolonial Indian education. Since the praxis and phronesis modes of inquiry are necessary to inform such a dialogue, they are joined with dialogos at the center of my new curriculum inquiry map (Figure 9.2). Techné would have a more peripheral position and would be informed by polis, theoria, and poesis.

The day-to-day enactment of this curriculum inquiry would pose a daunting challenge. Though educational stakeholders in school settings (the students, parents, teachers, and administrators) celebrate the contributions of Gandhi and Tagore annually during school assemblies, they often do not realize that their practices are not congruent with the philosophies of these visionary thinkers. They lack this critical awareness because they are too deeply embedded in a Western model that focuses on narrow educational aims.

I understand their predicament. Indian educators may understand very well the importance of integrating deep-seated inquiries into their everyday curricular work. However, many of their students come to them with the hope of mastering specific work skills in order to gain economic upward mobility. In effect, their students want an information-age techné, not a postcolonial dialogos, to be the central focus of curriculum work. What do educators do in such circumstances? How can educators engage their students with a "fuzzy" democratic morality that has no bearing on achieving a materialistic "better life?" The challenge in the Indian context would be to practice curriculum wisdom without marginalizing students who come with such economic expectations.

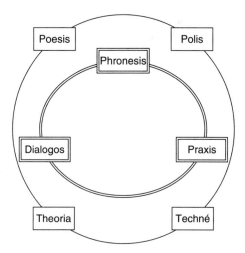

FIGURE 9.2

Curriculum inquiry from a postcolonial perspective

The regeneration and rejuvenation of the educational philosophies of Gandhi and Tagore with reference to the practice of democratic wisdom will only happen when Indian educators see the value of such curriculum work. As somebody wisely said, every journey starts with a single step; I am hopeful that there are individual teachers, principals, and others in India who would be willing to take this first step. However, for the immediate future, this curriculum wisdom would either be subservient to, or at best, co-exist with, current educational themes and aims. If Indian educators would begin to work with the inquiry map in Chapter 3, I am positive that many of them would embrace the curriculum wisdom challenge in their daily educational work. And if they were to do so, they would be rekindling India's rich wisdom heritage in a vital, democratic way.

References

Aké, C. (1990). *The case for democracy in African governance in the 1990's.* Atlanta: Carter Presidential Center.

Atweh, B., Kemmis, S., & Weeks, P. (1998). *Action research in practice: Partnerships for social justice in education.* London/New York: Routledge.

Australian Council of Deans of Education. (2001). *New learning: A charter for Australian education.* Canberra: Australian Council of Deans of Education.

Banks, J. A. (1991). A curriculum for empowerment, action and change. In C. E. Sleeter (Ed.), *Empowerment through multicultural education* (pp. 125–142). New York: State University of New York Press.

Bates, R. (1994). The impulse to reform in Africa. In J. Widner (Ed.), *Economic change and political liberalization in sub-Saharan Africa* (pp. 13–28). Baltimore: Johns Hopkins.

Bhattacharya, V. R. (1987). *Tagore's vision of a global family.* New Delhi: Enkay.

Boafo-Arthur, K. (1999). Ghana: Structural adjustment, democratisation, and the politics of continuity. *African Studies Review, 42,* 41–72.

Clark, J. F. (2002). The neo-colonial context of the democratic experiment of Congo-Brazzaville. *African Affairs: The Journal of the Royal African Society, 101,* 171–192.

Dewey, J. (1966). *Democracy and education.* New York: Free Press. (Original work published 1916)

Doll, W. E., Jr. (1993). *A post-modern perspective on curriculum.* New York: Teachers College Press.

Fafunwa, A. B., & Aisiku, J. U. (Eds.). (1982). *Education in Africa: A comparative survey.* London: Allen & Unwin.

Freire, P. (1985). *The politics of education: Culture, power, and liberation* (D. Macedo, Trans.). New York: Bergin & Garvey. (Original work published 1985)

Gado, I., & Verma, G. (2000). *Issues in international curriculum discourse: What does internationalization of curriculum discourse mean to scholars in the curriculum field?* Paper presented at the International Conference of the Curriculum Theory Project, Baton Rouge, LA.

Gandhi, K. (1977). *Issues and choices in higher education.* Delhi: B. R. Publishing.

Gandhi, M. K. (1937). *Harijan.* Ahmedabad: Navajivan Press.

Gandhi, M. K. (1951). *Basic education.* Ahmedabad: Navajivan Press.

Green, B. (Ed.). (1999). *Designs on learning: Essays on curriculum and teaching by Garth Boomer.* Canberra: Australian Curriculum Studies Association.

Green, B. (2001). "(Re-)Schooling Australia? Curriculum and the national imaginary." Keynote address at the Biennial Conference of the Australian Curriculum Studies Association. Australian National University, Canberra, Australia.

Greene, M. (1988). *The dialectic of freedom.* New York: Teachers College Press.

Grundy, S. (1987). *Curriculum: Product or praxis.* London: Falmer Press.

Henderson, J. G., & Hawthorne, R. D. (2000). *Transformative curriculum leadership* (2nd ed.). Upper Saddle River, NJ: Merrill/Prentice Hall.

Hinchliffe, K. (1987). *Higher education in sub-Saharan Africa.* Wolfeboro, NH: Croom Helm.

Kandeh, J. D. (1998). Transition without rupture: Sierra Leone's transfer election in 1996. *African Studies Review, 41,* 91–111.

Kincheloe, J. L., Slattery, P., & Steinberg, S. R. (2000). *Contextualizing teaching.* New York: Longman.

Macpherson, I. (Chair) (2002a). Proposal submitted for an interactive symposium at the annual American Educational Association conference, Chicago, 2003, entitled *Personal, cultural and moral discourses in ongoing critiques and reconstructions of curriculum leadership.*

Macpherson, I. (with Aspland, T., & Brooker, R.) (2002b). The place of curriculum studies in teacher education programs: A proposal. *Curriculum Perspectives, Newsletter Edition.* 22(2), 14–17.

Macpherson, I., & Aspland, T. (2002). *Moving outside the square: Shaping initial teacher education before 2010—A perspective from Queensland University of Technology.* Paper presented at the Annual Conference of the Australian Teacher Education Association, Brisbane.

Macpherson, I., Aspland, T., & Brooker, R. (2001). *Traversing a decade of curriculum thinking and practice: A conversational case study of curriculum leadership.* Paper presented at the Annual American Educational Research Association Conference, Seattle.

Macpherson, I., Aspland, T., Brooker, R., & Elliott, R. (1999). *Places and Spaces for Teachers in Curriculum Leadership.* Canberra: Australian Curriculum Studies Association and Goanna Print.

Macpherson, I., Aspland, T., Elliott, R., & Brooker, R. (2002). *A focus on places and spaces for teachers and other stakeholders in curriculum leadership—Seizing the global agendas at the local level.* Paper presented at the Annual American Educational Research Association conference, New Orleans.

McTaggart, R. (1991). *Action research: A short modern history.* Geelong, Australia: Deakin University Press.

Ministère de l'Education Nationale. (1983). *Programme Nationale d'Edification de L'Ecole Nouvelle* [National program for the edification of the new school]. Benin: INFRE.

Ministère de l'Education Nationale et de la Recherche Scientifique. (1990). *Actes des états généraux de l'éducation* [Acts of the General State of Education]. Benin: MENRS.

Ministry of Education. *Report of the study in the training of elementary teachers in India (1963).* New Delhi: Government of India Press.

Moumouni, A. (1968). *Education in Africa* (L. J. Lewis, Trans). London: Andre Deutsch. (Original work published 1964)

Mukherjee, H. B. (1962). *Education for fullness.* Bombay: Asia Publishing House.

Naik, J. P. (1975). *Equality, quality and quantity: The elusive triangle in Indian education.* New Delhi: Allied.

Patel, M. S. (1953). *The educational philosophy of Mahatma Gandhi.* Ahmedabad, India: Navajivan.

Perisaswamy, A. (1969). *School and society according to John Dewey and Mahatma Gandhi: A retrospective critique.* Masters of arts thesis, Loyola University, Chicago.

Perisaswamy, A. (1976). *Rabindranath Tagore's philosophy of international education.* PhD dissertation, Loyola University, Chicago.

Pinar, W. F. (2000). *Toward the internationalization of curriculum studies.* Paper presented to the Louisiana State University Conference on the Internationalization of Curriculum Studies, Baton Rouge, LA.

Pinar, W. F., Reynolds, W. M., Slattery, P., & Taubman, P. M., (1995). *Understanding curriculum: An introduction to the study of historical and complementary curriculum discourses.* New York: Peter Lang.

Reid, W. A. (2000). Curriculum as an expression of national identity. *Journal of Curriculum and Supervision, 15,* 113–122.

Saiyidain, K. G. (1967). *The humanist tradition in modern Indian educational thought.* Madison, WI: Dembar Educational Research Services.

Slattery, P. (1995). *Curriculum development in the postmodern era.* New York: Garland.

Tagore, R. (1917). *Personality.* Bombay: Macmillan.

Tagore, R. (1997). *Gitanjali: A collection of Indian poems by the Nobel Laureate Rabindranath Tagore.* New York: Scribner Poetry.

Urch, G. E. F. (1992). *Education in sub-Saharan Africa.* New York: Garland.

We have reached the end of this leg of the curriculum wisdom journey. On this voyage we have traveled through time, reaching back into the nineteenth century to the philosophy of American pragmatism for a conceptual and methodological platform. We have journeyed back even further, to the time of ancient Greece, to suggest the archetypal nature of the seven modes of inquiry (techné, poesis, praxis, dialogos, phronesis, polis, and theoria) that serve as a map for curriculum wisdom. We have examined personal and structural challenges and we have presented three implications for practicing these arts of inquiry: a paradigm shift, a way of professional living, and a systemic reform effort. Thanks to the thoughtful contributions of educators who took the time to share their unique viewpoints, we have explored this book's approach to curriculum work from different perspectives of practice. Two teachers, two teacher educators, a public school superintendent, a central office administrator, and a principal lend their voices to this book.

We ended our voyage by traveling not just through time, but also through geographic and cultural space to encounter the perspectives of an Australian, an African, and an Indian curriculum worker on the value of curriculum wisdom. Throughout this text we have also projected forward in time, imagining an educational future in which teachers, administrators, and educational policy leaders might exercise wise curriculum judgments in collaboration with the communities with which they hold a shared moral vision for a democratic future.

As we conclude our part of the journey with you and bring this book to a close, we want to pause and consider what has changed, in the world and in ourselves, over the three years that we've been working on this text. We want to take stock of our current educational circumstances and assess the extent to which we can expect a responsive environment for our ideas. We want to reiterate the importance of thinking long term and consider a career map for the development of wise curriculum judgment. Finally, we will close by thinking with you about concrete steps you can take to continue on this journey, both alone and in collaboration with your colleagues.

THE ACCELERATING CRISIS OF DEMOCRACY

In Chapter 2, which was written in the early phases of our work, we examined a well-documented crisis in democracy. Three years later, as we conclude our work, we find it troubling to acknowledge that this crisis has accelerated and reached proportions that neither of us would have imagined when we began. External threats to the United States, characterized most tragically by the events of September 11, 2001, have led to the accretion of power in the executive branch of the government. This power is perhaps best represented by the new National Security Strategy published in September, 2002, which allots to the president almost unilateral power to declare war without going through the historical channels that have characterized our democratic process. Further, according to this strategy, the decision to wage war through preemptive strikes may now be planned and executed in secret, without forewarning. Wendell Berry (2003), noted essayist, novelist, and farmer, warns us of the consequences of such policy in a convincing essay in *Orion* magazine:

> The idea of a government acting alone in preemptive war is inherently undemocratic, for it does not require or even permit the president to obtain the consent of the governed. As a policy, this new strategy depends on the acquiescence of a public kept fearful and ignorant, subject to manipulation by the executive power, and on the compliance of an intimidated and office-dependent legislature.... To the extent that a government is secret, it cannot be democratic or its people free. (p. 19)

Berry's concerns are echoed by Jonathan Schell, who writes in *The Nation* that this policy of unilateral preemption, coupled with the overthrow of governments and overall military supremacy constitute the foundations of a United States "imperial system," an assertion that is repeated by many thinkers on both ends of the political spectrum. Schell notes that the development of empire is

> incompatible with democracy, whether at home or abroad. Democracy is founded on the rule of law, empire on the rule of force. Democracy is a system of self-determination, empire a system of military conquest. (p. 17)

Educators should take heed of Berry's words: to paraphrase him, anti-democratic government policies and practices depend on a public kept fearful, ignorant, and compliant. We believe that it is our responsibility, as caretakers of the democratic tradition and mentors to succeeding generations of citizens, to educate a public that is knowledgeable, skeptical, and capable of the critical examination of the policies and practices of its leaders. Berry reminds us of Thomas Jefferson's justification for the expansion of general education, quoting him in reference to the obligation of citizens to be critical of their government: "for nothing can keep it right but their own vigilant and distrustful superintendence" (p. 23). We should heed these words, lest the crisis of democracy become the loss of democracy on our watch.

THE CRISIS IN DEMOCRACY AND THE CRISIS IN TEACHING

Although it is well beyond the scope of this book, we do want to note what we believe are some connections between the larger crisis in democracy and the crisis in teaching. When we talk about the crisis in teaching, we are not talking about the well-advertised, media-propagated "crisis in education" supposedly indicated by falling test scores and low levels of literacy. Please don't misunderstand us; we believe that there is a lot of room for improvement. It is true that many children are falling through the cracks, especially in deteriorating urban schools. But this "education crisis," which some noted scholars call a "manufactured crisis" (Berliner, Bell, & Biddle, 1996), seems orchestrated more to advance an agenda of privatization and national standardization than to advance the agenda of democratic education. The crisis in teaching that we are talking about is a crisis in the profession, a crisis that results from what curriculum theorists call "deskilling" and "disempowerment"—removing the decision-making power from teachers, students, and school communities and locating it in experts or policymakers who are far removed from the scene of implementation. This crisis is linked to the quality of students' academic achievement in a fundamental way. Disempowered teachers with underdeveloped curriculum inquiry capacities are not well positioned to facilitate students' inquiry learning.

To provide just one very concrete example of this disempowerment, let's examine a current educational policy that is being implemented in low-performing schools in urban areas. Rather than see the problems of low literacy and poor academic achievement in inner city schools as a crisis of interlocking factors (inexperienced teachers and high teacher turnover, lack of educational resources, poor facilities, dysfunctional leadership, lack of parental involvement, and impoverished communities), the problem is identified as a narrow curriculum problem, one that can be solved by the implementation of rigid, prescribed, even "scripted" curricula. Teachers are given a formula to follow: In literacy education, for example, they are told to allocate a certain number of minutes for reading aloud, a certain number for journal writing, a certain number for programmed phonics instruction, etc. Never mind if student interests or questions emerge in the context of teaching, if the prescribed texts hold no meaning for the students, or if the approved instructional methods do not resonate with the learning styles of the particular students; one must follow the preset curriculum and stick to the prescribed schedule or risk being "written up" and disciplined. In many schools teachers are regularly visited, unannounced, by supervisors, who are checking to see that the most trivial of directives are being followed to the letter. Teachers are even being criticized for not having their learning goals written on the board in the correct color of marker.

These sorts of mandates exemplify what we mean by disempowerment or deskilling and represent what we consider the triumph of the **standardized management paradigm**. In this paradigm, decisions are top-down, and teachers are expected to implement other people's ideas. Their work is closely monitored so that their behavior is aligned with standardized test mandates. As we noted in Chapter 1, in this paradigm teachers are not expected to envision the democratic good life and enact their professional judgments; they are only required to implement someone else's prescriptions. Although many experienced teachers, faced with such mandates, manage to meet the basic requirements and then close their doors and do good work, new teachers are likely to be more cautious about exercising their professional judgment in such an intimidating environment and just go along with the program. Many teachers, in some cases the most creative, independent, and effective ones, are simply leaving the profession rather than submit to decrees that limit their opportunities to teach in an authentic and meaningful way.

We are sure that you, the reader, can come up with many such instances in which the judgments of educators are constrained or inhibited by similarly oppressive policies and practices. We know that the present climate is not conducive to the pursuit of democratically liberating educational purposes. Rather, as in the larger society, the educational domain is marked by large-scale antidemocratic trends: federal consolidation of control over educational matters, represented by the massive "No Child Left Behind" policy (critics with a wry sense of humor call it "No Child Left Untested"); unprecedented state involvement with the content of university-based teacher certification programs; the control of information available about educational practices (the Department of Education has been instructed to remove research studies from its website that do not conform with the policies in "No Child Left Behind"); the imposition of national standards (states have developed their own frameworks of standards, but they are predictably similar); the increasing corporate presence in schools (e.g., Whittle's Channel One "News," which is mostly advertising); and continuing efforts to privatize education through vouchers and other schemes, hence removing education from public, democratic control. This is just a short list, and space constraints preclude our developing these ideas more fully. Taken together, these antidemocratic trends, coupled with the current dominance of the standardized management paradigm, do not create a supportive context for the development of curriculum wisdom. However, there are, within the seemingly monolithic efforts to standardize and control education and downsize democracy, opportunities to advance the cause of educators who care about the expansion of a democratic way of life.

WHERE DO WE GO FROM HERE?

We want to suggest that as you continue your professional study of the various important components of the field of education (teaching, learning, curriculum, content, school organization, etc.) you keep a love for curriculum wisdom, as enacted through the arts of inquiry, front and center. As you read from the literature in our field, try not to lose sight of the forest for the trees. There are vast numbers of trees in the educational forest: competing theories about how children learn, what knowledge matters most, how to organize and teach content, how to infuse the arts into the curriculum, how to teach from a multicultural perspective, how to discipline children, how to involve parents in the classroom, how to design service learning activities. Thousands of books and professional journal articles vie for your attention, and a multitude of experts and consultants hope you will adopt their methods and encourage your school or school district to purchase their services.

Let's just take the vast literature on teaching as an example. Current proposals for the reform of the teaching profession include some excellent ideas for its renewal and revitalization. These include things like more recognition for career achievements, more opportunities for teamwork and collaboration, more rigorous teacher preparation, mentoring of new teachers, and a clearly defined career ladder with opportunities for advancement (Troen & Boles, 2003). Sound as all of these proposals are, they are usually presented in isolation from other educational problems and solutions and outside the context of an organizing conceptual framework. Seldom do proposals for reform of the profession directly address the task of cultivating wise, democratic decision making. And yet, as we made the case in Chapter 1, the cultivation of curriculum wisdom is a key element of successful school reform. Whether we are trying to find our way through the thicket of information about testing or trying to sort out the various calls for accountability, if our work is informed by practicing the seven modes of inquiry, we will have a more publicly justifiable basis for our decisions. It is to this end—the development of a conceptual framework for thinking about the multitude of reform proposals and educational theories—that we have presented our multifaceted, holographic model of curriculum inquiry.

If the curriculum weren't such an important aspect of the culture, it would not be so hotly contested; and efforts to disempower teachers, by discouraging, suppressing, or even eliminating the crucial variable of teacher judgment from curriculum decisions, would not be so prevalent. What we teach our children embodies what we most value in our society.

The curriculum, in all its complexity, **is** the culture. Embedded in it are our values, our beliefs about human nature, our visions of the good life, and our hopes for the future. It represents the truths that we have identified as valued and worth passing on. Underneath this statement rumbles a host of debates: Who decides what knowledge is valuable? Whose interests are represented by the curriculum? Whose perspective will be dominant in the curriculum, and who benefits from a particular curriculum focus? These are educational questions, but they are also political questions.

Usually, adopting a political perspective as an educator requires that you affiliate yourself with conventional political categories: on the Right, conservative proposals often embody traditional cultural literacy, educational "basics," and private choice; on the Left, there is a focus on multicultural inclusiveness and solidarity; and in the technocratic center, there is conformity and bureaucratic procedure. We have tried to carve out a new space in this educational/political territory distinct from the libertarian Right, the egalitarian Left and the technocratic center, with our focus on the cultivation of wise judgments through multidimensional arts of inquiry. Working out of this "postideological" perspective is more challenging than working out of a clearly defined political position because it acknowledges the inherent ambiguity and essential uncertainty of situations. It recognizes that there aren't any formulae for decision making, clear-cut answers, or teacher-proof procedures. There are only pragmatic inquiries resulting in informed judgments. This professional freedom requires a high level of personal and professional responsibility. Not everyone is eager for this level of freedom or this level of responsibility, but we believe that both are crucial if the profession is going to demand of the public that their decisions be trusted.

As noted in our Preface, curriculum workers' professional freedom is bound up with students' personal and intellectual freedom. The practice of arts of curriculum inquiry is vital to the facilitation of student inquiry learning. We hope we have made this teacher/student reciprocity apparent. If there is a consistent theme in our book, perhaps it is the presumption that human freedom is best realized through the cultivation of the capacity for responsible judgment. In this sense, we have some very large purposes in mind while proposing this form of professional development. We are concerned with the future of freedom in our society and with the shape that our democracy will take as the current generation of children grow to maturity. We are concerned with the Big Questions—questions of knowledge and power and emancipation. Think about the educational/political questions posed in the previous paragraph. Has your capacity to both ask and address these important questions of value been enhanced through the exploration of the seven domains of inquiry that constitute our holographic model of inquiry? Has your sense of a critically informed moral vision been refined and thought through as a result of your encounter with these ideas? Do you have a stronger sense of mission and purpose from your engagement with a "love of wisdom" perspective?

Everyone who reads this book is at a different stage of his or her career and in a different place in terms of personal and professional development. Some of you are beginning teachers, while some of you are veteran educators who have already taken on leadership tasks in the field, such as mentoring, textbook selection, district-wide curriculum design and development, or participation on professional standards boards. Some of you may be in graduate school to become educational administrators, teacher educators, or educational researchers. You may be an education professor. In addition to these differences, you may be operating within any one, or some combination, of the three orders of "consciousness" (traditional, modern, postmodern) that we introduced in Chapter 4. In terms of this adult developmental model, we clearly have a bias toward the postmodern because it is positioned to be the most inclusive of all of the other orders of consciousness.

This developmental framework also holds the most potential for meta-cognitive development, that is, the capacity to become reflective about your own thinking. We think the postmodern order of consciousness best resonates with the playful hermeneutic spirit necessary for a multidimensional engagement with all seven modes of inquiry. But no matter where you position yourself on the psychological/developmental spectrum, and no matter where you are in terms of career development, there are multiple entry points and pathways into the curriculum wisdom journey.

Curriculum decision making takes place in many contexts: in interaction with an individual child, in lesson planning, in classroom instruction, in school committees, at community school board meetings, in district and state forums. One way to think about decision making is in terms of ever-widening spheres of influence. Think about where you are on the continuum of influence and to what extent you have experienced public trust in your judgments. What do you need to know and be able to do in order to exercise your capacities for wise decision making in an ever-widening sphere? How can you build alliances of educators who share your moral vision of a democratic society and democratic schools?

We feel there are a number of positive venues for engaging in the journey toward curriculum wisdom and a number of practices that can support this voyage. Let us briefly touch on a few of these. The emerging practice of teacher research is one promising development. Teacher researchers engage in systematic study of the particulars of their classrooms, gathering careful data about children's learning, social relationships, their own teaching practices, and classroom life. They document their observations and reflections in journals or more conventional research formats. They engage in analysis and action based on their findings. Many of them publish their narratives (see Burnaford, Fischer, & Hobson, 2001; Gallas, 1994; Himley, 2000; Hubbard & Power, 1999.)

Teacher research becomes an even more powerful tool of professional development and school change when it is carried out within a collaborative community of inquiry. When teachers engage in collective inquiry, as in the Descriptive Review processes developed at the Prospect School (Himley, 2002) or in Critical Friends groups (Nave, 2000), they together discover the power of knowledge-based advocacy. Teacher researchers, such as those in the Teachers Network Policy Institute, are working to gain an active voice in education policy making (Meyers & Rust, 2003). Engagement in collaborative inquiry-based processes such as these is linked to the potential for teachers to earn the public's trust in their decision-making. We want to suggest that our framework for the development of curriculum wisdom is particularly well suited to existing teacher inquiry processes and has the capacity to add important dimensions to these activities. As noted early in this book, although we have presented you with some complex theoretical perspectives, our focus is on action, experimentation, and the testing of ideas in the real world. In this sense, teacher research with its focus on the continuous improvement of practice is perfectly consistent with our inquiry model.

While teacher research groups are an important venue for the cultivation of sophisticated inquiry processes, schools will not be transformed until and unless the public comes to understand the larger democratic purposes that are at the heart of our inquiry model. If we are to move beyond the constricted vision of schooling that sees students merely as potential producers and consumers, as cogs in an economic machine, and that assesses their worth on the basis of test scores, to a vision of schooling grounded in human development, creativity, justice, caring, equity, and community, the public will need to be inspired with a sense of possibility. Teachers and other educational leaders, grounded in wise curriculum judgments and inspired by a democratic moral vision, will be well prepared for this public intellectual leadership.

There are many venues and opportunities for this sort of leadership: letters to the editor of your local paper, articles in organizational newsletters, speeches at community events, community/school committees, community-based social justice organizations, and churches, to suggest just a few. We are talking now about participation in genuine transformation, the social equivalent of moving from third-order to fourth-order (and beyond) consciousness. This may seem like a daunting proposition, given the snail-like pace of social change and the unfailing tendencies of society to regress, especially in the face of fear, uncertainty, and upheaval. Large-scale social transformations occur, we are convinced, as a result of a multitude of localized, individual transformations.

Though we might like to dictate change, we can really only be responsible for our own consciousness. As we move toward fourth- and fifth-order consciousness and exhibit the capacities outlined in this text (open-ended inquiry, the tolerance for complexity, the embrace of difference, and visionary intelligence), people will be attracted to our energy, for this is the consciousness of the postmodern world. Like it or not, this world is upon us. We can choose to cling to outmoded forms of consciousness and act out of habit, custom or coercive force. Or we can cultivate our inquiry capacities and choose to act in accordance with our most developed intelligence, working out of a commitment to deep democracy as a moral way of life.

In this quest, we will necessarily draw upon all of our best multi-intelligent capacities, as embodied in the seven modes of inquiry: our craft knowledge and skill, our imagination and creativity, our compassion and humor, our rational and ethical capacities, our collaborative and deliberative abilities, our empathy and diplomacy, our passionate and poetic sensibilities, and our critical and visionary insights. Things will not get easier as we go along; in fact, they will only become more complex, for that is the way of things. But we will find friends and traveling companions along the way, and we can take heart that we are moving in the stream of history, in the flow of human development that is oriented, like a compass, toward greater democratic freedoms and human possibilities...toward wisdom.

Remember, however, that wisdom is not something that can be finally attained. It is not a thing at all, but a dynamic process, a way of living, and a habit of mind. It requires cultivation and ongoing nurturance in order to come to fruition. It necessitates both inner work (reflection) and outer work (action). The exercise of wisdom has real, concrete consequences: as Kekes (1995) reminds us, "moral wisdom is a human psychological capacity to judge soundly what we should do in matters seriously affecting the goodness of our life" (p. 14). As educators, we are responsible for not just our personal "good life" but for the collective good life. We have a sacred trust to exercise our best judgment in matters that affect those entrusted to our care. Every day we make decisions that affect the lives of our students and their families in significant ways. Taken together, these decisions affect the quality of our communities and our society. We have tried to portray this decision-making responsibility as a moral activity; specifically, we have tried to show how the exercise of wise judgment is connected to the development of democracy and the expansion of human freedom. We hope that you have been inspired to take up the curriculum wisdom challenge, to travel with the inquiry map that we have laid out, and to use it to forge new trails and discover new terrain. The wisdom challenge is never finished, and no final map can ever be drawn. There will always be new problems-to-be-solved and emergent horizons to explore. And lest you get too focused on results, let us remind you, in the pragmatic and Socratic spirit of this book, that the journey is every bit as important, if not more important than the destination.

References

Berliner, D., Bell, J., & Biddle, B. (1996), *The manufactured crisis: Myths, fraud, and the attack on American schools*. Cambridge, MA: Perseus.

Berry, W. (2003, March/April). A citizen's response to the national security strategy of the United States of America. *Orion Magazine*, pp 18–27.

Burnaford, G., Fischer, J., Hobson, D. (2001). *Teachers doing research*. Mahwah, NJ: Lawrence Erlbaum.

Gallas, K. (1994). *The languages of learning: How children talk, write, dance, draw, and sing their understanding of the world*. New York: Teachers College Press.

Himley, M. (2000). *From another angle: Children's strengths and school standards*. New York: Teachers College Press.

Himley, M. (2002). *Prospect's descriptive processes: The child, the art of teaching, & the classroom & school*. North Bennington, VT: The Prospect Center.

Hubbard, R. S., & Power, B. M. (1999). *Living the questions: A guide for teacher-researchers*. York, ME: Stenhouse.

Kekes, J. (1995). *Moral wisdom and good lives*. Ithaca, NY: Cornell University Press.

Meyers, E., & Rust, F. (2003). *Taking action with teacher research*. Portsmouth, NH: Heinemann.

Nave, B. (2000). *Critical friends groups: Their impact on students, teachers, and schools*. Bloomington, IN: Annenberg Institute for School Reform.

Schell, J. (2003, March). The case against the war. *The Nation, 276*(8), 11–23.

Troen, V., & Boles, K. C. (2003). *Who's teaching your children? Why the teacher crisis is worse than you think and what can be done about it*. New Haven, CT: Yale University Press.

Glossary

3S education   carefully and consciously integrating subject matter understanding with democratic self and social learning.

arts of inquiry   practicing seven modes of curriculum questioning; ways of curriculum study that cannot be reduced to generally applicable rules; flexibility in case-by-case application; continuous modification and adjustment of democratic curriculum envisioning and enacting.

backward design   curriculum development that begins with the conceptualization of students' subject matter understanding and moves to the assessment of this understanding before turning to the design of specific instructional activities.

commodification   a general social trend whereby aspects of life that once were dealt with in the context of family or community (healing the sick, childcare, care for the elderly, food production, clothing making and shelter construction) are now part of the marketplace.

constructive developmental theory of adult development   describes orders of adult consciousness with reference to the complexity of adult knowing; examines adult meaning making and identity construction in light of traditional, modern, and postmodern ways of knowing.

curriculum   derived from the Latin *currere*, which literally means "the course to be run"; denotes the planning of the course, the course itself, and the running; that is, the envisioned educational program and the experiences of enacting that program.

curriculum enactment   A key dimension of curriculum work; the embodiment of a curriculum vision; creating educational experiences based on authentic student-teacher transactions; the power to engage in responsible decision making; connotes "grass roots" curriculum reform.

curriculum envisioning   A key dimension of curriculum work; the visionary side of curriculum decision making; the personal and professional power to conceive of educational journeys infused with enduring values; informed by caring imagination and social criticism.

curriculum implementation   A form of curriculum decision making in which teachers and their students base their educational actions on the judgments of others; complying with a prescribed change agenda; top-down curriculum reform, usually in a context of managing accountability for standardized student learning.

curriculum judgment   making informed, publicly defensible decisions about educational courses of action.

curriculum wisdom   the open-minded, inquiry-based challenge of approaching curriculum work as envisioning and enacting a good educational journey for all students.

dialogos   multiperspective inquiry, that is, knowing based on an open-ended play of perspectives; the recognition that truth is often best constructed through diverse, potentially conflicting interpretations.

fallibility   the pragmatic assumption that everyone is capable of making errors and, therefore, must be continually open to learning from experience.

hermeneutics   a method of philosophical inquiry that addresses the relationship between the part and the whole; the consideration of both the letter and the spirit of some matter; a balanced understanding open to both the mundane and the enchanted; the art of interpretation, especially in matters of practical judgment.

human agency   capacity to individually and collectively enact personal, social, and cultural goals.

modernism   the period of time roughly dating from the Renaissance in Western European culture, characterized by the broad emergence of rational thought, liberal democratic ideals, separation of church and state, and scientific epistemologies.

normative framework   a set of ideas, commitments, and practices around which to develop a moral approach to living.

orders of consciousness   hypothesizing qualitative distinctions in the capacity to understand complexity and embrace ambiguity; contrasting ways of knowing during meaning making; a basis for making distinctions between traditional, modern, and postmodern ways of knowing.

organization development   specific collaborative activities in an educational institution that create and sustain a supportive work culture for curriculum and professional development activities.

phenomenological   pertaining to matters of human perception, experience, and consciousness.

phronesis   the deliberative mode of inquiry; practicing a careful and broad consideration of how problems are defined and how solutions are enacted; the prudent side of practical reasoning.

poesis   a soulful, poetic, soul-searching mode of inquiry.

polis   the ethical-political mode of inquiry; examining and enacting the principled implications of one's moral imagination and feelings; sensitivity to the close relationship between virtue and power; addressing high-minded professional codes of behavior and social contracts.

postmodern ways of knowing   embracing paradox and contradiction; the celebration of differences and pluralities; the critical rejection of universal absolutes; skepticism about the universal value of modernist ideals.

pragmatism   a philosophical tradition based on a thoughtful, multi-intelligent and open-minded consideration of the consequences of one's actions; a context-specific and fluid decision making that is responsive to emerging contingencies; avoidance of ideologically rigid, formulaic ways of thinking; visionary, future-oriented actions.

praxis   the critical mode of curriculum inquiry; practicing social criticism; focusing on social change through educational activity.

relativist   the point of view that any one set of ideas is as good or as useful or as true as another.

six facets of understanding   subject-matter knowing demonstrated through explanation, interpretation, application, perspective, empathy, and/or self-knowledge.

techné   the craft of curriculum work characterized by action-based inquiry; identifies problems to be solved, hypothesizes solutions, and makes plans based on these hypotheses; enacts solutions and reflects upon the outcomes.

theoria   the contemplative mode of inquiry; envisioning and conceptualizing public morality; attuning to enduring values in education.

transformative curriculum leadership   collaborative, systemic reform activities that foster a deepening of curriculum judgments; denoting individuals who encourage and nurture curriculum wisdom; curriculum decision making that fosters personal and cultural change.

wisdom   the capacity of judging rightly in matters relating to life and conduct; soundness of judgment; in the Socratic and pragmatic tradition, practiced through arts of inquiry.

Subject Index

Note: f indicates figure.